WANDSWORTH
AND
BATTERSEA
BATTALIONS IN THE GREAT WAR

1915 – 1918

WANDSWORTH
AND
BATTERSEA
BATTALIONS IN THE GREAT WAR

The 13th (Service) Battalion (Wandsworth)
The East Surrey Regiment

The 10th (Service) Battalion (Battersea)
The Queen's (Royal West Surrey) Regiment

1915 – 1918

PAUL McCUE

Pen & Sword
MILITARY

Other titles by Paul McCue

Dunfold – Surrey's Most Secret Airfield
(first edition 1992, second edition 1996 ISBN 1-871187-12-5)

SAS operation Bulbasket
(hardback 1996 ISBN 0-85052-489-X)
(paperback 1996 ISBN 0-85052-534-9)

Behind Enemy Lines with the SAS
The Story of Amédée Maingard – SOE Agent
(hardback 2007 ISBN 978-1844-15618-4)

ISBN 9781848841949

The right of Paul McCue to be identified as Author of the Work
has been asserted by him in accordance with the Copyright, Designs and
Patents Act 1988.

A CIP catalogue record for this book is
available from the British Library.

Typeset in Palatino 10pt

Printed and bound in the United Kingdom by CPI

Pen & Sword Books Ltd incorporates the imprints of Pen & Sword Aviation, Pen & Sword
Maritime, Pen & Sword Military, Wharncliffe Local History, Pen and Sword Select, Pen and
Sword Military Classics and Leo Cooper.
For a complete list of Pen & Sword titles, please contact
Pen & Sword Books Limited
47 Church Street, Barnsley, South Yorkshire, S70 2AS, England
E-mail: enquiries@pen-and-sword.co.uk
Website: www.pen-and-sword.co.uk

Contents

FOREWORD

In November 1994 I travelled to the small community of Villers-Plouich in northern France. I was accompanied by two colleagues from Wandsworth Council and our aim was to visit this village where former Council employee Corporal Ted Foster had won his Victoria Cross in 1917. We also wished to pay our respects to the Wandsworth men and boys who lie in the cemeteries in the area. This we did, helped by the then Mayor of Villers-Plouich, Jean Leterme.

From this beginning, and as is so often the case, the project snowballed. Research on Ted Foster revealed the existence of an entire Wandsworth Battalion, the 13th (Service) Battalion (Wandsworth) of the East Surrey Regiment. Tom Miles, the son of a former soldier in the 13th East Surreys, made contact and was instrumental in persuading me to research and write the story. Thank you for your patience, Tom.

But as my study of this unit neared completion, another came to light – Battersea's 10th Battalion of the Queen's (Royal West Surrey) Regiment. Since the present-day borough of Wandsworth covers the former borough of Battersea, I would have told only half the story had I not extended the project.

The result, this book, has taken many years to produce as firstly another book, and then the demands of my 'day job', took over. But in the interim, interest has been rekindled in the exploits of the two battalions, leading to Wandsworth Council re-establishing its links with Villers-Plouich and exchanging Mayoral visits, the first being in 1995. In King George's Park, Wandsworth, a stone was unveiled in May of the same year, naming a new footpath 'Foster's Way' in memory of the Borough's VC winner. And in 1997 a new headstone was erected on Corporal Foster's grave, following public donations. More information was forthcoming as a result of these events, most importantly in the form of a personal account written in 1923, but never published, by Private A. L. Bonsey of the 13th East Surreys. I have therefore attempted to weave this fascinating first-hand account into what I discovered in the official records and from my own research.

The French communities where our troops fought and fell are no more than a day's trip from Britain, and the reader is encouraged to make the effort in order to appreciate the huge sacrifices made in the terrible struggle that was the First World War. For me, it was a sobering introduction to a type of conflict now largely, and thankfully, past. A conflict where the theories of military leadership had fallen far behind the enormous advances in weapon technology and destructive power. There could only be one loser - the front-line infantry soldier - and yet the men and boys of Wandsworth and Battersea had eagerly stepped forward to take their chance in precisely that role.

This book is dedicated to their memory.

PAUL McCUE Witley, Surrey, 2010

ACKNOWLEDGEMENTS

My thanks are due to Marion Simmons (word processing) and Catherine Parsons (proof reading) and the following individuals and organizations for their help with this book:

Alan Barrett; James Boys; Sidney Bragg; the late Jon Catleugh; Andy Clyro; Commonwealth War Graves Commission; Commune de Villers-Plouich; Sean Creighton; Alf Crichton; Ross Davies; East Sussex Record Office; Edinburgh City Council Libraries Service; Valerie Evans; E. Forlan; the late Denis Foster; Jean-Luc Gibot; Dominique Goubet; Guildford Local Studies Library; Priscilla Gwynne; Mrs Carole Henderson; the Imperial War Museum; Mrs Sabrina Harcourt-Smith; Alan Hibbs, Lewes Library; Mrs Diana Hucker; Tim Hucker; Trevor Hucker; Mrs Pat Hucker; Donald Inkster; Dan James; Mrs Penny James (former Curator) and staff of The Queen's Royal Surrey Regiment Museum; Hon. Alderman Mrs Beryl Jeffery; the late Charlie Jones; Jim Lees; Jean Leterme; the late Patrick Loobey; Raymond Machut; Chris Mason; Tom Miles; G.S. (Jim) Osborne; Eric Page; Stephen Page; Gordon Passmore MBE; Lord Petre; Brigadier John Pitt OBE; the late George Richardson; Neil Robson; The Royal Scots (The Royal Regiment); John Scott; Mrs Ivy Sharp; Tony Shaw and Meredith Davis of the former Wandsworth Local History Library; Liz Shaw; Terry Sims; Jim Sloane; Mrs Joyce Smith; Brian Spencer; Stadtarchiv Dülmen; Mrs Daphne Tullis; Gordon Tullis; the Wandsworth Borough News; Warden Bruce and Co.; the Western Front Association; A. White; Mrs Joanna Whitworth; the late John Young CBE and Helen Osborn, Young and Co's Brewery.

PART ONE

Chapter 1

'YOUR COUNTRY NEEDS YOU!'

By the spring of 1915 the First World War, or Great War as it was then known, had lasted some six months. The facile hope expressed by many, that it would "all be over by Christmas", had already died. The losses sustained by the Regular Army, joined by the mobilised Reservists and Territorials, were already eating into the volunteers which Lord Kitchener, Secretary of State for War, had initially called for in August 1914. Kitchener's first appeal had been for 100,000 men to form the 'service' battalions of his 'New Army'. His famous exhortation 'Your Country Needs You' had brought in some three quarters of a million men in

Field-Marshal Earl Kitchener, Secretary of State for War.

Recruiting stations frequently struggled to cope with the flood of recruits.

the first rush to volunteer, many spurred by patriotism, but others merely seeking adventure or relief from unemployment and the harsh social conditions of the time. For the latter, the lure of regular pay, food and clothing was incentive enough and as a result, recruiting stations frequently struggled to cope with the flood of recruits. Ultimately Kitchener's campaign produced not just one New Army, but five. Yet even so he had warned "I shall want more men and still more, until the enemy is crushed".

The magnitude of early losses had also made it clear that recruitment by voluntary enlistment would need to be pushed to its limits. In order to encourage volunteers it was widely publicised that groups who joined together could serve together. The war was portrayed as a great adventure for young men. the experiment of the so-called 'Pals' Battalions'. This led to many of the volunteer battalions being based on a locality, while others were linked to specific occupations (e.g. the Public Works Pioneers) or educational background (e.g. Universities and Public Schools). In the mood of optimism that still prevailed in expectation of a relatively short war, few paused to consider the highly concentrated local impact that would result should battalions suffer heavy losses.

Encouraged by the enthusiastic response to his initial appeal and the positive reaction to the idea of 'Pals' battalions, Kitchener turned his attention to London and in February 1915, approached the mayors of the capital's 28 local metropolitan borough councils. From the scale of the losses already being encountered by the British Expeditionary Force on the continent, it was clear that Field Marshal Sir Douglas Haig[1] would need the first of the New Armies that summer, as soon as they had finished their training. Kitchener's aim was therefore to recruit even more units for the New Armies which themselves could expect to be suffering losses in the not too distant future.

Several London mayors had already shown great enthusiasm in recruiting, particularly that of Fulham, Sir Henry Norris JP. Norris had served as an officer in the Volunteer Royal Garrison Artillery and was also well-known as a Director of Fulham and Arsenal Football Clubs. Through this latter aspect of his life, Norris had helped the Rt. Hon. Sir W. Johnson-Hicks, MP for Brentford, in raising the 17th Battalion, Middlesex Regiment (otherwise known as the 1st Football Battalion) in December 1914. Recruitment for this unit had been largely among fans at football matches. In the light of this earlier success, Norris was among those who had approached the War Office and suggested a general appeal to all the London boroughs.

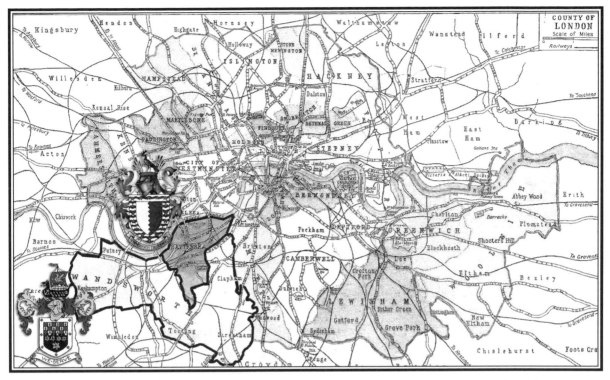

Wandsworth and Battersea had both at one time been communities within Surrey and chose that county to parent their battalions.

A first step was the 'Great Metropolitan Recruiting Campaign' of 11th-15th April 1915 and this was accompanied by a request for each mayor to raise a unit of local men for service overseas. There was some initial opposition to the plan from those civic leaders far-sighted enough to foresee the potentially disastrous impact which casualties in 'Pals' battalions might bring upon their communities. But all the boroughs nevertheless went ahead and appointed a committee or working party to agree upon the type of unit to be raised. The Boroughs of Fulham and Wimbledon each chose to raise artillery units, and this was also the original aim of Councillor T. W. Simmons JP, the Mayor of Battersea. Clapham Junction in Battersea was already the headquarters of the 23rd Battalion, County of London Regiment, the Territorial Force unit of part-time soldiers which had immediately been called up for active service in 1914 and which by 1915 was in the trenches in France. A second battalion, the 2/23rd, had then been raised and this had just departed for final training. Recruitment for a third battalion commenced in the spring of 1915. Battersea was also the home of Price's Candle Company. The company had formed a Volunteer Corps (the Volunteer Force was similar to the Home Guard of the Second World War) among its employees and these men had then volunteered en masse to form a Company in the 3rd (City of London) Battalion (Royal Fusiliers). There were therefore many men from Battersea and the surrounding district already in khaki. This was shown when the South Western Star newspaper published the following lines in 1915, an amateur poet's tribute to the efforts of the former masters and pupils of just one local school, Lavender Hill:

GOOD OLD LAVENDER HILL

We all know our country has now got to fight,
To teach the proud Germans that "might" is not "right"
Lord Kitchener now a huge army has got,
But of all the brave boys - why, the best of the lot
Come from good old Lavender Hill,
And they mean to knock spots off old Kaiser Bill.
They're hard and they're tough, and they're very hot stuff,
Are the boys of Lavender Hill.

Across there in Flanders, at a place they call "Wipers",
Mr Lamb is commanding a party of snipers.
And day after day they are making things hot,
But the Germans all say that the deadliest shot
Comes from good old Lavender Hill;
For each time he shoots he is certain to kill.
And they say "Oh mein Gott, vhat a terrible shot -
Gott strafe Lavender Hill".

Now somewhere in Flanders, midst the shot and shell,
In the thick of the fight you'll find Mr Snell.
He's filling the bombs for our soldiers to throw,
And he fills them so well that the enemy know
He's from good old Lavender Hill.
And we want him to know that we think of him still.
And his old Standard IV wants to see him once more
Back at good old Lavender Hill.

I want to have a po
at the Germans.

The war was portrayed as a great adventure for young men.
Author's collection.

I'm sorry to say that the time is too short
To tell you of all our brave boys, as I ought
I can't speak of one without mentioning all,
So I'll leave you to read down the list in the hall.
Of our good old Lavender Hill.
But at the sight of that list with sad tears our eyes fill,
There are some marked with black who will never come back
To their old place at Lavender Hill.

We're proud of our boys who fight out there:
Do you think that you and I, boys, are doing our share?
To fight in the wet and cold is no joke,
The least we can do is to send out a smoke
To an old boy of Lavender Hill.
So bring up your pence with a right down good will,
So that each old boy gets just a few cigarettes
From his schoolmates at Lavender Hill.

H.C.

Yet despite this local patriotic fervour and support, Battersea's Mayor felt it would be difficult to raise yet another large formation of local volunteers. Consequently, Councillor Simmons's first suggestion was to find only the 133 men that would be required for a battery of artillery, a unit similar to that being raised by Wimbledon and Fulham. But in Wandsworth, Alderman Archibald Davis Dawnay JP[2] was serving as Mayor and his Council agreed to support the raising of a full infantry battalion of over 1,000 men for the East Surrey Regiment. The local press subsequently commented scathingly on the small-scale proposals of Battersea Council, regardless of the thousands of men who had already volunteered from the community. This, coupled with the political rivalry which existed between the two neighbouring Councils, swayed Battersea into revising its plans. It too would raise an infantry battalion, not for the East Surreys, but for the county's other regiment, the Queen's (Royal West Surrey) Regiment. Prior to the growth and geographical expansion of London, Wandsworth and Battersea had both at one time been communities within Surrey and it was therefore fitting that the two boroughs chose that county to parent their battalions.

Despite the demands already made by the Army on the men of the two communities, there would still be many for whom the prospect of fighting was better than remaining in Wandsworth and Battersea. Poverty continued to be widespread, with up to 30% of urban populations struggling to survive and, with only one in ten boys remaining at school after the age of 14, education had yet to provide an escape. In the light of such hardship, and with so few other opportunities, the siren call of the recruiting Sergeant proved hard to resist.

Alderman Archibald Dawnay,
Mayor of Wandsworth. Author

Early losses had also made it clear that recruitment by voluntary enlistment would need to be pushed to its limits. British wounded being transfered from a French hospital train to a hospital ship.

PART TWO

THE 13TH (SERVICE) BATTALION (WANDSWORTH), THE EAST SURREY REGIMENT

Chapter 2

'WE SERVE'

The Metropolitan Borough of Wandsworth of the early 1900's had boundaries different to those of the present-day London borough. It took its name from the village astride Wandsworth High Street, an important coaching route from the city of London to Kingston-upon-Thames and then onwards to the coast, but it also encompassed another six quite distinct villages – Putney, Roehampton, Clapham, Tooting, Streatham and Balham.[3]

The recorded history of the village of Wandsworth stretches back as far as the Stone Age, when hunters camped along the River Wandle

Tooting Broadway. Author

and it is thought that the area derived its name from an ancient local chieftain, Wendle. The community had long been prominent in the field of commerce. There were commercial breweries from the 1500's, including a site in Ram Street from 1581, taken over by Young and Co. in 1831, and successfully operated by the late John Young and his family until brewing ceased in 2006. The Church was prominent in the area from very early times and there are records of services at All Saints Church in the High Street dating from 1234. During the Great Plague of 1665-1666, the village of Wandsworth suffered 344 deaths, the highest number compared with any other local community. In the 17th century the Wandsworth area had become home for Huguenots fleeing persecution in France, the Huguenot Burial Ground on East Hill, Wandsworth still today holds gravestones dating from 1687. In 1764 the Earls Spencer, ancestors of the late Diana, Princess of Wales, had become Lords of the Manor of Wandsworth after Sara, Duchess of Marlborough and widow of the Great Duke, died and left Wandsworth to her grandson John Spencer. Reminders of this can be found in street names such as Spencer Park and Althorpe Road. Commerce accelerated and by 1792 there were four Calico printing works, one of which employed some 250 people. Also established at the time were several iron smelting works, the largest of which was situated where Iron Mill Place is today. Wandsworth was also famous for its Bolting clothes (clothing without seams) which were produced by Benjamin Blackmore in Wandsworth High Street using a production method which was a closely guarded secret.

Wandsworth laid claim to the first public railway in the world when the Wandsworth Basin dock was built in 1803 at the junction of the Thames and the River Wandle. Using horse power to pull the trucks along a five foot gauge, the track closely followed the course of the Wandle from Wandsworth to Croydon and in its early days

Wandsworth, Trinity Road.

handled all types of cargo, though the two main loads were coal and dung. The railway went out of business in 1848 when it was no longer feasible to compete against the expanding steam railway network.

Yet although there had always been some industry by the Thames and the River Wandle, Wandsworth was still described as a quaint and old-fashioned village as late as the middle of the 19th century. Country lanes and byways spread out across the fields and along the banks of the Wandle and the Thames and the area consisted mainly of farmland, market gardens, parkland of the grand estates and the open heathland of Wimbledon, Putney and Wandsworth Commons. But over a period of some thirty years, all changed. The railways had already cut two routes across the fields, encouraging the arrival of more industries. This in turn led to more houses, shops and schools, until much of the open land disappeared. Wandsworth Common suffered too, with areas being divided by the railway or used for institutional buildings. As this expansion continued, Summerstown and Earlsfield (both along Garratt Lane) and Southfields emerged with identities of their own, especially Earlsfield and Southfields which developed as separate suburbs to Wandsworth.

In Earlsfield, Garratt Lane was an ancient road, following the course of the Wandle and providing communication among the many mills, as well as access to the farmland. The mills at Duntshill were used for a variety of purposes, including the manufacture of parchment, quill pens, the printing of Paisley shawls, dyes and fireworks. Nearby were cottages for the local workers. Although the railway line passed through in 1838, development of the area only took place from around 1877 onwards and Earlsfield station did not open until 1884. New shops sprang up and houses spread across the fields towards Wandsworth Common and Burntwood Lane.

Southfields took its name from the old manorial field system when the area was South Field, recorded as far back as 1247. In 1830 Southfields was still described as rural, consisting of parkland, farms and meadows and crossed by a few paths and tracks which were the forerunners of some of today's roads. Although there had already been development in the Wimbledon Park area and along Merton Road, it was not until the opening of Southfields station in June 1889 that rapid change took place. The Grid housing development was built between 1898 and 1907, with extensions taking place until the start of the First World War. Several parades of shops were included, the first being in Replingham Road which is still the main shopping area today.

Clapham had started life as a 9th century medieval village on the site of what is now Rectory Grove. It extended two miles south to the boundary with the lands of Streatham, the neighbouring parishes of Lambeth and Battersea also ran south from their villages on or close to the riverside. New houses were built in the late 17th century, around Clapham Old Town and the Common. These were mainly the 'country homes' (some three miles from central London) of wealthy merchants and politicians. Buildings increased in number in the 18th and early 19th century as the demand for housing in the area soared. As well as large mansions, many more large terraced and semi-detached houses were constructed and smaller terraces and cottages were built for poorer people. These developments continued for over 30 years, but by the 20th century the large houses were not manageable, the wealthy moved away and the area was ready for the redevelopment brought about by improvements in transport. These started with stagecoaches (for the well off) and later, from 1820, the omnibus, running between Clapham and the City. After that, the railways permitted faster and longer distance travel. Fares were still relatively expensive and this did not change until the introduction of the horse-drawn tram, with better operating costs. The first underground station opened in 1900, bringing lower paid workers to live in Clapham.

The name Streatham means the 'Hamlet on the Street' – Street Ham – the street being the ancient trackway that now forms part of the A23 London to Brighton road. For centuries the village remained a small and relatively insignificant community, situated roughly halfway on

Clapham old town. Author

Streatham. Author

the road between London and the Archbishop of Canterbury's palace at Croydon. By 1670 a local spa, Streatham Spa, had been developed into a major attraction and within a short space of time Streatham became a fashionable location. Several wealthy merchants established their 'country homes' in the parish and Streatham's popularity as a select residential area continued long after the fashion for medicinal waters had passed. By the mid-19th century a number of fine mansions had been built by wealthy residents who were attracted to the parish by its rural charms and close proximity to London. The opening of Streatham Hill railway station in 1856 brought the area within easy commuting distance of the capital (about five miles away) and led to an influx of a large number of middle-class residents. Roads of large Victorian villas provided these new inhabitants with comfortable homes and firmly established the neighbourhood as a much sought-after locality in which to live. Within the space of a generation the area changed almost beyond recognition and as the twentieth century dawned, Streatham too had been transformed from a small country village into a bustling southern suburb of London.

Balham, part of the parish of Streatham, started life as one or two farms situated on the old Roman road of Stane Street and did not

Balham High Road. Author

really start to expand until the second half of the 18th century when the London gentry started to build 'country retreats'. It was then another hundred years before the area began to develop as a London suburb. Its first railway station opened in 1856, the line dividing Balham into two with residential and commercial development proceeding to the north at a greater rate than to the south. The High Road became a mix of shops and flats and developers quickly bought up the remaining open land and created more streets of typical Victorian houses.

Tooting's origins are lost in antiquity, although Stane Street continued south through the area and there must have been some Roman buildings locally as Roman material was incorporated into the Saxon Church of St. Nicholas. It remained a village up until the mid Victorian period, a strip development along Mitcham Road and Tooting High Street near the Broadway and consisting of several grand houses, smaller dwellings and some farms. Development started in the 1870's between Mitcham Road and Longley Road, in the Fishponds Road area, and with extra impetus provided by the building of the Totterdown Estate by the London County Council in 1902-3. 1903 also saw the operation of the first electric tram service in London, which terminated at Tooting. The district was well provided with places of entertainment, such as public houses and from the very early 1900's there were a number of cinemas. Tooting also had its institutional buildings, such as police stations, the baths, the Tooting Bec Hospital and the Grove and Fountain Hospitals, the latter two now covered by the present-day St. George's Hospital complex.

In Putney, the River Thames had always been important in the development of the village, both commercially and for leisure activities. Watermen and ferrymen plied their trade from early times, though this declined with the building of the original wooden Putney Bridge in 1729. A new stone bridge opened in 1886, followed by the embankment which made the riverside a pleasant place to stroll, as well as a centre for rowing and sailing. Overlooking the river is St. Mary's Church, dating mainly from a re-build in 1836, although the tower is 15th century and inside is a Tudor chapel. Putney High Street has always been a busy thoroughfare and up to the mid-nineteenth century, it was lined by a mixture of substantial houses, inns, shops and cottages. After the arrival of the railway in 1844 and the sale of the large estates, new streets spread out from both sides of the High Street and the lower end of Putney Hill. Market gardens and orchards disappeared as more and more houses were built. By 1914, Putney had completely altered, though the large houses around Putney Heath did not start to disappear until during the First World War. Putney Heath, with its ponds and woodland, was protected as a tranquil breathing space for the local population.

Close by and in the same parish, Roehampton was for many centuries only a small village, a medieval offshoot of Putney. The early 16th century saw the formation of Putney Park, a royal hunting preserve, and it is likely that the village was moved at that time to its present site on the edge of the common. By 1617 it boasted 33 houses and two inns, the Kings Head and the Angel, with a population of about 200. By the 18th century a number of grand residences had been built, surrounded by park-like grounds. Only with the advent of the

Putney High Street. Author

Roehampton. Author

20th century did the first real expansion of the village take place, when new streets were created just north of the High Street.

Together, the former Surrey villages of Wandsworth, Putney, Roehampton, Balham, Tooting, Clapham and Streatham formed the Metropolitan Borough of Wandsworth and when the Borough looked to choose a parent regiment for its Council-raised battalion, the history of the East Surrey Regiment made it a natural choice.

The origins of the Regiment lay in the 31st (Huntingdonshire) and the 70th (Surrey) Regiments of Foot which in 1881 amalgamated to become the 1st and 2nd Battalions of the newly-created East Surrey Regiment. These units had long looked to the population concentrations just south of London for recruitment, since the more sparsely-populated country areas of Surrey were not so productive of men. Traditionally, the rural areas were better covered by the Queen's (Royal West Surrey) Regiment, whose regimental headquarters were in Guildford. With its regimental depot being in the county town of Kingston-upon-Thames, however, the East Surrey Regiment's recruitment naturally evolved most fruitfully in the towns south of, and reaching up to, the River Thames. On the outbreak of war in 1914 the Regiment's strength consisted of two Regular infantry battalions (the 1st and 2nd), two Reserve battalions (the 3rd and 4th) and two Territorial battalions (the 5th and 6th). Of these, the 1st and 2nd Battalions were the only professional front-line units. The 3rd and 4th were the home defence and training battalions, responsible for supplying the Regiment's fighting units with drafts of trained men. The 5th and 6th Battalions provided part-time volunteer soldiers for the Territorial Force that had been created in 1908. These two battalions had been undergoing their summer training exercises when war broke out in August 1914, and were immediately mobilised. As the first year of the war progressed, both Territorial units expanded into three battalions apiece, the 1/5th, 2/5th and 3/5th and the 1/6th, 2/6th and 3/6th respectively. And when Lord Kitchener made his first appeal in 1914 for a New Army of 100,000 volunteers, the East Surrey Regiment initially succeeded in raising five new 'Service' battalions from its traditional recruitment areas of north Surrey. These were the 7th, 8th, 9th, 10th and 11th Battalions.

The 1st Battalion in particular had a strong contingent of Wandsworth men already serving as regular soldiers. Indeed, this unit was to lose more Wandsworth men killed in action during the First World War than any other of the East Surrey Regiment, including the Borough's own 13th Battalion. The 3rd and 4th (Reserve) Battalions also had historical links with the Wandsworth area. Their roots lay with the Surrey Militia, which as long ago as 1697 had based a company in Putney and by 1759 had a battalion quartered in Fulham, Putney and Wandsworth. An earlier 4th (Volunteer) Battalion of the East Surrey Regiment had been based at the Drill Hall at Clapham Junction in St John's Hill, Battersea, on land granted to the Army by Lord Wandsworth.[4] The 5th (Territorial) Battalion, though based in Wimbledon, also maintained one of its companies in Streatham.

Wandsworth Council therefore had strong historical reasons for preferring to recruit on behalf of the East Surrey Regiment. Another

Basic military coomunication, by flag waving, practised by volunteers on Wandsworth Common. Author

Metropolitan London borough to do so was Bermondsey. There, Mayor Councillor Hart was no less enthusiastic than Alderman Dawnay and had already set about raising a unit of local men. He was helped by the popular public figure of Harry Lauder, the celebrated singer, and his Pipers who gave several concerts and performances in aid of the call for volunteers. Recruitment centred on Rotherhithe and on 24 May, 1915, the 12th (Service) Battalion (Bermondsey) of the East Surrey Regiment was officially formed there from the new recruits.

In Wandsworth a considerable number of men had already been recruited for the Regular and Territorial battalions of the Army, but a full volunteer battalion had not been raised locally since the Napoleonic wars. The East Surrey Regiment therefore made additional efforts in the borough as part of the 'Great Metropolitan Recruiting Campaign' which commenced on Sunday, 11th April 1915. To support this initiative, Alderman Dawnay was determined that his Council should now lend every assistance and fulfil its patriotic duty to answer Lord Kitchener's latest appeal. On 7th May Dawnay therefore made the first appeal for 36 officers and 1,314 men, between the ages of 19 and 38, to form Wandsworth's own battalion and on the 20th he chaired the first meeting of 27 interested parties, consisting of Councillors, Aldermen, Mr Samuel Samuel (the local M.P.), other borough notables and Army district representatives. The Mayor explained that he had been authorised by Lord Kitchener to raise a Wandsworth Battalion and that an initial recruiting poster had already been produced and circulated throughout Wandsworth. It was agreed that a General Committee (consisting of those already present, plus 16 others who had been unable to attend), be formed to oversee the task, and that the Mayor should choose an Executive Committee and Sub-Committee to carry out the detailed work involved. A resolution was also passed that the battalion's officers should only be Wandsworth men.

On 2nd June the Executive Committee held its first meeting and Dawnay reported that he had met with officials of the War Office who had agreed that all recruiting matters should be left in his hands. Since, however, almost all the borough fell under the jurisdiction of the Army's 31st Regimental Recruiting District, Dawnay had invited Major Parmenter of the 31st District to attend and advise the Executive Committee. Parmenter was accompanied by Captain Clay of Eastern Command and, together, they spelled out the recruiting process for raising an infantry battalion. It was accepted that a commanding officer, in the rank of Lieutenant-Colonel, would be appointed by the

Committee, and that the priorities thereafter would be the selection of an Adjutant and a Quartermaster. The second in command, a Major, would then be responsible for picking four Captains as company commanders, and in turn, the four Captains would each select four subalterns, that is junior officers with the rank of Lieutenant or Second Lieutenant. It was agreed that, in particular, suitable local young men of the required calibre should be encouraged to apply for commissions as junior officers. In principle, each subaltern granted a commission would then be expected to raise at least 50 men, though this was seen not to be practicable in the borough. Instead, volunteers were to be pursued through a system of Recruiting Offices, with those of the 31st Regimental Recruiting District being made available, where geographically appropriate. Foremost among these was the office in Wandsworth Town Hall, which was now designated the Central Recruiting Office for the whole borough. Other 31st District facilities to be used included 6 Bemish Road and 25 High Street in Putney where Wandsworth Battalion recruiters were to be immediately stationed from 9 a.m. to 9 p.m., supplied with quantities of a distinctive ribbon that was to be handed out to every volunteer signing up. The District's offices in Tooting and Streatham were likewise made available, while the Council added 380 Streatham High Road and started to look for additional premises. A Council sub-committee of four members, again headed by the Mayor and dealing solely with recruitment and suitable offices, was created. A battalion orderly room was to be set up in the Town Hall and Mr Duncan Milligan FRAS was confirmed as the borough's Recruiting Officer.

Milligan's aim was that each of the Borough's five parishes of Wandsworth, Putney (including Roehampton), Streatham (including Balham), Clapham and Tooting should provide 200 volunteers each. The Council produced over 50,000 handbills and posters which were distributed throughout the Borough, encouraging enlistment and quoting the rates of pay which could be enjoyed by those still living at home. The Executive Sub-Committee met for its inaugural meeting on 14th June 1915 and Mayor Dawnay commenced proceedings with the news that the 31st District recruiting personnel at 380 Streatham High Road

G. R.

ENLIST WITH YOUR LOCAL FRIENDS

IN THE

Wandsworth Regulars

(13th [Service] Battalion East Surrey Regiment).

COMMANDING OFFICER, LIEUT.-COL. ALFRED BURTON.

While the present rates of pay and allowances are in force, men enlisting in the above Regiment (who live in the London Area) will receive for themselves and families while living and messing at Home pay at the following rates, viz :—

	Sergt.	Corpl.	Private.
With Wife only ...	£2/1/11	£1/16/5	£1/11/9
,, Wife & 1 Child	£2/6/11	£2/1/5	£1/16/9
,, Wife & 2 Children	£2/10/5	£2/4/11	£2/0,3

And **2/-** shillings extra per week for every other Child

Unmarried Sergeants receive	£1/10/4 per week.
,, Corporals ,,	£1/5/8 ,, ,,
,, Privates ,,	£1/1/0 ,, ,,

Proficiency pay will be issued where applicable. Uniforms at once.

The various separation allowances will be issued to **ALL** dependants of Soldiers.

By enlisting you are doing your Duty to your King and Country.

ARCHIBALD D. DAWNAY, *Mayor.*

Recruits were originally paid special rates if they still lived at home. A. Clyro

had recruited, inadvertently, the first volunteer for the Wandsworth Battalion on 3rd June. Appropriately, Private (very soon to be Sergeant) Ayers was a Council employee, working at Streatham Library. Another library worker among the very first volunteers was Private Herbert Davis, an assistant at the Garratt Lane Library and youngest son of Mr Cecil Davis, the Council's long-serving and kindly Borough Librarian. Mr Davis had already seen his three older sons join up and Herbert, the only one not to be commissioned, must have falsified his age, as he was only 18 years old at the time and therefore a year too young. The youngster, who had also recently signed up as a Special Constable, had in fact just been attested for another battalion of the East Surreys, but quickly obtained a transfer.

Lt-Col Alfred Burton, first Commanding Officer of the 13th.
Author

Nor had Dawnay wasted any time in finding candidates for the position of the Battalion's commanding officer, indeed he had brought two applicants to the meeting for consideration. Captain Alfred T.W. Burton was a 47-year-old bachelor with extensive experience in both the Regular, Reserve and Territorial forces. He had seen active service in the South African wars, after which he had helped form the 3rd County of London Yeomanry where he had been Adjutant and Machine Gun commander. He had then served in the Army Service Corps, the Coldstream Guards and the Berkshire Regiment where he had continued a machine gun specialisation. He had been serving in the Paymaster's Office for the first nine months of the war before he had been chosen as second in command, temporary Major, of the 12th (Bermondsey) East Surreys. Though presently residing at the Charing Cross Hotel, he expressed his willingness to become a Wandsworth resident.

The alternative to Burton was every inch a Wandsworth borough man, but suffered from the potential drawback of being 64 years of age. This was Captain Gethen, an old soldier of the Boer War and retired both from the Territorial Force's 4th Battalion of the Queen's (Royal West Surrey) Regiment and his civilian occupation of stockbroker. He was nevertheless still militarily active, being then in command of a unit of Clapham Volunteers, and was respected as an experienced Quartermaster.

Not surprisingly, Gethen's age counted against him and Burton was chosen, subject to the approval of the War Office. The choice of a second in command, Adjutant and Quartermaster, was deferred for future consideration and just one candidate for a captaincy, 54-year-old Captain Hallett, a Clapham resident who had retired from the Royal Sussex Regiment in 1892, was seen. Hallett's only real advantage was that he had recent experience as Recruiting Officer for the Public Schools and Universities Men's Force, where he had recruited some 4,000 men for four Fusilier battalions. He would clearly not, however, be suitable for active service and again, a decision on his application was deferred.

Five local candidates were then interviewed for appointments as Lieutenants or Second Lieutenants: Second Lieutenant Hoare of Nicosia Road, Wandsworth; Mr Robert Harker of Haldon Road, Wandsworth; Mr Courtney Bishop of Victoria Road, Clapham; Second Lieutenant Greene of Cautley Road, Clapham; and Mr G. W. Buchanan

Wandsworth Town Hall (since rebuilt) was the first recruiting office.
Author

of Trinity Road, Upper Tooting. All had military experience to some extent, in addition to being borough residents, but both Hoare and Greene would be dependent on the often-difficult task of obtaining transfers from their current regiments, the 4th Royal Irish and the 7th Dorsets respectively. Bishop was an Engineer by profession and had served with the 1st Battalion of the Surrey Volunteer Force[5] in Croydon, but as a widower with one child, his commitments were onerous. Buchanan, a director of the family business of building contractors, had served with the London Scottish territorials until six years before, but had only reached the rank of Corporal. Harker was then the Sub-Commandant of the Wandsworth and Earlsfield Athletic Volunteer Force, and came with a strong recommendation. A 28-year-old married man with two children, he was also a journalist with the Wandsworth Borough News and though no decision was taken there and then, Harker later proved to be the only candidate from this group to be appointed.

Finally, Sergeant-Major Eggleton, late of the Household Cavalry, presented himself for consideration, albeit with the proviso that he

Many young officers came through OTC's - the band of one is seen here on Clapham Common, helping the recruitment drive. Author

would sign on for home service only. In view of this stipulation, his application was not entertained, though he still offered to help with drilling of the Battalion if needed.

The meeting ended with news that the Mayor had obtained use of an empty shop at 489 Garratt Lane, on the corner of Earlsfield Road, as another recruiting office and that donations continued to flow in to help with the unit's setting-up costs, pending the arrival of any governmental financial assistance. The largest donations to date were £500 from the Mayor himself, £100 from Dr. Longstaff (who had since joined the Executive Committee) and £100 from Young's Brewery. Finally, Dawnay also put before the Sub-Committee several designs for a cap badge unique to the Battalion.

The Executive Sub-committee's second meeting took place on 14th July when it was announced that a series of recruitment marches had commenced earlier that week in order to attract more men, there having been no more than a trickle throughout June and a total of only 55 had signed up by the end of that month. As part of a programme of regular and high-profile church parades, the Battalion would also attend a service on the coming Sunday morning at Putney Parish Church. The Mayor had obtained the services of the Wandsworth Borough Brass Band for such marches and church parades. Dawnay also reported that he had approached the War Office with his suggested variation of the regimental cap badge, that this had been submitted to Lord Kitchener and that the matter was now before the Army Council.

The Regiment's standard badge consisted of the coat of arms of Guildford, surmounted by a crown and superimposed upon the star of the Order of the Garter, both emblems dating from the badges of

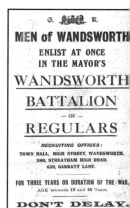

G. R.

MEN of WANDSWORTH

ENLIST AT ONCE
IN THE MAYOR'S

WANDSWORTH

BATTALION

— OF —

REGULARS

RECRUITING OFFICES :

TOWN HALL, HIGH STREET, WANDSWORTH.
380, STREATHAM HIGH ROAD.
439, GARRATT LANE.

FOR THREE YEARS OR DURATION OF THE WAR.
AGE between 19 and 40 Years.

DON'T DELAY.

The recruiting offices first expanded to Streatham. Author

The Battalion's unique version of the East Surrey Regimental badge.
S. Page

the 1st and 3rd Royal Surrey Militia.[6] Now, Dawnay proposed that the Wandsworth unit should have its own version of the badge with the Guildford arms replaced by those of Wandsworth and the borough's motto 'We Serve'. Somewhat unexpectedly, the grateful Army Council agreed to the request and the Wandsworth Battalion was permitted a unique change to the regimental badge. The Mayor and Council much appreciated the changes and the badges, produced by the Putney firm of George Starr and Co., were proudly worn by the volunteers, strengthening the camaraderie of the 'Pals' battalion.[7] Despite a request for a similar variation of badge, Bermondsey's 12th Battalion was not permitted any change. This was due to that unit's first commanding officer, Lieutenant-Colonel Beatson, being a firm respecter of tradition and refusing to support Bermondsey Council's wish to modify the East Surreys' badge. As a compromise Beatson did, however, permit the wearing of Bermondsey's coat of arms as a uniform collar badge.

Together with approval of the unit badge came confirmation from the War Office and the East Surrey Regiment that, with no deference to the superstitious, the new unit was numbered the 13th (Service) Battalion (Wandsworth) of the East Surrey Regiment.

Sergeant Billy Barton
A.White via C. Mason

The local press was then of great influence in encouraging the appeal to arms, an extensive campaign calling for volunteers between the ages of 19 and 38 to serve for three years or the duration of the war. Journalist Robert Harker of the *Wandsworth Borough News* had already led by example, while on the *Tooting and Balham Gazette* Mr A. J. Hartley did much to promote enlistment, especially among the local sporting personalities. To these a special appeal was made and among those who responded was Billy Barton of Iron Mill Road, Wandsworth, a well-known local boxer and footballer who had played for Fulham and Plymouth Argyle. Appointed as a Sergeant, Barton was to prove himself a popular NCO.

Route marches and parades around the borough continued as the main means of attracting recruits. Parades were held on Wandsworth, Clapham, Streatham and Tooting Bec commons, at East Hill, Wandsworth and at Southfields station. An appeal was made to local tradesmen, industrialists and residents to assist with the funds necessary to initially equip the Battalion and Dawnay used his own wide-ranging contacts and force of personality to persuade employers to let their staff volunteer. The Mayor also made sure that proper uniforms and other kit were obtained as soon as possible through the early appointment of an efficient Quartermaster. This served to ensure that the recruits at least looked soldier-like as they began their training before the public's gaze.

On Saturday, 10 July, the Battalion's existing strength marched from Wandsworth to Tooting Bec via Clapham and Balham. They were led by the Wandsworth Borough Brass Band and were followed in a motorcar by the Mayor and Mayoress, the Mayor also having generously provided cigarettes for the men. At Tooting Bec the members of the lawn tennis club entertained the Battalion's officers to tea before the march back to the Town Hall. On the return trip, 30 new recruits tagged along and were immediately issued with uniforms in Wandsworth before their fervour cooled.

Perhaps the greatest asset to the East Surreys' recruitment drive at this crucial point was Lance-Corporal Edward Dwyer of the Regiment's 1st Battalion. Dwyer had concealed his true age of only 16 years when he joined the Army in 1912 and he had gone to France early in the war with the Expeditionary Force, fighting in the retreat from Mons. In April 1915, while still a Private and only 19 years old, he had won the Victoria Cross at Hill 60 near Ypres in Belgium and returned to Britain for his investiture at Buckingham Palace on 28 June 1915. The timing of Dwyer's award could not have been better. By early July the 13th Battalion was still less than half way to its manpower target, but on the 17th, wearing his medal, the country's youngest VC holder joined the fledgling unit on another recruiting march through the streets of Wandsworth. Dwyer knew the area well, having been born and brought up in neighbouring Fulham, and then courting a Red Cross nurse (later to become his wife) from Balham. Dwyer accompanied the march to where it finished in

Lance-Corporal Edward Dwyer VC addressing a meeting in Trafalgar Square. Right, flanked by fellow NCOs after a recruitment meeting in Putney.

a field in Buckhold Road, Wandsworth. The field had been patriotically loaned by its owner Mr A. Rawlings for drill and parade purposes, with an adjacent field for a camp, on the understanding that a grant would later be made by the War Office to cover the cost of tents etc. At the field Lieutenant-Colonel Burton introduced the young hero to a large and admiring crowd and the next day Dwyer gave another address in Putney where his theme towards the young men who had yet to volunteer was "Make up your mind before you're fetched!" One of Dwyer's recruitment rally speeches, indeed perhaps one of those made in Wandsworth, was recorded and in it, Dwyer expressed his determination to return to France for another crack at the Germans. This wish was granted all too soon and when Dwyer failed to arrive for another parade in

Wandsworth it was learned he had been suddenly recalled to his unit. Later promoted to full Corporal, Dwyer was to die in action on the Somme in September 1916.

By the third week of July 1915, and after just three months of recruitment, the Battalion's complement of volunteers had been greatly enlarged. At the end of June only 55 men had been attested, but by 14 July there were 300 recruits. There had been no less than 157 applications for commissions, Burton and the Mayor had interviewed over 100 and 33 had been chosen, with only eight not coming from the borough, but deemed to have special qualifications. Of the local men, brothers Jim and Tom Hucker, formerly of 7 Dault Road and then of 20 Allfarthing Lane, Wandsworth, responded to the press appeal together and were both commissioned.[8] One of the exceptions to the 'local' rule was Ernest "Frank" Buckland who had returned to fight for his country from Argentina to where his family had emigrated to farm sheep on an estancia south of Buenos Aries. Joining the East Surrey Regiment, Buckland was posted as a Lieutenant to the 13th Battalion where he joined 'D' company.

Lt Jim Hucker, B Company.
Mrs P. Hucker
Lt Tom Hucker   Mrs P. Hucker

This boost in recruitment was thanks not only to parades and marches, helped by the attendance of Lance-Corporal Dwyer VC, but also to the extensive network of recruiting offices which the Council had set up throughout the borough. The main centre was still at Wandsworth Town Hall where, assisted by Sergeants Cavell and Rowe, another Victoria Cross holder directed efforts. Colour Sergeant James Smith was a quiet and unassuming Regular Army soldier who had gained his award with the Buffs (East Kent Regiment) in India in 1897. Normally making little of his honour, he had nevertheless worn it proudly during Lance-Corporal Dwyer's visit so that the East Surreys could display two heroes among their ranks. Under Sergeant Smith's supervision, branch recruiting offices had also been established at:

Lt Frank Buckland returned from Argentina to volunteer.
Mrs D. Hucker

- 489 Garratt Lane;
- adjacent to the L. C. & W. Bank,
	Wimbledon Park Road, Southfields;
- 8 Clapham Common South Side;
- 509 Wandsworth Road, Clapham;
- 25/27 High Street, Putney;[9]
- 380 Streatham High Road, (later
	transferred to 75/77 Streatham High Road);
- 157 Tooting High Street;
- 133 Upper Tooting Road;
- 121 Balham High Road.

After another week 630 recruits had enlisted and a week later this rose to a strength of nearly 900, swollen by a programme of Saturday-night recruiting visits to the borough's entertainment venues. On 24 July Lieutenant-Colonel Burton gained another 30 recruits at King's Hall, Tooting where the proprietor had helped considerably by offering a half sovereign to all who joined up. The following weekend the impetus was maintained when Alderman Dawnay, Lieutenant-Colonel Burton and other officers of the Battalion visited the Empire Picture Palace in Streatham. In a stirring speech made before the start of the evening's programme, Burton urged:

Lt George Head, another of the early officer recruits.
Mrs P. Hucker

"Now boys, remember that your girls will squeeze your hands and look into your eyes much more lovingly if you join the ranks. Girls, don't go out with him on Bank Holiday unless he puts on khaki."
One can imagine the response from a modern-day cinema audience.

The *Wandsworth Borough News* of 30 July 1915 trumpeted several news items covering the Battalion: a donation by Young's Brewery; Mr Rawlings's long-term loan of his Buckhold Road field as a training ground; and Wandsworth Council's agreement to provide free swimming facilities at the Borough's swimming baths. The *South Western Star* added the news that the 13th Battalion had also been granted free use of public paths, presumably for marching, 'by the generosity of the Wandsworth Borough Council.'

Further assistance came from the formation by the Mayoress, Mrs Dawnay, of a Women's Recruiting Committee in the Borough, with branches in each ward. One of the most energetic organisers was Mrs Melhuish of Tooting, wife of Alderman Melhuish, and the Committee pledged not just to encourage men to enlist, but also to raise money and help with munitions work. Sensibly, the ladies voted not to adopt the relatively common practice at that time of handing white feathers to young men not in uniform, though some instances were subsequently reported in Garratt Lane, Wandsworth.

The recruitment campaign had indeed become so successful that the only problem now came from coping with the scale of the response. Many of the earliest and most enthusiastic volunteers were either adventurous youngsters or men well over military age and unfit for service. It was the duty of the recruiting sergeants and doctors to weed these men out, but in July's rush to join up, many slipped through the net. This would later cause

Alderman and Mrs W P Mellhuish played a prominent part in recruiting in the Tooting area. Melhuish family

problems when the older men's fitness was found wanting during training and they had to be replaced before the Battalion went into action. The young boys, however, once over the initial induction hurdle, stood a much better chance of passing unnoticed through the rigorous physical demands of training. A number of under-age recruits consequently managed to stay with the Battalion and continue on to active service. One typical example was Walter Catchpole, originally from Manville Road, Balham. Although just 16 years old, young Catchpole was subsequently discovered not to be the youngest recruit to make

G. 👥 R.

MEN OF TOOTING!
FALL IN!!

THE LADIES' RECRUITING COMMITTEE FOR TOOTING, under the Chairmanship of Mrs. W. P. MELLHUISH, of 22, Totterdown Street, Tooting, is authorised by the Mayor of Wandsworth, to recruit a

TOOTING COMPANY
OF THE WANDSWORTH REGULARS.
(13th Service Battalion East Surrey Regiment).
Commanding Officer: LIEUT.-COL. ALFRED BURTON.

WILL YOU ANSWER THE CALL?
MEN BILLETED AT HOME.   EQUIPMENT READY.
JOIN AT ONCE.

Nearest Recruiting Offices:—
157, HIGH ST., TOOTING, and 133, UPPER TOOTING ROAD.

Ladies willing to assist the Committee are cordially invited to communicate with Mrs. W. P. MELLHUISH.

The recruiting staff were often ready to accept under-age boys.
T. Sims

it through initial training, but he was as enthusiastic as any man.[10]

Overall, so efficient were the Borough's efforts that Mayor Dawnay was able to claim that of the 115 Service battalions so far raised by individuals and other bodies, the one raised by Wandsworth was completed in the shortest time. Indeed, far more men came forward than were needed and the Mayor had already been warned by the War Office to order the formation of a depot company. He had consequently negotiated the use of 76 East Hill, Wandsworth, at a nominal rent, but it was soon clear that another battalion could be formed to take the excess. This 14th (Reserve) Battalion (Wandsworth) had between 500 and 600 men by November 1915, when it moved to Gravesend in Kent to await calls for any replacements needed by the parent 13th Battalion.

Now that full strength was reached for the 13th Battalion, training could begin in earnest and was carried out by NCO's from the 3rd (Reserve) Battalion and the East Surrey Regiment's Kingston depot. Lieutenant-Colonel Burton wasted no time in using the exercise and parade ground on the land donated by Mr Rawlings by the viaduct in Buckhold Road, Wandsworth. Previously, drill and parades had been carried out in the cramped confines of the Young's Brewery yard off Wandsworth High Street, a venue where the aroma of hops and fermentation would surely have not been conducive to good

Early parades in 1915 were held in the yard of Young and Co Brewery. Young & Co.

soldiering. Some of the companies also undertook training on Wandsworth Common and during the warm, sunny days, local residents often gave free refreshments to the men, most of whom still lived at home or in local billets when not training. The Buckhold Road parade ground provided the local population with the opportunity to observe the various aspects of training and considerable amusement was provided in the early days as the raw recruits struggled with the demands of drill.

With time now running short before the expected call to leave Wandsworth for a proper military camp, August was taken up with a round of social and fund-raising events. On Wednesday, 4 August, the Battalion paraded at Buckhold Road with a strength of 1,020 men to mark the first anniversary of the start of the war. At the ceremony Alderman Dawnay presented Lieutenant-Colonel Burton with a handsome chestnut charger while the Mayoress gave him a revolver.[11] On the 12th a very successful concert was held, attended by Major General Sir Francis Lloyd,

Private Tom Miles of the Transport Section, an early recruit. T. Miles

officer commanding 31st District, and Mr Samuel, the local MP. Both dignitaries addressed the men and the Mayor took the opportunity to announce that, as the War Office would not grant funds for Service battalions to have bands, he had purchased the required instruments himself and a Battalion band had been formed from men already recruited.[12] Alderman Dawnay also reported that the new badges were being made at his request locally and would shortly be distributed.

In anticipation of the Army calling the Battalion away, a series of Farewell Route Marches was undertaken, culminating with the final one on Saturday, 21st August 1915, which finished at the Buckhold Road parade ground. There, at 3 p.m., the Mayor and Councillors of Wandsworth entertained the Battalion to a 'Farewell Tea and Send Off', attended by some 2,000 guests and a huge crowd of the public who had been invited via handbills given out during the route march. The entire Battalion paraded and its smart appearance and bearing showed that a fine standard of morale and spirit had been achieved in what was still a relatively short period of time. In his speech, Alderman Dawnay led the crowd in a rousing "Farewell and God's Speed" and stressed how proud he and his Council were of what he termed 'Wandsworth's Own' or the 'Wandsworth Regulars', so-called

The Mayor's 'Farewell Tea and Send Off', 21st August 1915 at the Buckhold Road parade ground.
Author

in the belief that, coming from Wandsworth, they were bound to be as good as soldiers of the regular professional Army. It was also the occasion for a number of presentations by Alderman Dawnay. Sergeant Ayers, as the Battalion's first recruit, received a special badge and Captain Alexander and Lieutenant Tabrum, who had helped form the Battalion, were given inscribed silver cigarette cases. The Mayor revealed that he had also commissioned a silver sword to be presented that day to Lieutenant-Colonel Burton, but he had been let down by the makers and it would have to be forwarded later.[13] A final parting gift from the Borough came in the form of a regimental mascot, a Harlequin Great Dane that enjoyed the impressive name of 'Mac Os Aberarder'.

After the 'Farewell Tea', as many men as possible were granted a free weekend in expectation of a move to training camp. Yet it proved to be some time before such orders were received and so local training continued until, in September 1915, the Battalion paraded for the last time in Wandsworth. It was on this occasion that one of the training NCO's, Lance-Corporal Pavey, left upon becoming the Battalion's first NCO to be promoted to commissioned rank, being posted to the 9th Battalion, Bedfordshire Regiment. Lieutenant-Colonel Burton congratulated Pavey and acknowledged that he had transferred to the Battalion from another unit at the special request of the Mayor. He had been promoted to Lance-Corporal on his first day of service with the 13th Battalion and had been instrumental in recruiting and training the newcomers.

From their final parade, the Battalion left for its first camp at Witley, in Surrey. The journey was to be by train from Barnes and together with their transport,[14] the men marched there through Wandsworth and Putney, cheered everywhere on the way. The transport section was already shaping up well, there having been little difficulty in those days of attracting men with experience of, and a liking for, managing horses. One such recruit had been Private Tom Miles of Wandsworth, but on the journey to Barnes his horse had thrown him after putting a hoof down a drain. Dazed from his fall, 34-years-old

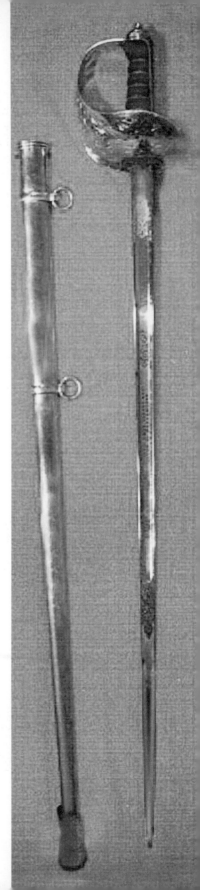

Sword presented to Lieutenant-Colonel Buton by Alderman Dawnay.
Via author

Miles was immediately the centre of attention for a group of local people lining the road and brandy was swiftly produced to revive the brave warrior off to war. Unfortunately the liberal drafts of spirit revived the soldier all too well and when Miles caught up with his comrades he was put on a charge for singing and being under the influence of alcohol. At Barnes families, friends and well-wishers swamped the little station to bid an emotional farewell to their men folk as they steamed off down the line.

On arrival at Milford station, just south of Godalming, the Battalion detrained and formed up for the march along Surrey's leafy lanes to Witley Camp. This was conveniently close to Aldershot, home of the British Army and only ten miles away just over the Hampshire border. Many of the men had rarely seen anything of the countryside beyond London, except perhaps on Bank Holidays when family visits were made to a popular heath or common in the suburbs. The training establishment at Witley, set up in the pine-wooded heathland that ran along both sides of the London to Portsmouth road, was unlike anything they had seen. Pre-war, Witley had been a well-known beauty spot, but now a bewildering assortment of wooden barrack huts, canteens and all the other institutions of an army under

In the Great War troops were encouraged to write home using postcards of their army camps.   Author

Morning wash at Witley Camp. Author

instruction overwhelmed the area. The huts, each holding a platoon, were raised above the ground with a short flight of steps leading to the entrance. Inside, long wooden tables, forms and trestle beds were ranged down both sides and a single stove for heating dominated the centre of the hut. The trestle beds consisted of three boards and there was an issue of two blankets in the summer and three in the winter. After local home billets in Wandsworth, this spartan standard of comfort was most unwelcome. But generally, camp life in this beautiful part of Surrey was a wonderful change for the Wandsworth men. When the day's duties were finished they would walk to the surrounding villages where some were intent on drinking as much beer as possible before returning. Others inevitably searched for the female company denied them in camp.

Adjacent to the huts each company had its own small parade ground, while a much larger area, for drilling the entire Battalion, was sited opposite the Battalion Orderly Room. Training now began in earnest and at last came the issue of proper bayonets and rifles, the short magazine Lee-Enfield Mark III. As infantry, the Wandsworth men had to learn that their rifles were the most precious of

possessions, "Care for your rifle as you would your wife" the NCO's were fond of saying, "….rub it with an oily rag every day". Pay books and identity discs were issued and ominously, the men were given instructions on how to make out their wills on the relevant page of their pay book.

About this time there had been considerable national press coverage about waste in Army camps and Witley was particularly mentioned when it was alleged that best quality food had been thrown away. Whatever the truth of the matter, there certainly was a plentiful supply of good food. Best Irish butter was readily available and among the extras not easily obtained at home, cake and canned fish were frequently to be had. Eating under camp conditions was a novelty to most, but everyone became used to it in time. Less attractive was early morning reveille with hurried ablutions which included the necessity of shaving in cold water. Another part of the daily routine was bayonet fighting, when the camp would echo to blood-curdling yells as men charged at hanging sacks. Elsewhere, specialists began to develop their skills, including signallers, Lewis machine-gunners and bombers.[15] The drum and fife band reached an impressive standard and last, but not least, the Battalion's transport continued to improve in efficiency and was brought up to strength including a full complement of officers' horses. Consequently, many of the officers learned to ride for the first time and after a spell of intensive tuition it was not unusual to see an officer carefully arranging two cushions before sitting down in the mess. It was said there was also a marked increase among those who preferred to remain standing at the bar. Sunday was normally the day for riding practice and the following narrative[16] from an unnamed officer of the 13th Battalion gives a humorous description of the trials and tribulations involved:

'I remember one such day when Captain Linge, [Linge had arrived to replace Captain Alexander as Adjutant] *who was a keen learner, and I, went for a ride over Thursley Common. Linge was riding a rather fractious pony he called Ginger (partly on account of its colour and partly on account of its nature). It was a lovely day, and we were both eager to get to the open country, where we could stretch our horses' limbs.*

Just after leaving camp, Linge dismounted to adjust his stirrup lengths and I went onto the Common thinking he would catch me up, as he knew the path I would take. Arriving on the Common I took my horse for a good stretch gallop of about a mile and then slowed up to

The Lee-Enfield Mk. III rifle.

Lt Buckland and men at Witley. Mrs D. Hucker

Lt Deacon and men at Witley. T. Sims

a canter. The air was keen, the sun was shining, and I was enjoying myself so thoroughly that the passing of time and the absence of Linge did not occur to me for half an hour, as I alternately cantered, trotted and galloped over the springy turf of Thursley Common.

Then I came back to Earth. Where was Linge? He must have been thrown and probably hurt. I put heels to my horse and galloped back the way I had come and the way Linge should have come, scanning the country for a riderless horse, or the inert figure that I felt sure I would find. At last I arrived back at the clearing where I had left him, and there he was – he and the horse both perspiring freely, Linge hopping on one leg and trying to reach the stirrup with the other, swearing volubly the while, whilst Ginger was prancing always just away from the raised foot. The picture presented such an anti-climax to my expectations that I laughed so much that I could barely hold Ginger whilst Linge mounted. He had been trying to mount ever since I had left him nearly three quarters of an hour ago, and he was in a mighty bad temper about it.'

Another unusual experience for many came when the enemy airship Zeppelin *L13* passed close to Witley Camp soon after 10 p.m. on Wednesday, 15 October 1915. The night sky was clear and the cigar-shaped airship was easily seen and heard cruising at about 10,000 feet. *Kapitanleutnant* Mathy and his crew dropped a number of bombs on the outskirts of nearby Guildford, but fortunately the Germans did not spot the attractive target of Witley Camp's row upon row of undefended barrack huts and the Zeppelin continued on its way.

Successful raider over England L13 under the command of Kapitanleutnant Mathy.

At Witley the 13th Battalion initially found itself part of the 41st Division, the very last of the new Kitchener divisions, and while the recruits continued their basic training their officers attended various classes on the theory of the job that lay ahead. In October, when Bermondsey's 12th East Surreys arrived at Witley and were also posted to the 41st Division,[17] the 13th Battalion was switched to the 39th Division commanded by Major-General Barnardiston. A move was made to the permanent brick-built Barrossa Barracks in Aldershot and further organisation of company, platoon and section structures was carried out there. While the total establishment of a battalion was around 36 officers and 1000 men, there would always be men on leave, undergoing training, or otherwise unavailable for front-line duties. A reserve was also normally kept at the battalion's transport lines in order to provide reinforcements in the event of losses. 'Trench strength' in the front line could therefore fall to about 20 officers and 600 men. A battalion was usually commanded by a lieutenant-colonel with a small headquarters staff including a major as second-in-command and an adjutant, usually a captain. Four rifle companies, A, B, C and D, were each commanded by a captain and held the unit's fighting soldiers. Companies were in turn sub-divided into four platoons, each led by a junior officer.

At Aldershot, some of the gaps created by drop-outs from initial training at Witley were filled. Among the replacements was newly-commissioned Second Lieutenant Courtney Embley, a Wandsworth man from Eglantine Road. Embley, a former pupil of Battersea Grammar School, had enlisted as a Private in the Queen's Westminsters on the day war broke out. He had been in the front line ever since and was home on leave when he learned of the new local unit then shaping up at Aldershot. Applying for a commission, Embley was immediately accepted on the strength of his active service to date and was swiftly despatched to catch up with the Battalion.

Letters home during this period show that at least some of the officers had to be billeted in civilian accommodation in Aldershot and this may have been a contributing factor to a march back to Witley Camp being ordered in early November. This time the training at Witley and on the surrounding heaths was to be on a brigade basis, the 13th East Surreys then being one of the four battalions of 118 Infantry Brigade of the 39th Division.

Brigade training involved day and night operations in the field. Trench digging began and for this purpose the area around Hindhead and in particular the Devil's Punch Bowl, was used. Normal practice was to train in open warfare during the day and to perfect the relief and occupation of trenches at night. Gradually, instruction in trench warfare extended to holding a trench position for about 48 hours. As welcome relief from the hard slog of training, weekend leave was usually available and although the cost of a return ticket to London used up two days' pay (at a shilling per day), there was always a demand for passes.

While training progressed, the weeding-out process of older men and young boys continued. Most of those rejected were returned to the 14th and 3rd (Reserve) Battalions and in return these units, along with the 10th and 11th Battalions, were responsible for providing replacements. More men came from the 'Derby Scheme', named after Lord Derby who was responsible for Army recruitment. In July 1915, the National Registration Act had been passed and the Local Government Board had been given the task of registering all men between the ages of 18 and 41 who had not yet enlisted. The Derby Scheme had then commenced in October 1915, when these men were contacted individually and asked to volunteer. Those who did volunteer were attested and then returned to their jobs until called up for service. Single men were the first to be called up, according to age, and married men were not called upon until the lists of single men had been exhausted. By mid-December of 1915 two million men had been processed under the Scheme, of whom half were married.[18] In practice, very little time was lost in calling up the single men after they had been attested and many of those in the replacement drafts which joined the 13th Battalion in late 1915 and early 1916 came from the Derby Scheme. They were to prove every bit as courageous and determined as the earlier volunteers.

Fresh drafts of men were also brought in from Wandsworth's 'overspill' battalion, the 14th East Surreys who had been undergoing basic training at Shoreham-on-Sea in Sussex. One such newcomer who transferred from the 14th to the 13th Battalion was Private Bonsey, originally from West Hoathly in Sussex, who recorded many of his wartime impressions in a document 'My War Services', now held by the The Queen's Royal Surrey Regiment Museum. Of his arrival at Witley Camp, Bonsey wrote:

> 'We entrained [sic] at Milford Station and then marched to the camp which was about a mile and a half from the station on the top of the hill going towards Hindhead. This camp was much larger than Shoreham Camp. Artillery as well as Infantry troops, numbering twenty thousand as far as I can remember. There were three long Y.M.C.A. huts as well as the Salvation Army huts, and a little row of shops where we could buy almost anything that we wanted. All these shops were made of galvanised iron which went by the name of 'Tintown'.
>
> At the Y.M.C.A. huts in this camp we used to have some fine concerts, one and sometimes two every week, amateur concert parties coming from London and Guildford. And during the intervals the party would throw us packets of cigarettes and tobacco which we used to scramble to catch. This part of the programme we used to look

forward to. These concerts were always well attended, sometimes it was impossible to get in after waiting for half-an-hour or so, so then you would hear once again, "Coming up Tintown?" And that was how we used to pass the evenings away, as it was so far to go down to Godalming, the nearest town and not much to see when you got there. It was in a public hall here that I first heard that well-known song "A Perfect Day" sung by a woman whose name I have forgotten. She was loudly applauded by singing this which she sang again as an encore to satisfy the audience which was chiefly soldiers.

Apart from a few general shops, there was nothing else to attract our attention. Training in this camp was much harder, the route marches were longer and our service kit was added to; we also had to carry iron weights, something like ninety two pounds in all. Our marches used to be anything from fifteen to eighteen and twenty miles a day all around the surrounding villages. We would sometimes go out three or four miles from camp and then practice skirmishing for an hour or two across Witley Common, perhaps some places ankle deep with water which made it heavy going, up steep banks and down the other side and so on, make a hard day's training. And then there were the forced route marches which used to be very trying. We would start out in the morning fresh and strong, fit for anything. On these marches we had to march four miles per hour and keep this up without one single halt, mile in and mile out.

The longest of these forced route marches that I have done was a twenty two mile march and on this occasion there was about half of the Battalion fell out, could not do any more of it. From about eleven in the morning they began to fall out, ones, twos and threes at a time, some looked fair done up, shirt and tunic collars undone to keep as cool as possible. It was not altogether the distance that beat us, it was the time in which we had to do it in, and how the Battalion got back to camp I hardly know, only about half of the Battalion marched in together, or rather walked in was more the word, we could not march, and the other half came in as best their legs would let them. Little batches of cripples, footsore, blistered backs and shoulders. Always, after these marches the Regimental Doctor was kept busy attending to sore feet and shoulders, which would mean some of the chaps being sick for about a week until their sores healed up again. It was on this march that we threw away our iron weights. I did for one. We had been marching for so long that we were almost done up. We kept asking for a halt but the O.C. would not halt us and so we started throwing away these iron weights to make our packs lighter. When we got in camp again at night all those that *threw away their weights were crimed. And then the next morning we were all outside the Battalion Orderly Room waiting to hear of our sentences of punishment. But we all got let off with a reprimand, the C.O. told us this training was for our own good, but we could not see that at all. We thought it was a bit stiff, but there it was, we got through that part of the training'.*

On 15 December 1915 a first change of commanding officer came when Lieutenant-Colonel Burton was posted to reserve duties with Wandsworth's 14th Battalion, then at Gravesend. In his place, Major W. C. Newton, a Regular Army officer who had served since 1902 with the Middlesex Regiment, took over and was promoted to Lieutenant-Colonel. Newton, who had recent experience of active service, arrived to find he had inherited a fast-improving unit. After several months the combined effect of healthy living and hard training had certainly begun to show itself in the 13th Battalion. The early route marches, as described by Private Bonsey, had resulted in many men dropping out along the way, but gradually, up to 20 miles were regularly mastered, even with full pack, rifle and equipment and the Battalion would return to camp, still at full strength and in high spirits, to the accompaniment of their band.

The training process also meant that the officers came to know

Lt-Col Newton replaced Lt-Colonel Burton in December 1915 at Witley Camp.
Mrs P. Hucker

Lieutenants George Head, Victor Scott, Reginald 'Jim' Hucker and Geoffrey Deacon, December 1915. Mrs P. Hucker

their NCO's and men much better. Talks to platoon members during halts in route marches, or during last visits to the huts just before 'Lights Out', gradually became something more personal. As time went on it was known which men were going to be short of kit at the kit inspection, and what their excuses would be. The young subalterns also learned that behind the gruff and forbidding exterior of an old Corporal might lurk one of the best, and kindest, of natures. And even if a certain Private Smith had not held down a decent job in civilian life, he was none the worse a soldier for that. Nor did the officers' growing appreciation of their men extend only to their characters. At foot inspection after a route march, the corn on a Private's little toe could be a matter of the greatest concern to his platoon commander. And a Sergeant's three-year-old daughter, who one day came to visit her father in camp, became a personal acquaintance of all who met her.

For their part, the men learned that their officers were not the superior types they had at first supposed. They learned to know that the officers used a certain amount of discrimination in the manner in which they berated them when they were at fault. Most also learned that straight dealings met with straight treatment. A violent and powerful string of language meted out by the Sergeant-Major, or some seemingly drastic punishment by the company commander for nothing more than a dirty button on parade, was not the mark of a permanent or personal vendetta. Rather, it was just another step along the road to greater efficiency and the important goal of *esprit de corps*. For the Christmas of 1915, as many men as possible were allowed to go home on leave, but those remaining in camp shared the festive occasion without regard to rank. On the evening of Christmas Day, officers visited both the Sergeants' Mess and the huts and canteens of the men to socialise over a pint of beer. On a more sombre note Witley Camp was where Private William Brackwell contracted a serious illness at that time and was returned to No. 3 General Hospital, Wandsworth Common.

Though many of the men enjoyed their time at Witley, over-exhuberance sometimes brought them into conflict with the local population. On one occasion, Lieutenant-Colonel Newton called the whole battalion out on parade to announce that he had received complaints from local farmers about damage the troops had done to property, including breaking down holly trees and hedges. The farmers had sent in a claim for damages and Newton had decided that the entire Battalion should collectively foot the bill by being stopped one shilling a week until the total was paid off. This move was particularly resented by the new arrivals, since the damage had been done before they joined the battalion. Consequently, the draft of some 100 men from the 14th Battalion protested to Newton, but he countered that they were now all part of the same unit and therefore they had no option but to comply with battalion orders. The shilling per week stoppage lasted some three months in total.

In January 1916 the 13th East Surreys underwent their shooting course on the rifle ranges at Ash, just to the north-east of Aldershot. It is not clear from the records whether there was any link to this, but the Battalion's first loss occurred on 25th February with the death of Private Stanley Neale, a 40 year old from Huntsmoor Road, Wandsworth, who was buried in Aldershot military cemetery. Neale achieved this unenviable distinction before the seriously-ill Private Brackwell died in hospital, back in Wandsworth, in April.

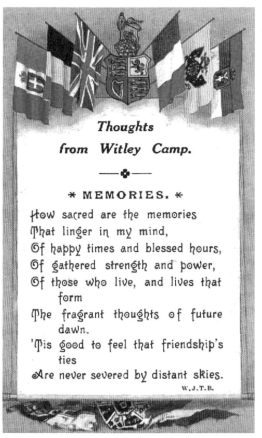

Distant skies' pressaged departure for the Western Front.

Despite its achievement of marksmanship, the Battalion had found itself left behind when the 39th Division departed for active service in February. Divisional command was not confident that all four battalions of 118 Brigade were adequately trained, while at the same time the 40th Division was in need of additional, fit and full-strength battalions. Units were moved accordingly.

The 40th Division was still training at Blackdown, near Aldershot, and was under the command of Major-General Harold Ruggles-Brise, formerly of the Grenadier Guards. Typically, a Division of the British Army consisted of some 20,000 men, 64 artillery guns, 54 machine guns, a squadron of cavalry, engineers, supporting transport and medical services. The bulk of the strength was in infantry, which at that time was organised into three brigades, each of four battalions. The three infantry brigades of the 40th Division were the 119th, 120th and 121st, commanded by Brigadier-Generals Cunliffe-Owen, the Hon. C. S. H. Drummond

B Company while at Blackdown Camp, spring 1916.   Mrs D. Hucker

Willoughby and J. Campbell respectively. 119 Brigade was entirely
Welsh in composition, the 120th a mixture of English and Scottish
units and the 121st completely English. In joining the 40th Division,
the 13th East Surreys transferred with the 14th Battalion, Argyll and
Sutherland Highlanders to the 120th Brigade of Brigadier-General
Drummond Willoughby where they joined the 11th Battalion, King's
Own Royal Lancaster Regiment and the 14th Battalion, Highland
Light Infantry. [19]

Making use of the battalion's newly-gained proficiency in route
marching, the move to Blackdown was conducted on foot, as
recounted by Private Bonsey:

*'We marched to this camp, a long march too, taking us all day from
eight in the morning until five o'clock in the afternoon, landing this
time at Blackdown, a camp near Frimley. These moving days were hard
work, having to carry everything with us. The regimental cooks getting
our meals ready on the field kitchens which always meant stew for
dinner, which was the usual thing on these marches. Then the cooks
would make us some tea. This would be poured in our greasy mess tins
as we had no hot water to wash them out, so you see our tea was
something like beef tea. We used to laugh about it. Perhaps we had had
mutton stew for dinner and that would make our tea nice and greasy,
quite a skin on top, especially if we let our tea get cold before we drank
it, which was the case sometimes, as it would soon get cold in our Dixies
standing on the ground, as we had to use the ground for our chairs as
well as our tables on these marches. Well, this part of the camp where
we were billeted in was a new part, all new huts and fixtures, spotlessly
clean and we had to keep it like this too…This division had one Brigade
of Bantams [troops of short stature], all Welsh troops, in it. They were
all short fellows, about five feet in height, but still well built. They had*

a white goat for a mascot which wore a red rug with their regimental badge and coat-of-arms on it. It always walked at the head of the battalion, just behind the Commanding Officer...There was also a German prisoner-of-war camp here while I was at this camp. It was at this camp that I had my first firing course. We fired our course on the Pirbright ranges adjoining this camp. This took us three or four days firing at different distances, and I remember only too well we had it wet every day and a driving cross rain and wind which took our bullets off the mark. At this course I did well, getting a second class shot, and for another three or four days we would be in the butts at the targets, marking for the other regiment that would be firing. The targets were different sizes, the largest about seven feet square and the smallest about four feet square. These were used for grouping the others for hitting the bullseye, but these targets were longer range firing up to one thousand yards. This firing course finished, we marched off to North Camp, Aldershot for our final course of firing. This lasted ten days. We used to be up early in the morning and start off at half past six for Ash ranges. Almost the same as on the other ranges, only much larger, so

The Battalion's officers at Witley, as depicted in The Tatler magazine. Mrs D. Hucker

that two battalions could fire their course at the same time. I never did so well at this course, but I did not mind that as afterwards I found out they picked the best shots out for snipers. This meant more dangerous work when we got overseas, although the snipers got sixpence a day extra for passing out as a first class shot. We were firing all day on Sunday just the same as on weekdays on account of the other battalions that wanted the ranges after us. We also handed our billets over to the relieving troops, that was how it worked, we then had to march back to Blackdown Camp again'.

Blackdown was generally enjoyed apart from the mud (and later the dust) and was enlivened by the opportunity to pass ribald comment on German prisoners of war housed in a nearby camp at Frith Hill . Training and hard physical exercise had continued the weeding out process through the winter of 1915-1916 and into the early spring. Another battalion which joined the 40th Division at this time with over 1,000 men was reduced to only a little over 200 following medical examinations, but the 13th Battalion was now fit and ready for action. As confidence grew, the Wandsworth men prepared to demonstrate their ability on the first occasion of a General's visit. Again, the Battalion's anonymous chronicler recorded[20] the episode:

'The officers polished up their 'Infantry Drill'; the non-commissioned officers busied themselves sorting out the men who were most efficient in forming fours, in order that on the parade itself they should be found in the front ranks of their companies; buttons were polished vigorously, equipment fitted; and the Battalion bugler betook himself to the fastness of the hills to add the 'General Salute' to his somewhat shaky repertoire, which at present was composed of 'Reveille', 'Cook House', 'Last Post', and a very confused idea of 'Orderly Room'.

The day arrived, the Battalion paraded fully 20 minutes too soon, and the General was fully 20 minutes late. It was, of course, at this moment that the General approached along the one road upon which we had not posted a look-out, and instantly there was dire confusion. The Colonel hurriedly gave the command "Shun! Slope-Arms!" followed by a short pause, during which the Great One himself left the road and approached us, then by "General Salute, Present-Arms!", a long drawn-out rustle of unaccustomed hands juggling with rifles, and out of the tail of my eye I saw Regimental Sergeant-Major Birch[21] rushing stealthily towards the bugler, who was apparently overawed by the situation, saw him whisper hoarsely in the manner of all Sergeant-Majors, saw that worthy bugler waver, gather together his scattered faculties, raise the bugle falteringly to his lips, and then the cloud

BlackdownCamp – the gymnasium was an essential tool in getting recruits fit for active service.
Author

seemed to pass from his mind and with a magnificent flourish he blared forth, and bugled as he had never bugled before – the 'Last Post'.

The face of the General for a few moments was a study. But, thank heavens, he saw the humour of the situation, and what seemed to us at the time to be a tragedy passed by as one of the many such humorous little incidents that marked the progress of the Battalion where we were all learners, but enthusiastic ones at that.'

120 Brigade was now assessed as being up to war strength. The final stages of training were undertaken, including the divisional route march in which all battalions of the 40th Division participated and carried full overseas kit. In March 1916, word spread that the Division might be sent to Ireland as a result of the rebellion in Dublin. This was discounted, however, when several of the senior staff and regimental officers began trips to France to observe front-line conditions. Early in May, His Majesty King George V inspected the Division. He pronounced himself pleased with the martial bearing of the men paraded before him and added he was sure their steadfast discipline would serve them well in the trials to come. His Majesty was not to be disappointed.

At last, news arrived to confirm that the Battalion would proceed overseas. Final embarkation leave was granted, but only four days could be spared for the men to settle matters at home. Consequently, several found themselves on a charge after overstaying their leave and two men did not return at all in time for departure. They were later brought to France under armed escort to rejoin the Battalion, but not before serving 96 days field punishment, as well as paying for their escort. This meant soldiering for months without any pay and field punishment included the humiliation of being strapped to the wheels of a transport limber for two hours in the morning and two hours in the afternoon every day.

Families and friends made their way down to Blackdown in the days preceding departure. As was to be expected, numerous rumours still abounded as to the Battalion's destination, but as helmets and gas masks were finally issued, there could be no doubt – the Western Front.

On 28 May 1916 an advance party left Blackdown and crossed from Folkstone to Boulogne that night in order to make arrangements for the arrival of the remainder of the 40th Division and movement orders were received for 3rd June. The night before, the last in England for some time and perhaps for ever, brought out high spirits as the men used up their secret caches of beer and spirits, dressed up in what old clothes they could find and set off on a torch-lit procession through the camp, beating a tune on old biscuit tins. As they passed through neighbouring battalions' lines, men from other units joined them and even the officers left their quarters to watch good-humouredly and laugh.

On the morning of 3 June 1916, exactly a year after receiving its first recruit, the 13th Battalion marched to near-by Frimley railway station. There the total strength of 34 officers and 970 men was split into two parties and entrained for the docks at Southampton. The docks contained many large ships which were of great interest to the men, most of who had not seen their like or size before. Lieutenant-Colonel Newton took one group aboard the 'Queen Alexandria' troop ship while Major Johnson, the Battalion's second in command, led the other detachment onto a black-painted liner, the 'Hunscraft', so-called as it had been captured from the Germans. The famed liner the *Acquitania* was berthed nearby, fitted out as a hospital ship and dwarfing the Battalion's two ships. Private Bonsey's journal gives a detailed and colourful description of the train and sea journey:

'*This was a morning. Some of the chaps were up early in the*

France - and for most units, the route to the Front entailed much marching. G. Richardson

morning singing about and woke up the others. We got no more sleep that night. We had an early breakfast, somewhere about five o'clock I think it was. After breakfast all the huts had to be cleaned out, so we all got our packs outside and some of us had to get on with the cleaning of them up. Well after we had finished clearing our huts out, it soon came time for us all to fall in on parade, this time to say "Goodbye" to Old England, for a while anyway. We all fell in on parade and stood there with our heavy packs on, waiting for the order to quick march while the other Brigades were already marching past us going down to the station. Then came our turn to move off. We were all fairly happy, some looking a bit down, those with wives and children at home whom they were leaving behind I expect.

This entraining took us a good while this time on account of all the transport horses and limbers that had to be put in the trucks behind, but we were all on rail and started off before midday. We had a lovely send off from the people when we started, they all wished us good luck and those that were farther away we could see them waving their handkerchiefs to us. This was the reception we got all the way down the line and until we could see the sea and the big boats waiting to take us.

We stayed in the trains until they took us right on to the quay quite close to where the boats were at anchor. We then got out of the trains. We were all numbered off to see that we were all present and then we were marched down to the boats where we marched straight on in two ranks. When we got aboard the ship [the Hunscraft] we were taken down to the bottom deck so that they could load the old boat up alright. This was quite a small boat compared with the other one that brought

Troops lining up to board their transport for France are able to view at close-hand the hostital ship Aquitania.

the other two companies and the whole of our transport besides some of another Brigade. It was in the afternoon, near tea time, that we got aboard and when tea time came around we were told that we could get a drink of tea at the canteen on the ship, but there was such a crowd that I could not get anywhere near it, but I managed to get a drop from one of the others that had been more fortunate than me. Our tea consisted of biscuits and jam, while others had cheese. We sat down on the deck and had our tea and when we had emptied our jam jars we threw them overboard. We soon made the ship look untidy at anchor in the docks, this was about seven o'clock at night and we began to wonder what the Captain was waiting for. Afterwards we found out he was waiting for it to get dusk so that the enemy submarines would not be able to see us quite so easy. About eight o'clock they loosened her from her moorings and we began drifting out down Southampton waters right through the Solent. The sea was very calm through here and we could see the coast both sides of us for miles up the Solent. By the time we were nearing the English Channel it was almost dark. Here three of our torpedo boat destroyers joined us as well as another big liner which was by our side right through the Channel in case anything happened so that they could take us aboard that ship. It was here that we had orders to put our life belts on, we each had one of these belts aboard. We began to think that something was waiting for us farther out but they did not catch us. Our destroyers were very busy, one going well ahead and the other two circling our boats all the way across, but we managed to get across alright, going at full speed all the way as the sailors told us we were being chased by a German submarine. Ours being a fast boat we could keep ahead of the submarine but the other boat with all the other troops and transport had to stop in home waters. As we were getting near the French coast we could see the lights in the distance and for eight or nine miles from Le Havre we were guided in with lights at about every hundred yards it seemed, until we got right into the quayside and anchored down. This was about two o'clock in the morning. They did not let us get off then, not until the next day about dinner time, so we just laid down to get an hour or two's sleep. When we woke up were just in time to see our boys coming in on the other boat, it had taken them twelve hours to come over, we got across in six hours.'

Though the sailors may have exaggerated the submarine threat, it was nevertheless real, for the Battalion war diary records that German submarines were known to be operating at the time, everyone had to wear a lifebelt and an escort of destroyers was provided as soon as they were clear of the Solent.

As dawn broke on the 4th, the men gathered on the upper decks, eager to gain what was, for the vast majority, their first impression of a foreign land. They called across to a number of old Frenchmen on the quayside who tried to reply as best they could, but only managed to raise laughter. For most of the troops, this was their first experience of a foreign land and a foreign language. For the moment, all was fun. Many dangers undoubtedly lay ahead, but morale was high. The men had heard a good deal of the fine work already accomplished by the other regular and service battalions of the Regiment in the field. As the last unit of the East Surreys to be sent overseas, there was fierce determination that the 13th Battalion should live up to the Regiment's proud record.

Souvenirs sent home to Wandsworth by Pte. T. Miles. T. Miles.

Chapter 3

FRANCE

T he 13th Battalion's initial destination proved to be Le Havre and after coming ashore the men formed up on the quayside and marched out of the docks. Reaching the town's wider streets and better houses, they turned onto the seafront and marched north for about a mile before starting to climb a long hill. They passed the headquarters of the Belgian Government in exile, housed in a large hotel, and a camp of wooden huts until, after another mile or so, the Battalion reached No 1 Rest Camp just outside the town. By now much of the excitement of foreign shores had worn off as most of the men had found it impossible to sleep onboard ship and had soon become weary on the uphill march. The road was uneven and muddy and at the camp itself there was little in the way of comfort. Accommodation was in the form of tents deep in mud and into which as many men as possible were crammed. On a more positive note one officer, no doubt with more spacious accommodation than many, wrote of the 'splendid view over the bay and Channel.' Later in the day exploration of the town was permitted and when the men returned to camp they found considerable excitement from the first English newspaper reports covering the great sea battle at Jutland.

After the poor conditions in camp the men were relieved to march back down into Le Havre early the next morning. But at the railway station more discomfort awaited. There, two typical French troop trains stood, their carriages with the unwelcoming inscription *Hommes 40 – Chevaux 8*. As far as the men were concerned the vans were much more suitable for animals, yet forty, or even fifty troops with all their equipment and kit were herded into each of these draughty and spartan trucks. It was impossible to lie down and rest, even on long journeys, and in order to get a breath of fresh air the sliding doors were normally kept open. Good humour was nevertheless still the order of the day and as the troops awaited orders to climb aboard, the railway carriages were chalked over with ribald comments. The men were issued with a day's rations of biscuits, cheese, jam and bully beef, but it then seemed to take hours before, at last, the engine started whistling, the command was given to climb aboard and Lieutenant-Colonel Newton paced down the length of the train to make sure all

HOMMES 32 40
CHEVAUX (EN LONG) 8

WE ARE GOING TO STRIKE

British troops give a hearty cheer from one of the infamous French carriages.

was well. It has been said that troop trains travelled so slowly that it was possible to get out and pick flowers in the course of a journey. In reality the men did find it possible, as some relief from the cramped conditions, to periodically jump down to stretch their legs in a gentle jog alongside the train. At a stop it was the usual practice to obtain hot water from the engine to make tea and if a halt were made near habitation, swarms of French children would descend on the train, clamouring for "beeskeet" and "boulibif".

The train took the Battalion through Rouen and as far as Lillers, not far from Béthune, from where the men then marched to billets in the nearby villages of Faucquenhem and Lières. Generally, NCO's and other ranks slept in barns, while officers shared spare rooms in cottages. Private Bonsey recalled:

We all got out and paraded in the street, all the French people stopping to look at us. We then had to march to our different villages where we were to be billeted, the first time amongst French people. Our billets were empty sheds and barns, just wherever the officer could find us room. This village was inhabited, as it was some thirty or forty kilometres from the firing line (about 25 miles), so we were practically safe here. We were not allowed any lights at night owing to the danger of catching alight the old buildings. We could get sweets and tobacco here in some of the shops, and also bread from bakers if we kept it quiet, as these French people were all rationed with food stuffs, so we just tucked it under our tunics until we got to our billets. It was surprising how some of these old French people still stayed on, even in these conditions. We had to do parades just the same here, as if we were at home, and also keep ourselves just as clean, although this was a job here, laying rough in these sheds and barns. We soon found a few lice as well as rats and mice to keep us company, but we soon got used to them too. We were issued with more kit here, a different kind of gas helmet adapted for tear gas shells and then came what was known as our iron rations. These were one tin of bully beef and some hard biscuits which were put in calico bags. These we had to carry with us everywhere; we were not allowed to eat these without orders, they were meant for in cases of emergencies when no other food could be got to us, so it was up to us to look after these iron rations as they were called.

Although the Battalion was still at a safe distance from the front lines, most men spent at least part of their first night here listening to the distant thunder of artillery and wondering what lay ahead. Yet for the next ten days, only field training and route marching were undertaken, interrupted by the task of filling in old trenches at

The 13th East Surreys received their first experience of trench life in the devastated Lens area.
G. Richardson

Ecquedecques on 12 June and a memorial service the following day for the late Field Marshal Lord Kitchener.[22]

A new arrival who joined the Battalion at this point in order to make up a full complement of officers was Second Lieutenant Gordon Alexander, also newly-commissioned, but whose new officer's 'pip' did not reflect the valuable front-line experience he had already gained in the ranks. Indeed, there was more to Alexander than first met the eye. Despite his Scottish name, the 30 year old came from a Jewish family in south-west London and was an urbane Old Harrovian with an international reputation as a fencer, having become Amateur Foils Champion of Great Britain in 1913. Giving up a lucrative career in the City as a stockbroker (having followed in his father's career footsteps), he had volunteered in August 1914 as soon as war was declared and enlisted as a humble Private in the 10th Battalion, Royal Fusiliers. He had gone to France with them the following year and saw active service before returning to England for a commission in the East Surrey Regiment in January 1916. Perversely first posted out of the regiment to the 14th Royal Sussex, he was nevertheless soon transferred back to the 13th East Surreys on their arrival in France in June 1916 to fill a gap in the numbers of the subalterns, bringing maturity in both years and experience. He quickly fitted in with his new unit and enjoyed not only a warm relationship with his brother officers who nick-named him, for some forgotten reason, 'Togo', but also, perhaps because of his previous service in the ranks, with his platoon Sergeant and men who knew him as Alec.

On the 16th, the entire 40th Division (part of First Army) moved to Sailly-Labourse and Noyelles. From there the Division's three brigades were sent up to the front line for instruction by the 15th Division which was holding the Hulluch and Hohenzollern Redoubt sectors, north of the coal-mining town of Lens.

The Western Front, of which the Wandsworth men now found themselves a part, consisted of two huge opposing forces interlocked in battle on a frontage of several hundred miles. This front had no exposed side flanks since to the east the border with neutral Switzerland provided one barrier, while to the west the front ended on the North Sea coast. The conflict was, with air power still in its infancy, primarily one of infantry and artillery. The war's first winter, in 1914, brought torrential rain and mud, making offensive operations extremely difficult, and had caused each side to dig in. The result was the greatest trench system ever dug with just a narrow strip of

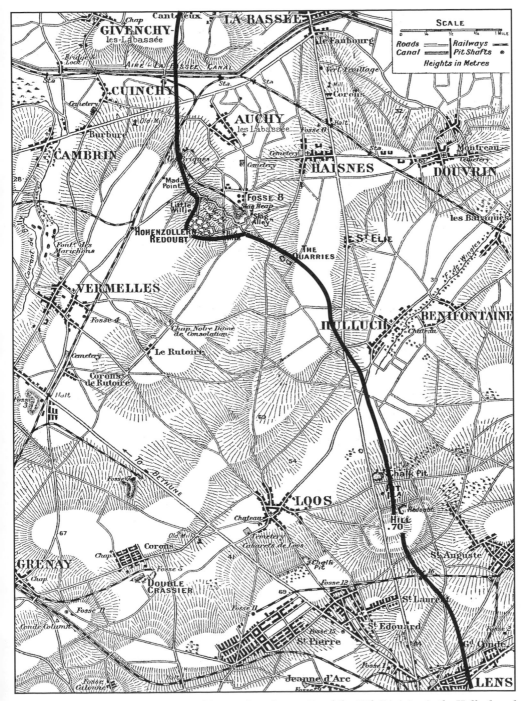

The 13th East Surreys received instructions from units of the 15th Division in the Hulluch and Hohenzollern Redoubt sectors.

British trench near Hulluch.

territory, known as No Man's Land, separating the two sides. By June 1916, the trenches were well and truly consolidated. The communication trenches were all named and the fire trenches systematically numbered from right to left of sector. Some dug-outs were very deep and bomb proof against all but the larger shells. Trenches became named after the streets and places of the localities in Britain from which the occupying units were drawn, so it became possible to know who had first improved certain sectors.

For their introduction to the grim reality of the trenches, the 13th Battalion joined 44 Brigade of the 15th Division and each company of the East Surreys was then attached to a battalion of the brigade. As this attachment commenced, Private Moorey became the 13th Battalion's first active-service casualty on 16 June 1916, when he was wounded by shrapnel. The next day saw a further four men wounded and another admitted to hospital with shock. On the 18th three more men were wounded and Private James Norris, a 34 year old from Alfred

Cottages, Tooting Grove, gained the sad distinction of becoming the first soldier of the Battalion to be killed in action when he was hit by enemy shelling. Grimly, there were no remains to be buried and Norris is therefore commemorated on the Loos Memorial as having no known grave.

Contrary to the record of the Battalion's war diary, Private Bonsey recalled a different incident leading to the unit's first active service fatality:

The battalion was in the trenches here at a village by the name of Hulluch and around the Hohenzollern Redoubt just north of the town of Loos [Loos-en-Gohelle, generally abbreviated to Loos]. *The front trench here in places was only fifty yards from the Germans who could be heard quite plainly. I used to go up the line every night with the water carts from here. We would get them filled during the day ready for going up at night with the rest of the other battalion rations. There used to be four limbers and our two water carts. We used to start off just before it got dark. All these limber wheels were covered with old motor tyres to stop them from making so much noise. These old tyres had to be cut asunder and then wired on round the fellies. All the main roads were made of granite sets here, so we had to be careful not to make too much noise. We would open out to one hundred yard intervals when we were within a mile from the line in case they started shelling us. We used to bomb one another here as it was fairly easy to throw a bomb into their front line trench. Our first casualty with our men happened here. A German aeroplane came over head dropping aerial darts. These were steel pins about six inches long. It was impossible to see, or even hear, these darts falling, and one of these struck one of our fellows in the thigh. He was sitting on the fire bay taking a rest, but the poor fellow died soon afterwards. These darts were deadly things, they would easily go clean through you without a sound.*

After four days of this graphic introduction to war the East Surreys moved back to Bruay, five miles south-west of Béthune and battalion headquarters were established at 555 (and later at 525 bis) Rue Maréchal French, Les Brebis, only some eight kilometres from the front line. The men were billeted in empty houses that had been badly damaged, hardly any doors or windows, fire places or grates remained. Many of the houses were really only a heap of ruins, yet still some of the local French people, especially the older inhabitants, had stayed on to brave the regular shelling and aerial bombing. Private Bonsey had his first encounter with good fortune here:

I once had a large piece of shrapnel from a shell just miss my head and stick in the bank where I was sitting...I was only about ten yards away from where the shell exploded, and two Royal Army Medical men were sitting just close here too on an empty box which they had just emptied into the incinerator to burn. They were from a small hospital in the village of Les Brebis. Well, these two RAMC men both stopped a packet. This was an expression we used amongst ourselves out there. One poor chap had one of his feet cut clean off by a piece of shrapnel from it, and the other chap had a big slice cut clean off one of his buttocks, but this poor chap soon bled to death although they were only about one hundred yards from the back of the hospital, the other chap we never heard how he got on as we soon moved from here after this happened, and once again they missed me. One other time I was walking through a road in a village up the line, the enemy was shelling it as usual, when a piece of shrapnel from one of the shells cut my identity disc clean off my left wrist and never touched my arm. All I felt of this was a sudden faint snatch at my wrist. And several other shaves, but of course other chaps had the same experiences many a time. Some of the chaps longed to get a Blighty wound as they called them, just to get away from the line for a change as it got very tiring, month after month the same routine.

It was here, too, that the Battalion first saw tunnellers at work, preparing a shaft in order to place a mine under the Germans' positions. The tunnellers were all short, sturdy men, peace-time coal miners, and the Wandsworth soldiers helped by emptying out the soil and stone spoil, carried out in sandbags, along the top of the trenches.

More training followed until, on 11th July, the time finally came when the men of Wandsworth were deemed ready for the war in earnest. Moving up to the front line, the 13th Battalion relieved the 12th Battalion, Suffolk Regiment in the Maroc sector, just north of the village of Loos and opposite the Hohenzollern Redoubt. With the ordinary soldier's eye for everyday issues, Bonsey remembered this dangerous move for other reasons:

We stayed around here for several weeks, to and fro to the lines, a few days in the line and a few days out in these billets. As reserves, our part in the line here ran through the village by the name of Maroc; quite a small village. We would be in support here. At one time it had been a very pretty place as there were still flowers in the garden of some of the houses. The houses were all of the same pattern and the roads were all straight. We used to billet in the cellars of these houses and the cellar, I was in one that had an old box mattress in it, so we four watermen were in luck's way for once. This district around here was a coal mining district, three mines quite close. We got to know this part very well as we were to and fro the line from these surrounding villages for about

The German caption reads: Bei Hulluch (nordich v. Lens) Graben-Spiegel. Using a trench mirror near Hulluch, north of Lens.

four months. It was up the line here that I saw a whole cheese out on the ground, it looked as if it had been there some time as we could see where the rats had been at it. Rations became too scarce to see anything like this again.

Initially, the Battalion enjoyed a relatively peaceful existence in the Hulluch, Maroc and Calonne trench sectors, alternating with rest periods which were spent in billets in or around Bully and Grenay. The weather was generally warm and fine and while the complement of officers was still being brought up to full strength, there were as yet few demands on the Battalion to leave the protection of their trenches. On 13 July, however, after rifle grenades and artillery bombardments had been exchanged with the enemy, a small party from B Company crept out at night to place notice boards in the enemy's wire. A crude but effective form of front-line propaganda, the boards gave, in German, news of the Allies' successes on both the Western and Eastern Fronts.

Another incident of note during this period came on the 23rd of the month when, during a foray to repair the wire defences, Second Lieutenant C. J. Noakes, one of the officer reinforcements who had only arrived four days before, was hit and slightly wounded. More positively, Second Lieutenants Deacon and Thompson led the Battalion's first raiding party from the Calonne sector over to the German lines. While they did not succeed in capturing a prisoner as hoped, the raiders nevertheless managed to cause considerable commotion and inflicted a number of casualties on the enemy.[23]

Although not engaged in any major actions, the Battalion was nevertheless exposed to considerable danger while holding the front-line trenches. Enemy snipers and artillery bombardments maintained a steady, if small-scale, drain on resources. One such enemy shelling came on 8 August 1916, in retaliation for an Allied bombardment by rifle grenades, Stokes guns and trench mortars which had been ordered purely in order to test the Germans' response. Unfortunately for the 13th East Surreys, the response was only too vigorous. Although the return fire and shelling was eventually subdued by Allied artillery, the Battalion suffered ten men wounded and five killed. All were subsequently buried in the Philosophe British War Cemetery on the outskirts of the nearby village of Mazingarbe. They lie in a rare sward of green in the shadow of the now-defunct coal industry's brooding spoil heaps which still blight this part of the countryside today. There, the cemetery's register reveals a heart-rending statistic. Of those killed on the 8th one is recorded in plot I B 26 as:

> Pte. Reginald Albert TWYFORD, 13064. A Company, 13th Bn. East Surrey Regiment. Killed in action 8.8.16. Age 15. Son of John William Twyford, 70 Merton Road, Wandsworth.

Somehow, young Reginald (originally from 80 Pirbright Road, Wandsworth) had succeeded in concealing his true age when he was among the first to volunteer, at the age of just 14, for his local battalion in 1915. His great adventure had come to a tragic end just two months after arriving in France.[24]

For the remainder of August, the 13th East Surreys alternated between front-line trenches and reserve billets in the Loos area, the latter not being popular with the men on account of the stench of dead bodies trapped beneath the ruins from the battle there in September 1915. The odour could be detected some way outside the shattered town, but despite this, Battalion headquarters were first established in the ruins of Loos itself, and then at 209 Rue de Mazingarbe, Petit Sain. It was therefore a welcome move when the 40th Division was relieved by another formation and was sent out of the line for a rest. The

An early tragedy – the grave of Pte Reginald Twyford, killed in action 8 August 1916, aged 15.

Battalion marched back, stopping at villages for two or three days at a time, cleaning themselves up and carrying out a variety of drills to keep the men as fit as possible. Yet, even well away from the front, danger still stalked the Battalion, as Private Bonsey recorded:

It was while we were at this village that one of our dispatch riders got hit from a German long-range gun, while he was going through the village on his motorcycle. It blew a large hole in the road almost blocking it, and also killing the fellow. I expect the enemy could see us at this village from their observation balloons as we had several shells over after that. We were about ten miles from the line here at a village called Barlin. We could just see their balloons above the trees.

On the 18th the first officer to be lost, Lieutenant Wilfred Chambers, was one of two men killed, while among another four who were wounded was B Company's commander, Captain Max Pemberton. Chambers was a recent arrival, but had served with the East Surreys since 1914. He survived just under a month with the 13th Battalion and two days later another officer was killed when C Company's commander Captain Leopold Merryfield, a 34 year old married man from Madeira Road, Streatham, was fatally wounded.

A steady trickle of killed, wounded and sick continued throughout September although, despite heavy artillery bombardments from both sides, the Battalion's war diary considered this to be a period of relative inactivity. Nevertheless, and even without any direct contact with the enemy, the Battalion had already suffered around a hundred casualties by the time it left the Lens and Loos sector. Total unit fighting strength at this time was some 620 officers and men and therefore, after just three months in the front line, casualties amounted to over 16%. Without any real fighting having yet been encountered, this did not bode well for the future. More worrying still was the fact that three officers had already been killed and a further three wounded, representing approximately 30% of the commissioned strength. Such losses also excluded accidental injuries and sickness which further weakened front-line resources. On 2 September one soldier had inadvertently wounded another when aiming at a low-flying enemy aeroplane and on the same day Lieutenant-Colonel Newton had to be evacuated to the Corps Rest Station for three weeks with a recurrence of trench fever, a legacy of his previous front-line service with the Middlesex Regiment. His latest bout would have been aggravated by the deteriorating weather, heavy rains having started to once again turn the battlefield into a quagmire and a noticeable chill giving advance warning of the approach of a harsh winter. From a command point of view, sanitation, second only to the care of weapons, was a great priority in the trenches and the British Army prided itself on its arrangements, which they considered superior to those of their French allies. Nevertheless, a new type of fever, trench fever, had developed from infections brought about by the bites of lice. The disease itself was not serious to the individual, but was enough to remove a man from the front line as a casualty.

For the average 'Tommy', however, priorities were usually clothing-related, as shown by the following brief letter, written to his mother in Wimbledon, by Private Herbert Bell:

> Pte. H. Bell
> 13th E. Surrey Regt.
> attd 120 Inf. Bde.
> 16/9/16
> Dear Mother
> Just a few lines to let you know I am quite well. It is rather a long time since I heard from you. Well, I am just asking you if possible to send out at once, 1 shirt, 1 pr. pants, 1 pr. socks, please. Also you know, the winter is coming on so if you would send me out my grey sweater, a scarf, and a pr. of fur lined kid gloves. I know it is rather a long list but you see they are absolutely essential. I am still in the best of health, as I hope it leaves you at present. How are all the boys, and Dorothy, are they all right?
> Well I must close now, with love from your loving son, Bert[25]

An officer of the battalion, writing home to his family at the same time, was full of praise for this spirit of getting on with the job and not grumbling, 'the men are simply magnificent' he wrote.

In late September and early October 1916, the Battalion moved onto a more aggressive footing, back in the Loos sector, as the weather continued to worsen. The enemy was known to be tunnelling close to the 13th Battalion's lines and one night guttural conversations could even be heard. In a letter to his family in Argentina, Lieutenant Frank Buckland recorded:

> The Germans have dug an underground post very near to this trench. Last night I listened to them talking. I couldn't help wishing that I had learnt more from Miss Beck [Buckland's childhood German governess] when I had the chance.

Private Bonsey also noted this novel form of warfare:

> It was in this village (Loos) that we started tunnelling. These men were miners, picked out from different regiments as they were used to

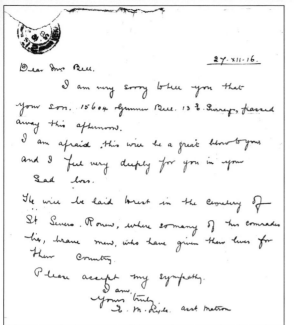

News of Pte Bell's death, dated 27.12.16. Mrs C. Henderson

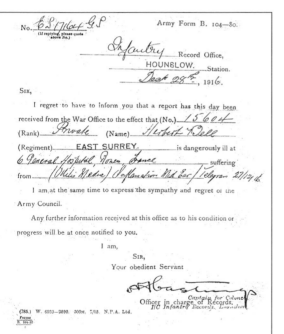

News of Pte Bell's wounding, dated 28.12.16. Mrs C. Henderson

this kind of work. Afterwards they were known as the tunnelling company. They used to work under the supervision of the Royal Engineers.[9] They would start digging a tunnel from our trenches and burrow right under the enemies' trenches, taking care to go well below them. The enemy also started to mine when they heard we were at it so it was a race to who could get finished first. As it happened, we did this time, so our engineers blew it up. We managed to take the portion of ground that was blown up and a little more with it, but we had a few casualties over this I remember. As it upset the Germans for a time, they made a raid once or twice on our lines to try to get it back again, but they never did.

The British retaliated by sending out their own patrols and raiding parties across No Man's Land. Such activities were a frequent and hazardous aspect of trench warfare, whereby small parties of men from both sides would regularly slip out of their positions at night and creep, hearts in mouths, across the devastated landscape. Sometimes the aim was to actually enter and raid the enemy's trenches, looking to take prisoners and capture documents. More often, the purpose was merely to reconnoitre the enemy's barbed wire defences or strongpoints. The following report details the 13th Battalion's second such operation, carried out by a party from D Company and led by Lieutenant Buckland. The objective was to enter an enemy sap, an exposed outpost leading from the opposing front-line trench into No Man's Land. The account shows how, all too often, there was little to be gained from these dangerous undertakings:

REPORT ON MINOR OPERATION CARRIED OUT BY THE 13TH BATTALION EAST SURREY REGIMENT ON THE NIGHT OF THE 29/30TH SEPTEMBER 1916.

1. The party responsible for laying of line from Boyau 63 to enemy's sap head left at time appointed and experienced no difficulty in executing the duty allotted to them.

2. The Bangalore[26] Party left Boyau 63 at 10 p.m. and arrived with the torpedo at the mouth of the enemy's sap without being discovered by the enemy. This party experienced some difficulty in getting the torpedo into position. Lieut F.N. CORBEN returned to Boyau 63 and reported the matter to Capt L.B. MILLS. The Corporal of the R.E. then proceeded to the sap head and succeeded, after taking one section out of the torpedo, in placing it in position. He then returned to Boyau 63.

3. The Raiding and Covering Parties left Boyau 63 at the time appointed.

4. The Artillery appeared to be a couple of minutes late in opening fire. The torpedo was sprung immediately the bombardment commenced.

5. Immediately the torpedo was sprung the Raiding Party rushed forward and entered the enemy's sap. They found that the torpedo had done its work with great efficiency. The concertina wire which had previously filled the sap and the wire which had stretched across the top of it had disappeared and the way was clear. On proceeding down the sap it was found that a corner existed in it and from this corner to the enemy's fire trench the sap was filled with a second lot of wire both in and over it and that their further progress was barred. The Party spent 40 minutes in and about the sap, endeavouring to find a gap through which to enter the enemy's lines, but were unsuccessful.

6. The whole operation was carried through without any hitch whatever and the existence of the second line of wire was, in my opinion, the only bar to bringing the raid to a successful issue. It appears to have been a complete surprise and our movements were unhindered by hostile fire. No casualties were sustained during the operations, nor did the enemy retaliate on my line afterwards.

7. I consider that the R.E. Corporal (Cpl BAMBER) did his work in a very efficient and praiseworthy manner which I wish to bring to your notice.

(signed) W. Newton Lieut-Col.
Commanding 13th Bn. East Surrey Regiment.
1/10/16.

This time the Battalion had escaped without casualties, but Lieutenant Davis's patrol was not so fortunate a few days later.

On the night of 4/5th October Davis and three men slipped over the parapet half an hour after midnight. During the previous day the lines opposite the 13th Battalion had been subjected to extensive trench mortar fire, which had succeeded in cutting the enemy's wire in a number of places. It was expected that the Germans would send out repair parties and Davis's job was therefore to lie in wait and observe the enemy's wire. If a repair party did emerge, it was to be prevented from accomplishing its task and if possible, a prisoner was to be taken for Intelligence purposes.

When Davis's party reached the enemy's wire it looked as if their ambush plan had been well conceived. Already, fresh coils of concertina wire had been put out and Davis expected the Germans to return at any moment to complete the job. The party lay low in the scant cover of shell holes and waited.

Several hours later the four men were still waiting as the night sky perceptibly began to lighten. The new wire lay untouched and a disappointed Davis realised he would quickly have to make his way back to his own lines. As this was attempted, however, an enemy machine gun opened up and caught the party just short of safety. From the Battalion's trenches, anxious comrades peered out, but none of the four men appeared out of the gloom. The patrol was posted as missing and the worst feared.

Out in No Man's Land the situation was, in reality, somewhat better. While all the party had been hit, Davis and two of his men were

The forbidding landscape of no-man's-land, looking towards the German Second Line.

fortunate to suffer only slight wounds, though the fourth man was killed outright. The three wounded men had managed to find refuge in a shell crater, but the enemy machine gun had their range and knew exactly where they were. To have ventured out of the crater would have been suicidal and Davis therefore resigned his men to a long wait throughout the daylight hours to come. All day the three lay without food and water, not daring to make any noise or movement for fear of attracting the attention of the enemy's snipers who were very active, as evidenced by an incident back in the 13th Battalion's trenches, where one of the sentries on the trench fire step was having difficulty in working his rifle. When Lieutenant Buckland stepped up to try to help, he showed himself briefly, but tragically, above the parapet. Even as the crack of the enemy sniper's rifle was heard, Buckland was falling into the bottom of the trench, killed instantly by a shot to the head.[27]

Thus, as night fell on the 5th, there was considerable despondency over the losses in the 13th Battalion's front line, but spirits revived when, at 7 p.m., Davis and his two remaining men scrambled back into the Battalion's positions, undetected by the enemy and much to the surprise of their comrades who had given them up for dead. For his coolness and resourcefulness Davis was commended in Lieutenant-Colonel Newton's official report to Brigade. The following night the body of the man killed during Davis's patrol was recovered from No Man's Land for decent burial and the enemy successfully completed their wire repairs.

Snipers, such as the one responsible for the death of Lieutenant Buckland, were a persistent and deadly nuisance. One in particular had been achieving such success that the 13th Battalion received orders to keep a special watch to see if they could locate him. Fortunately, one Battalion soldier was alert enough to spot a muzzle flash at the top of a disued coal mine shaft. It was swiftly reported to the British artillery and a response awaited. Two ranging shells soon came over, and the second of these was so close to the target that only a final minute adjustment needed to be relayed back. Almost immediately afterwards, a salvo of high explosive screamed over and onto the exact spot, obliterating the mine shaft and the sniper.

As autumn set in, the weather continued to deteriorate and the Battalion came to know the misery of trenches at least ankle deep with mud and water. There was always a store of gumboots kept handy so that the men could try to keep their feet from getting wet, but while these came right up over the legs to fasten onto trouser buttons, they usually made one's legs swell after a time and offered no protection against the cold at night. The potential result, brought about by constant exposure to damp and lack of circulation, was the condition known as trench foot, often considered more of a danger than the Germans in the winter months. The gumboots gave some protection, but discipline and hard work, assisted by medical precautions, were better safeguards and by 1917 this condition was almost unknown in some of the more rigorous units.

Later in October, Major Johnson's departure came on the 23rd when he was posted and promoted to take over command of the 17th Battalion, Welsh Regiment. For the moment, his position as Battalion second in command passed to Major Taylor of A Company, though the latter was already waiting to be posted as Camp Commandant of the 40th Division. While Taylor prepared to leave, the East Surreys moved back to Averdoingt when the 40th Division was relieved in the line. For the next few days the men then marched south-westwards, being billeted overnight in and around Rebreuve and then in Mézerolles, near Doullens. On 5 November they reached Vacquerie, near Candas, where a halt was called for a week's training and they were joined by Major E. B. Poole, formerly of the 3rd Battalion, Dorsetshire Regiment, who temporarily took over as second in command.

Once out of the front lines, the men made the most of their relaxation time, as Private Bonsey again recorded in admirable detail:

October 1916 – transport details near Doullens.
G. Richardson

When we came out of the line for a few days rest, we used to go to the 'Estaminets' pubs in the evenings where we could enjoy ourselves a little. The beer used to be sold in bottles here, about the size of a pint and half, which we could get for half a franc. These public houses used to get packed in the evenings as there was nowhere else to go. One of our favourite games here was the game of 'House'. This is a card game played with large cards something like the pattern of a draught board, divided into squares, some of these being numbered. What we had to do was

*to cover these numbers as they were
called out and the first one to fill his
card would be the winner. The prize
depended on the number of players. If
it was what is known as double house,
it would be about five or six francs and
if a single house, two or three francs.
The rule was to charge fourpence for a
full house, a twopence for a single
house, but in a single house you would
only have to fill up one line of figures
instead of the whole card full; so if we
won we would be alright but, of course,
if we lost we would only be a few pence
out. This game is the only gambling
game that the army authorities will
allow the soldiers to play.*

Still not permitted to remain for any
length of time in one place, the Battalion
next moved on to Doullens itself and
then to Souastre where it arrived on 14th
November. It was in one of these
supposedly safe rear areas that the
Battalion was lucky to avoid casualties
among the troops from their first air raid,
although the transport section's horses
were less fortunate. A German aeroplane
had droned over in the afternoon and
was thought only to be on a
reconnaissance flight until it dropped
two bombs among the horses, killing two
and severely wounding a mule which
had to be shot. Those horses that were
not wounded broke loose and ran wild
until they were caught and re-tethered,
while half a dozen men were detailed to
dig a huge grave for the three dead
beasts. It proved no easy task to drag the
bodies into the pit and many an unkind
oath passed the lips of the toiling troops,
showing a distinct lack of gratitude that
it was not their own corpses being

*The autumn of 1916 brought rain, flooding
and trench foot.*   G. Richardson

lowered into the ground.

By now the 40th Division had been transferred to the XIII Corps of Fifth Army. The East Surreys, however, learned that along with the other units of 120 Brigade, they were being temporarily attached to the 49th Division within Third Army. The next day they therefore returned to the trenches and relieved the 4th Battalion, King's Own Yorkshire Light Infantry (KOYLI) at Hébuterne, eight miles north of Albert. For six days the Battalion held this sector on the left flank of Fifth Army. Again the period was relatively quiet, though on 19th November Company Sergeant-Major R. T. Padget won the Distinguished Conduct Medal during an enemy bombardment. Padget was in an advanced post with seven of his men when a shell fell, blowing in their dugout and killing two men outright. The survivors, including Padget, were all wounded, but the Sergeant-Major managed to extricate himself and one of the wounded, whom he took to the regimental first aid post. There, Padget got his own wounds dressed before returning to the blown-in dugout to start digging out the other wounded. He subsequently got them all back to the aid post, despite the Germans continuing their heavy shelling.

On 21st November 120 Brigade's temporary attachment to the 49th Division ended and the East Surreys marched out of the line to camp at Couin, near Souastre, where they rejoined the rest of the 40th Division. For three days the Battalion then moved westwards, reaching Bussus-Bussuel, near Abbéville, where it moved into billets. Training continued until 14th December when, in readiness for a return to the front line, the Battalion marched to the railway at Pont Rémy and entrained for Dernancourt, near Albert, on the 15th. From there the Battalion continued on foot to Camp 112 between Bray and Méaulte and on 20th December, Company Sergeant-Major Padget was presented with the ribbon of his DCM by 120 Brigade's Commanding Officer, Brigadier-General Drummond Willoughby, this being the Battalion's first gallantry award.

Another spell of front-line duty then began when 120 Brigade relieved the 108 Brigade in the Bouchavesnes area, to the north of Péronne in the Somme valley. A short period as brigade support followed, occupying dugouts in a valley near Maurepas and it was there that Christmas 1916 was celebrated. For many men it was their first Christmas away from home, yet the occasion was marked with the usual good humour and comradeship typical of the 13th Battalion, helped by cigarettes and other small gifts from families, old schools and clubs in Wandsworth.

The Battalion next moved into the Bouchavesnes North sector of the line to relieve the 14th Battalion, Highland Light Infantry on 30 December. This sector was arguably the most miserable in France. Part of the Somme battlefield, the countryside was a devastated mass of mud as a result of the atrocious weather and the heavy fighting and shelling which had continued since the great Somme offensive of July 1916. Constant rain was varied only by spells of intense cold and very heavy snow falls. Even rear-area camps were miserable collections of dirty, wet and decrepit huts, which gave no comfort to troops 'resting' from trench duties in and around High Wood. The front line consisted of a lunar landscape of shell holes in a general sea of mud and pools of icy water. Trenches were very few and far between, except on high ground, and front-line troops were reduced to making the best of those shell holes which were least full of water and decaying bodies from the earlier fighting. Trench foot increased, depleting the ranks as many men were sent back for medical attention. The Battalion's remaining strength of 20 officers and 600 men was then further

By December 1916, trenches fell apart under the atrocious weather and exposed the men to more danger. G. Richardson

diluted by one company being attached to the 14th Battalion, Argyll and Sutherland Highlanders, also in the front line. After only a day's duty, New Year's Eve of 1916 brought the welcome order to move out from the line, but owing to muddy conditions and flooding it was almost impossible to negotiate the communication trenches. Seven miserable hours were spent reaching Maurepas, only four miles to the rear. There lorries were waiting, but enemy shelling caught the East Surreys as they set off, killing one man and wounding another.

The first elements of the Battalion arrived at Camp 21 near Maricourt during the early hours of New Year's Day 1917, but the last

company, exhausted and wet through, did not arrive until 9 a.m. The men had barely rested and scraped off the clinging mud from this last spell of trench duty when, on 4th January, they moved into the Rancourt Sector, north of Bouchavesnes. Front-line conditions here were again atrocious, the weather being exceptionally poor and freezing cold. For men from the urban and suburban environment of Wandsworth, it was all the more difficult to bear. No matter how many layers of clothing and newspaper were worn, the all-pervading cold seeped through. The line itself consisted of only a series of detached and precarious posts held by guns and a few rifles, there were therefore few substantial earthworks to protect against the elements. It was said that the British soldier's greatest opponents were the weather, mud, lice, rats and the enemy - in that order of priority.

The transport of all supplies to this sector proved extremely difficult, owing not only to the exposed positions, but also to the treacherous mud, which was often waist-high. Lorries were of no use in such conditions and 120 Brigade was therefore obliged to organise a nightly mule train of some eighty drivers and animals. Under cover of darkness these struggled up to the front line with food, ammunition, water rations and clothing throughout the following month. Each journey took up to 15 hours and invariably exhausted both man and beast. If either fell into a mud-filled shell hole, it was only with the greatest difficulty and speed that they could be pulled out alive.

The Battalion held this sector until it was relieved on 8th January and was fortunate in only suffering one man killed and one wounded in such a perilous area. Sickness, however, continued to take its toll. By 1917, military hospital 'severe' admissions unrelated to enemy action were most frequently due to venereal disease[28] (50%), frostbite (22%), inflammation of the kidneys (16%), dysentery (6%) and pneumonia (2%). The balance of cases was made up by tuberculosis, enteric fever and meningitis.

Major Poole was one of those suffering ill-health and was evacuated to a Casualty Clearing Station as the East Surreys came out of the trenches. For the moment, the lack of a second in command posed a problem. Major Taylor had left for divisional headquarters on 9th December and although Captain L. B. Mills was being groomed to take over, he had not yet returned from his senior officer's course in England. With Lieutenant-Colonel Newton also still not in the best of health, manpower among the ranks of the Battalion's senior officers was becoming severely stretched and to make matters worse, only a brief spell was spent in brigade reserve at Maurepas. All too soon came a return to the same bleak Bouchavesnes North sector on 18 January for more front-line duty. This time the tour lasted four days and considerable shelling had to be endured, particularly on the night of the 19th. The enemy hit the East Surreys' reserve positions with some 500-600 gas shells and the Wandsworth men were fortunate to suffer only four casualties. At last, on the 22nd, a final return was made to brigade support duties in dugouts at Asquith Flats, named after the former British Prime Minister.[29] On this day, two movements of officers occurred. On the debit side, Lieutenant Davis departed for his training as an Observer, having been the first of the 13th Battalion's officers to be accepted by the Royal Flying Corps. On the credit side, 46-year-old Lieutenant-Colonel E. C. Atkins[30] was attached from the Leicestershire Regiment to serve as second in command. To have a Lieutenant-Colonel as a second in command was unusual, and was probably recognition of Lieutenant-Colonel Newton's continuing health problems. For the moment, however, there were no taxing demands as 120 Brigade was relieved on 26 January. The East Surreys were driven back by lorry to a camp near Sailly-Laurette and the next day marched to billets at Corbie, near Amiens. There, they gratefully became part of GHQ Reserve.

The entire month of February 1917 brought welcome respite from the front line. Initially the men remained in the camp at Corbie, undertaking shooting on the range, bayonet fighting, PT and other such training. On 10 and 11 February the Battalion left Corbie and camped at Bray-sur-Somme, from where working parties were provided to work at a nearby rail head. Yet even here the peaceful existence was interrupted by an accident on the 14th in which three men were killed while unloading ammunition from a train. On 24 February the East Surreys returned to Camp 21 near Maricourt where training continued until 6 March when, after six weeks' break, the

A working party arrives to unload a train in the winter of 1916-17.
Taylor Libray

Battalion returned to the front line just south of Bouchavesnes. Three day tours of trench duty were carried out, alternating with another unit of 120 Brigade, the 14th Battalion, Argyll and Sutherland Highlanders. In between front-line duties the 13th Battalion rotated back to spells in support positions at Road Wood, just to the south-west of Bouchavesnes, or as brigade reserve at Howitzer Wood. It was at the latter position, on the afternoon of 11 March, that a sudden enemy barrage of some 200 shells rained down, rudely interrupting the men's rest from the front line. Fortunately no casualties were suffered, but great was the consternation over a direct hit on D Company's cooker, which was blown to pieces.

It was back in the forward trench positions, however, that a much more serious and sad loss was experienced two days later. Due to the very poor condition of the trenches, movement in daylight was much restricted and consequently rations were again brought up at night by mule to within 100 yards of battalion headquarters. On 13/14 March the mule train had just arrived shortly after midnight and was being unloaded when enemy shells began to fall on the position. Somehow, not a single animal was injured, but one shell burst at the entrance to the headquarters' dugout. Three visiting soldiers from the Argyll and Sutherland Highlanders were killed while the 13th Battalion's only loss was, tragically, Regimental Sergeant-Major Seymour. The death of Seymour, one of the Battalion's stalwarts, was keenly felt by all.

General von Hindenburg.

On a more positive note, the middle of March 1917 brought exciting news. Intelligence sources were convinced that the Germans were about to fall back on the Arras-Soissons front to a new defensive position which came to be known as the Hindenburg Line, a vast and carefully constructed system of trenches, wire and gun posts stretching nearly 160 kilometres from Lens to the Aisne River. The decision to build the line was made by Generals von Hindenburg and Ludendorff and it was to extend across a costly salient between Arras and Le Transloy, enabling the Germans to husband their strength in a well-prepared, yet shorter, line of defence. The total length of the front was reduced by 50 kilometres and enabled the German Army to release no fewer than thirteen divisions for service in reserve. A gradual withdrawal to the line had begun in February 1917 and the territory between the old front and the new line was left devastated as the Germans employed scorched earth tactics, leaving nothing untouched that might help the Allies. On 15 March,

The heavily-fortified Hindenburg Line seen from the air.

120 Brigade received instructions to move forward when it was thought that the enemy's positions in front of them were being vacated as part of this withdrawal, but patrols by the East Surreys initially found the Germans still present. It was then to the frustration of the 13th Battalion that they were not in the front line when the German retreat actually commenced on the 17th. Instead, it was the Argyll and Sutherland Highlanders who were able to push forward and take over the enemy's abandoned forward positions and it was not until the following day that the Wandsworth men were also ordered to advance. Consequently, for the first time since its arrival in France, the Battalion was able to briefly break out from the mind-numbing monotony of static trench warfare. Its war diary noted that 'keenness and enthusiasm was very marked in having passed over trenches and through villages occupied by the enemy only 24 hours before.'

Lt Beecroft, the Battalion's transport officer who entered Peronne hard on the heels of the Germans.
Mrs P. Hucker.

While the fighting troops of the 13th East Surreys were disappointed at not being in the forefront of the advance, other elements of the Battalion were finding all the excitement they could handle. This began on the morning of 18 March when the Battalion's Transport Officer, Lieutenant Beecroft, had been ordered to report to Brigade Headquarters. There he was told that the enemy had withdrawn and that the 13th Battalion was pursuing as closely as possible. Beecroft was ordered to follow up the advance with ammunition and supplies as soon as he could. Though communications had broken down and it was impossible to say with any degree of certainty where the Battalion was to be found, it was nevertheless assumed that the troops would be following a general line towards the crucial German-occupied town of Péronne. The transport details therefore started and made their way up to the last known location of the Battalion. On arrival there it was found that headquarters had apparently already moved on and Beecroft decided to continue along the main road to Péronne. Towards dusk the transport came within sight of the town and while the convoy of men and animals took cover in the roadside hedges and ditches, Lieutenant Beecroft, Corporal Bull and Private Burrell tentatively went forward. Together they found a British officer, only to receive the discouraging news that it was thought that the Germans still held the town. This posed a difficult choice, as it was clearly not desirable to take the transport convoy close to an enemy position, but it was equally important to find the Battalion's fighting units and deliver their much-needed ammunition and supplies. After careful thought Beecroft decided to risk continuing on into Péronne, trusting that if the enemy were still in the town they would only be there in small numbers. The town presented an unforgettable sight as night fell. The retreating Germans had set most of the houses on fire and the streets were full of blazing heaps of furniture, bedding and other household contents, which had been thrown out of the windows of dwellings. Many buildings had also had their frontage pulled down in an orgy of wanton destruction. It was impossible to determine whether the enemy had completely left, but the transport's cautious advance through the streets met with no opposition. A worrying moment came when suddenly, above the noise of the crackling flames, the distinctive sound of approaching cavalry was heard. Men and animals took as much cover as possible while Lieutenant Beecroft bravely went forward alone to investigate. Happily, he came across a squadron of British cavalry which had been sent forward to discover whether the enemy had yet pulled out of Péronne. The cavalry's commanding officer could scarcely believe, until he saw the evidence with his own eyes, that the 13th Battalion's entire transport column had already come through the town.

Breathing a little more easily, Beecroft marshalled his charges and set off towards Allaines where the cavalry had reported seeing other British troops. After much wandering in the dark and with the ever-present danger of running into the enemy, a village was seen in the distance. Again the Lieutenant went forward alone, leaving Corporal Bull to take charge if he did not return within ten minutes. The village appeared deserted, but Beecroft eventually discovered a barn from which came light and the noise of voices. He crept up to the door in an attempt to identify the language and was considerably relieved to hear a voice saying "Where the 'ell have the rations gone?" By the greatest good fortune not only were the troops British, but they were none other than the 13th East Surreys. The supplies were quickly brought up and the rations distributed to the hungry men. The village was indeed Allaines and many of the Battalion enjoyed their meal in lavishly-furnished dugouts which had been abandoned by the Germans. Some had walls lined with polished wood and in another a table was laid with crockery, cutlery and napkins of a quality which the East Surreys had not seen since leaving England.

From Allaines, the Battalion established an advanced line to the east, between the 14th Battalion, Argyll and Sutherland Highlanders and the 20th Battalion, Middlesex Regiment. After pushing up just

Moving up supplies on the Western Front using transport horses.

three miles, however, a new system of trenches was dug and the war settled back into its familiar pattern. On 20 March the Battalion was relieved from the line as the 40th Division moved back to Curlu.

After the mud and filth of the Somme battlefield it was almost a relief to return to the bureaucracy of the rear areas, as the 13th East Surreys found when it came to handing over the pack saddles of their transport horses. Up to 90 saddles had been in constant use each night for a long time, but when the Battalion was relieved from the front line, these had to be handed in. By then many were badly worn and incomplete and many more had disappeared under several feet of mud. Only 30 complete sets were made up by cannibalising what was left and the problem then lay before Lieutenant Beecroft as to how to make 30 saddles appear to number 90. His solution, a variation of 'Here we go round the mulberry bush', was ingeniously simple. First he displayed nine wagons before the Ordnance Officer, each capable of holding ten saddles. The first wagon holding ten saddles was then driven past the Ordnance Officer who counted and recorded ten saddles loaded in it. While wagons 2 and 3 then held the attention of the Ordnance Officer, the driver of No. 1 wagon turned the corner of some convenient houses where colleagues hurriedly changed the mules and a fresh driver took up the reins. Circling around to join the back of the procession of wagons, saddles 1-10 then became saddles 31-40. Repeating the trick soon brought the total to the desired 90 and a receipt was given to the satisfaction of all concerned. The 13th Battalion was justified in considering itself as astute as any regular Army unit.

Men hitching ride back to reserve quarters after a spell in the trenches.

Chapter 4

VILLERS-PLOUICH

The first two weeks of April 1917 found the 13th Battalion toiling on the Maricourt-Péronne railway under the orders of Fourth Army's Construction Engineer. This was an urgent need at the time, for without adequate communications and transport the British Army's advances could not be maintained and the Germans had done everything they could to slow their enemy down by damaging and destroying roads and railways. While the manual labour was therefore not to everyone's liking, as commented upon by Private Bonsey below, the work at least represented a break from the dangers of the front line and the Battalion's base remained at Curlu, close by the River Somme:

It was to our own interest to get this line through so that the engines could get up with train loads of material and food supplies, as well as all kinds of ammunition that was badly wanted to enable us to hold this part of the line. So our division had to put in six weeks with the RE's [Royal Engineers] and the whole of the division being at it, we covered a few miles. We all had to work ten hours a day, digging and levelling the ground ready for the RE's to lay the rails, and every day the old

A period of rest from the trenches often meant hours of back-breaking work. Here men help the Royal Engineers construct a light railway.

engine was able to go a little farther up. We were supposed to be out from the line on rest. A good rest, too, doing this navvy work for the RE's. After our six weeks at this job with the RE's we were relieved by another division to carry on and we had to go up the line again.

During this period Lieutenant-Colonel Atkins departed for a course in England while Captain L. B. Mills returned to take over as second in command and on 15 April, Mills was given temporary command while Lieutenant-Colonel Newton left to attend a commanding officers' conference held by the Fourth Army School at Flixecourt.

The next day the Battalion was once again on the march, moving north-east via Allaines to the shattered village of Equancourt. Here the Germans had destroyed almost every building during their retreat to the Hindenburg Line and the Wandsworth men had no option but to camp in the ruins while they halted for two days in reserve.

The Battalion left this bleak and blasted landscape to relieve the 20th Battalion, Middlesex Regiment at Gouzeaucourt Wood. In this area of the front line, some ten miles south-west of Cambrai, the troops enjoyed little cover by way of trenches. Instead, the line was formed by a series of mutually-supporting machine-gun positions and isolated outposts with rough shelters. The trees of Gouzeaucourt Wood itself offered more protection, but on the 19th, enemy artillery

Gouzeaucourt village under German occupation. The church is being used as a hospital and the furthermost cottage on the right serves as a canteen.

zeroed in on this haven and one man was killed. The same danger was faced the next day, but the Battalion managed to ignore most of the shell fire by concentrating on the building of a new strongpoint just south of a sunken road which ran through the wood.

Shortly after midnight on 21 April patrols were sent forward, but found no sign of the enemy to the immediate front. The remainder of the Battalion therefore moved up about a mile north-eastwards towards the next village of Villers-Plouich. This position was known to be strongly held by the Germans and the Battalion's advance was halted about a thousand yards short of the enemy while a detailed plan of attack was prepared. A series of strongpoints was established along the new forward line by elements of A, C and D Companies, while the remainder of these companies held a second line further back along the north-east border of Gouzeaucourt Wood and B Company remained in reserve. So far, the only casualties were three wounded.

For the remainder of the 21st and the 22nd the Battalion waited, strung out in a line from Fifteen Ravine on the right to Beaucamp Ridge on the left flank. Fifteen Ravine derived its name from fifteen trees which had bordered it until destroyed by the Germans who doubtless realised their value as ranging marks for the British artillery. In reality the so-called 'ravine' was nowhere more than ten feet deep.

Sporadic shelling was still proving a nuisance, but of more concern were the German snipers who were now well within range. Three officers and four men were hit on the 22nd alone, including Second Lieutenant Forster Johnston, a young Scot returned from his job in South Africa in order to fight, who died from his wounds the following day. On the 23rd the enemy's artillery fire increased as the Germans recognised the build up of British troops in Gouzeaucourt Wood and other areas immediately behind the front line. Again the East Surreys suffered, losing one man killed and nine wounded.

At last 120 Brigade received its orders to attack, aiming to capture both Villers-Plouich and adjacent high ground. The terrain over which the advance was to take place was open and undulating, but crossed by numerous shallow gullies, characteristic of this sector of the front. All crossroads had been cratered by the enemy, but generally it was considered good fighting country with natural cover and many opportunities for observation. The enemy were using what was left of buildings as strongpoints, but the ground was fairly free from shell holes. One of the more observant officers waiting to attack noted that partridges were plentiful and there were many nests of young birds.

The village itself was already in ruins, having been a German headquarters for some time and therefore having attracted considerable attention from Allied artillery. Other than this, Villers-Plouich's other claim to fame in the war had come when, on 17th September 1916, a shot-up F.E.2b of the Royal Flying Corps had carried out a forced landing on the outskirts of the village. While German troops lifted out the mortally wounded pilot and already dead observer, the German pilot responsible for downing the British aeroplane landed close by. The eager young flyer was determined to see his prey at close quarters, as it was his first confirmed 'kill'. His name was Baron Manfred von Richtofen - soon to become the feared 'Red Baron' of air fighting over the Western Front.

The attack on Villers-Plouich in April 1917 represented the south-eastern limit to the Battle of Arras, a major Allied offensive which, although limited in its eventual gains, was to include the heroic Canadian assault which captured Vimy Ridge some 25 miles to the north-west. For their part in the battle the 13th East Surreys had the village of Villers-Plouich as their initial objective and the plan then called for the Battalion to hold a line beyond the village, extending from Highland Ridge on the eastern flank, across a railway line and as far as the Cambrai road to the west. At 2.00 a.m. on Tuesday 24 April, with a strength of 24 officers and 600 other ranks, Captain Mills moved forward and occupied a new trench running north-west from Fifteen Ravine. The order of attack was that A and B Companies should be in the front line, supported respectively by C and D Companies. The men, fortified by a tot of rum to counter any anxiety over what was to be their first major 'push', settled down to wait.

Zero hour was at 4.15 a.m. when a terrific artillery barrage roared overhead to crash down upon No Man's Land before rolling forward towards the enemy's lines. On cue, the 13th East Surreys climbed from their trenches, urged on by the shrill whistle blasts of their officers. They advanced in four waves towards the German wire, helped by the the glare of exploding shells ahead which turned the still-dark sky into an inferno of light. Captain Crocker lead B Company on the right, with support from Captain L. I. Deacon's D Company. On the left, Lieutenant Hann urged A Company on, backed up by Captain Naunton and C Company. As well as rifles and packs, every man carried two Mills bombs each and also two sandbags, so as to be ready to create shelter if needed. In addition, one platoon of 'D' company and one of 'C' company carried picks and shovels. As the troops moved, forward German artillery began to search them out, but for the

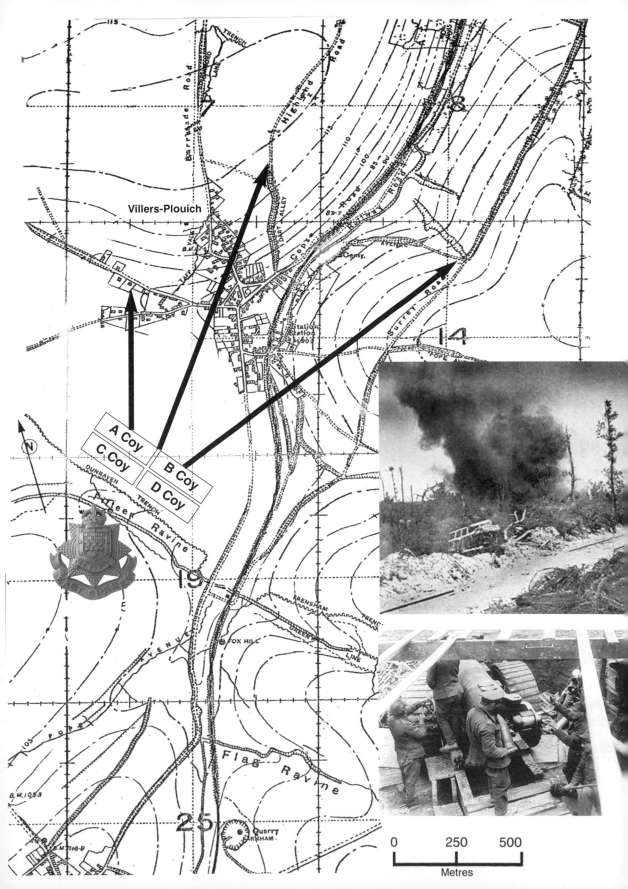

Villers-Plouich

A Coy

C Coy

B Coy

D Coy

N

0   250   500

Metres

moment the enemy's aim was poor and did little to slow the advance. The 14th Highland Light Infantry, however, were not so lucky. They had formed up in the rear of the 13th Battalion and received the 'overs', losing eight men immediately.

After only seven minutes the first German trenches were reached and the 13th Battalion leapt down upon the enemy. A short but vicious struggle followed until the Germans were either dead or had surrendered and the Wandsworth men then pressed on towards the village. During this stage of the attack the Battalion came under accurate enemy machine-gun fire from concealed strongpoints and emplacements, but supported by Lewis gun fire, parties of men rushed forward with great daring and hurled their bombs on the enemy's positions. Soon the attack was able to progress again and by 5.30 a.m. the outskirts of the village were reached. There the Battalion split into three parties. The group led by Captain Naunton swung to the left and soon came upon a German strongpoint on the sunken road leading to Beaucamp. The position was stormed and quickly taken, yielding over a hundred enemy prisoners who were sent back to the rear positions. But as Naunton then prepared to continue, enemy fire from the direction of Beaucamp revealed that another attacking battalion had failed to take the hamlet. Recognising the futility of trying to advance further, Naunton consolidated the captured enemy post and set out his men in a defensive arc to protect the flank of the other 13th Battalion

attacks. The nearest was that of the central group, led by Second Lieutenant Alexander after Captain Deacon had been wounded. This party had successfully negotiated the western flank of Villers-Plouich and pushed on out of the other side of the village. Reaching Highland Ridge, the high ground that was their objective, they dug in and awaited developments.

The third party, consisting of men from A and B Companies and led by Captain Crocker, was meanwhile finding the going much tougher beyond the eastern outskirts of Villers-Plouich. Strong opposition met them every inch of the way, but

German machine gunners with a MG 08/15 light machine gun.

92

undeterred they continued to push forward. Their object was a ravine some 700 yards north-east of the village, yet as they reached it, tragedy struck. A strong force of Germans held the ravine and as the East Surreys appeared the enemy opened up with murderous machine-gun fire. Young Captain Edward Crocker, just 23 years old, fell dead at the head of his men and, leaderless, the attack stalled while Lieutenant Hann took over and attempted to rally the troops. As he did so, a fresh chapter was added to the East Surrey Regiment's illustrious history.

Corporal Edward Foster

Ted or Tiny to all who knew him, was typical of many of the 13th Battalion's men. A Tooting man born and bred, he had benefited from schooling at Tooting Graveney School only until the age of fourteen when he had started work with Wandsworth Council at their destructor site in Tooting. A re-organisation of his department then saw Foster transferred to the Council's 'dusting' ('dusting' then being the term for refuse collection) contractor, the firm of F. W. Surridge. The job, despite its unglamorous nature, was nevertheless a coveted one due to the pickings which could be had from 'totting'. This was the sifting of household waste for saleable items, which could then be taken to one of the three local scrap companies, Jones and Perry, Bill Webb or Jimmy Wood. Other additions to basic pay came from private transactions to remove bulky items, but best of all were the Christmas tips. Charlie Jones, then a ninety-two year old lifelong Tooting resident, was the son of the Jones half of Jones and Perry and in 1995 recalled for the author how 'Tiny' and the other dustmen would deliver their seasonal 'Merry Christmas, Madam', while waiting to record the tip given in a black book. "Only the bravest refused to 'drop'!" recalled Charlie.

For such opportunities of relatively rich rewards, a vacancy on a dustcart was normally a matter of internal resolution and the crew members would choose their own new recruits, frequently from family or close friends. Legendary were the tales of baby boys having their names put down at birth for a particular crew, the expectation being that the son would follow in his father's footsteps, perhaps even working together. So, for the young Ted Foster, breaking into the close-knit 'dust' fraternity was something of an achievement and a job to be respected. Ted therefore made sure he merited his chance, working hard and growing into a strapping young man over six feet tall and powerfully built. By the outbreak of the war in 1914 Foster was living at 92 Fountain Road, Tooting, with his wife and young niece, Alice.

When Wandsworth Council announced its intention of forming the 13th Battalion in 1915, Ted Foster had decided that now was the time to serve his country. The men of Tooting in particular were quick to volunteer and Foster found himself in a company of the Battalion which held many local acquaintances and former colleagues from the 'dust'. His commanding presence and relative maturity of twenty-seven years of age meant that Foster was soon singled out for promotion to Lance-Corporal and by 1917 he had progressed to full Corporal. When Lieutenant Hann therefore called for his men to rally at Villers-Plouich, it was no surprise that Ted Foster dashed forward.

The worst of the enemy's fire was coming from two machine guns sited in a trench and protected with dense barbed wire. Foster, himself in charge of a team of two Lewis guns, charged the position carrying his own heavy gun and, followed by Lance-Corporal Reed, managed to enter the enemy trench. Hand-to-hand fighting led to one of Foster's Lewis guns being lost, but the Corporal was determined to win it back. Throwing his bombs he succeeded in killing or forcing back the Germans who had taken the Lewis and with both guns now available, Foster quickly set them up and opened fire on the enemy's own two machine guns, killing the crews and capturing their weapons.

Corporal Edward Foster who won his Victoria Cross at Villers-Plouich on 24.4.17.
(the late) D. Foster

Confronted with such daring, German resistance collapsed and twenty of the enemy stepped forward in surrender. With this thorn removed from their side, the easternmost party of East Surreys continued their advance, secured the ravine and halted at their objective, on the right flank of Second Lieutenant Alexander's party. It was still only two hours since the attack had started and the 13th Battalion busied itself in consolidating positions while awaiting reinforcements from the 14th Battalion, Highland Light Infantry.

At 6.30 a.m. the British artillery barrage ceased, but after only ten minutes of relative peace and quiet, the enemy opened up with its own

The small ravine where Foster won his VC. Arrow denotes drection of attack on German machine guns.
Author

4.2" and 5.9" guns, having spotted the exposed parties of Second Lieutenant Alexander and Lieutenant Hann to the north of Villers-Plouich. In such lightly-protected positions these two groups were in grave danger of annihilation and had little option but to withdraw into cover on the eastern outskirts of the village. This they did, securing the northern entrances to the village with Lewis gun teams. A quarter of an hour later, however, the expected reinforcements arrived in the shape of the Highlanders and the 13th Battalion received orders to push their line north of the village again. Captain Mills came forward to lead this hazardous venture, knowing that the enemy's artillery spotters already had the range and would be waiting for the British to emerge from the cover of the village. Sure enough, the 13th Battalion faced a determined onslaught as they moved forward again. Second Lieutenant Alexander, who had done so well earlier with the centre party, was killed and so too was Second Lieutenant Goodyear, a recent arrival from the 6th East Surreys. The loss of Alexander, the former Private in the Royal Fusiliers who had joined the Battalion on its arrival in France, was especially keenly-felt. He was leading a small party of men forward when fire from an enemy machine gun found them, but Alexander rushed ahead and captured it and the crew. Swinging the gun round he trained it on the enemy's positions and opened fire, but then noticed one of his men wounded and lying out in the open. Leaving the German gun to others, he went out to the wounded man, but as he reached him a shell burst killed him instantly.

There were many who witnessed his actions who thought that Alexander had merited a Victoria Cross, rather than the simple posthumous Mention in Despatches that eventually followed. One Battalion officer wrote to his father:

> If it be any consolation to you, you may know that he died the death of a hero and deserved the V.C. ...he was a man absolutely without fear, who commanded the affections and respect of his Company to such an extent that I think, without hesitation, every man would cheerfully have died for him.

Another brother-officer confirmed that Alexander 'did most marvellous work in the battle, and people say everywhere that he is worthy of the VC.' It was Alexander's platoon

Lt Gordon Alexander, kia 24.4.17. T.Miles.

95

Sergeant who attempted to express to the grieving parents the loss felt, rather than the bravery and valour of their son's death

I am sure it will help you in your grief if you could hear how well the men speak of him. I was greeted with the words "Sergeant, your old pal Alec is gone," and tears stood out in eyes that were quite unused to them.

Mills's advance had managed to establish a line some 300 yards from the village, but still a quarter of a mile short of the extent of the morning's earlier attack and the scene of Corporal Foster's bravery. At 8.30 a.m. another fierce enemy artillery barrage fell on the new positions and continued relentlessly for six hours. Captain Mills was himself hit and wounded, but the line held until the shelling eased off to harassing fire in the afternoon.

For the remainder of the day the Battalion was left to lick its wounds. Three officers and 36 men were dead, while eight officers and 152 other ranks were wounded – some 32% of the Battalion's front-line strength. On the credit side, however, the village of Villers-Plouich had been taken and held and over 300 of the enemy captured, along with ten machine guns and some 500 rifles. The Germans were estimated to have suffered 52 killed and 304 wounded. Many deeds of great individual heroism and bravery had been performed during the day and a number of men were recommended for decorations. In due course, the number of awards received was a clear indication of the esteem in which the 13th Battalion's assault on Villers-Plouich had been held. No fewer than six men received the Military Medal: Sergeants Briggs and Knight, Corporals Morgan, Jennings and Richards and Private Brooker. For the wounded Captain Mills came a Military Cross and for Captain Naunton, who had assumed command after Mills was put out of action, a Distinguished Service Order. Lance-Corporal Reed, who had so valiantly accompanied Corporal Foster's charge, was awarded a well-deserved Distinguished Conduct Medal. For 'Tiny' Foster, the former Tooting dustman, Britain reserved its very highest award for valour in action, the Victoria Cross.[31] Posted home to receive the award at the hands of the King, Foster arrived unaccompanied in Tooting on the Tuesday night of 17 July 1917, but found great difficulty in reaching his house in Fountain Road due to the large, cheering, crowd that awaited him. Once indoors, he found a telegram from the Mayor, Alderman Dawnay, which read

'Wandsworth welcomes you home. Hearty congratulations on winning the VC. Our town and Council are proud of you. May you win further honours.'

Pte Albert Pryke kia 24.4.17.
G. Richardson.

At a meeting of the Council on the following evening, Wednesday 18 July, Foster received an illuminated scroll of appreciation from the Borough. Mr A.D. Robinson, Vice-Chairman of the quaintly-named Officers and Servants Committee, moved that the seal of the Council be attached to the document and Foster himself then arrived and was greeted with hearty applause as the entire Council rose to their feet to welcome him. The address on the scroll listed Foster's service with the Council, the official account of his winning the VC and the following address from the Council:

'We, the Mayor, Aldermen, and Councillors of the Metropolitan Borough of Wandsworth, having heard with sincere gratification that his Majesty has awarded Corporal Foster the Victoria Cross for conspicuous bravery in the face of the enemy, congratulate him heartily on the honour conferred on him and express our admiration for the act of gallantry which earned him the distinction.'

King George V pins the Victoria Cross on Corporal Foster at Buckingham Palace.
(the late) D. Foster

Foster, invited to reply, managed "I am not much of a spokesman. What I did I did for my King and country". A storm of applause greeted this simple statement and it was unanimously agreed that he be offered re-employment with the Coucil after the war with uninterrupted service, so as to boost his pension rights. The following week saw Foster collect his medal from King George V at a Buckingham Palace investiture on 21 July 1917. Tiny's Victoria Cross was the only such decoration to be granted to the 13th Battalion, and one of only nine won by the East Surrey Regiment throughout its history.

The award of a V.C. was greeted with great pride throughout the Battalion and served to lift morale after the recent bitter fighting and heavy losses.[32] For while Foster enjoyed his leave and fame in England, his comrades continued very much as before. On 25th April 1917, the enemy's resistance at Beaucamp, which had threatened Captain Naunton's left flank on the previous morning, was broken by the 11th Battalion, King's Own Royal Lancaster Regiment. With the East Surreys' line then extended and securely held, the 13th Battalion was relieved from the front line that evening and marched back to Equancourt. The next day Lieutenant-Colonel Newton rejoined his unit, proud to learn of its tenacious achievements during his absence. The end of the month was seen out at Equancourt, where the only disruption to a well-earned rest came from the enemy's long-range shelling which caused three casualties.

May 1917 saw the Battalion remaining in the Villers-Plouich area, alternating between front-line duties in the Villers-Plouich, Gouzeaucourt and Gonnelieu sectors, with spells in reserve at Queen's Cross, Sorrel-le-Grand and Dessart Wood. In this sector, No Man's Land was relatively wide in places and the thick, high grass greatly assisted patrolling in relative safety. For much of the period Lieutenant-Colonel Newton was again absent since, less than two weeks after his return from the Fourth Army Training School, he left on 6th May for the XV Corps Rest Station near Abbeville. Surviving records suggest that the commanding officer's health was showing further signs of deterioration at this time and Newton was clearly failing to throw off his recurrent trench fever. To cover his absence, Major J. H. Foster of the 14th Highland Light Infantry was temporarily attached for command duties.

While Newton was away the Battalion enjoyed a comparatively peaceful month, but May was not entirely without incident. On the night of the 9th, in the trenches covering Villers-Plouich, the Battalion's alert sentries opened fire on an enemy patrol, which was spotted probing the barbed wire defences. Two of the Germans were killed and a patrol was quickly sent out to bring in their papers, revealing the useful information that the men belonged to the enemy's 162nd Regiment.

On 23 May it was the Battalion's turn to take this type of warfare back to the enemy. That night a patrol led by twenty-year-old Second Lieutenant Trevor Mills slipped out of the East Surrey positions, looking to observe the enemy's wire directly opposite them. In the pitch darkness, however, Mills lost his bearings and eventually reached the outskirts of the enemy-occupied village of Banteux. Appreciating his error, the young Lieutenant went forward alone to inspect the German defences. As he did so, the remainder of the patrol was spotted and heavy fire from rifles and machine guns followed. The patrol was forced to beat a hasty retreat without their officer and though a search party was later sent out, there was no sign of him. Much later the Battalion received notification that Mills, from Sutton, had been badly wounded and captured on the night of the 23rd and had died of his wounds the following day. The young Lieutenant was one of the four men killed and two wounded in May, but on the last day of the month Lieutenant-Colonel Newton returned from his spell

Lieutenants James (left) and Corben in the ruins of Villers-Plouich.   Mrs P. Hucker

at the Rest Centre and while still not in the best of health, he was able to take some comfort from his Mention in Despatches, which had been announced in *The Times* on the 23rd. The award dated from 9 April and recognised Newton's fine command work, the same distinction being bestowed upon Lieutenant Ainger, (who had replaced Linge as Adjutant), Hon. Lieutenant Mr Foster (Quartermaster) and Sergeant Holmes. The 13th Battalion, along with the entire 40th Division, was now transferred to III Corps, and enjoyed a brief respite from front-line sector duties while still remaining in the locality of Villers-Plouich. Private Bonsey was to later recall the enjoyable sports that Brigade organized for the troops:

About the end of May we were brought back out of the line for a break for a while. This time we stayed in Gouzeaucourt Wood near Fins. Here we stayed eight weeks doing nothing only a few drills during the day. The brigade here organised some sports lasting all day, so we were practising for this. The sports lasted all day and the weather kept fine so it went off alright. We had nearly every kind of sport they could think of including wrestling and boxing on the mules' backs. This caused some fun, and so it did when they had a race riding all the mules. I think the race was a quarter-of-a-mile. They all got in line ready to start but when the time came for them to start, they would not go. Some made a start alright and others turned round to come back. One of the Officers that was riding one of these mules got thrown off and he had to finish the race by pulling the old mule behind him. The mules seemed very stubborn that day. They had a job to get them to do anything or go anywhere. They whacked them but they took no notice at all. This day's sport was real treat for us all. It was quite a change from the usual routine work up the line.

Yet even during this lull, the enemy's artillery presented a continuing threat. On 24 June Captain Naunton (who had received the DSO on the

99

16th) and two other men were wounded by shelling while in reserve positions and on the 27th two more men were wounded and two killed after a return to the front line. A further eight men were wounded when an enemy raid upon an exposed position was thwarted on the night of the 29th/30th. The Germans, twenty to thirty strong, were spotted by one of the Battalion's sentries and immediately engaged with heavy Lewis gun and rifle fire. Caught by surprise, the enemy soldiers wasted no time in throwing their stick bombs and withdrawing, but being at extreme range the Battalion escaped any fatalities. Not so lucky were the Germans, evidenced by the groaning of their wounded out in No Man's Land for the remainder of the night.

The advent of July saw Lieutenant-Colonel Newton granted short leave in England, the Battalion being commanded in his absence by Major W. G. West. Formerly with the Notts and Derby Regiment, West had been promoted and transferred to the 13th East Surreys in mid-May as second-in-command (releasing Major Foster to return to the Highlanders) and now held the reins until Newton's return on 12 July. There had been little activity for West to report on his superior's return. Lieutenant Scott's snipers had scored a number of hits on the 3rd against several of the enemy spotted walking against the skyline. Two days later, however, the enemy's shelling had killed Second Lieutenant MacEwan (attached from the 5th East Surreys) and another man on 5 July, wounding ten others.

On the 20th the pace of life quickened with orders to mount two raids on the enemy's trenches. Both parties, the first of twenty men and a Lewis gun led by Second Lieutenant Wilson, and the second of thirty men under Lieutenants Scott and Anderson, were ultimately forced back by intense enemy fire. Despite this disappointment, both groups had made great efforts and Wilson in particular had shown fine leadership which was recognised with the award of a Military Cross. In the other party Lieutenant Anderson and three men were wounded, the officer only being brought in with great difficulty.

The steady trickle of killed and wounded was again proving a drain on the Battalion's resources. Even a quiet month like July resulted in 54 casualties, at a time when the Battalion's total strength was down to 29 officers and approximately 500 other ranks. A rate of attrition of over 10% per month, even without any major engagements, did not require a mathematician to forecast the future and the situation was exacerbated by the Germans' regular use of gas in the sector, as described in Private Bonsey's journal:

The Germans were fond of gassing us here; they tried it several times when the wind was in their favour. I know at one time we had to keep our gas masks on for two hours and it was awkward for breathing. Until you got fairly used to the helmets with these masks on we had to breathe through our mouths as there was a clip that used to clip on our noses to stop us from inhaling the gas. These gases were always scented very strong and most pleasant to smell, and directly we smelt anything like this on would go our gas helmets and then we could withstand it alright. He also used to shell us with tear gas shells. This gas we could not smell at all. The first effects were that our eyes would start itching and smarting and then they would start running water. For this we had what was known as gas goggles just for wearing over our eyes. They used to be padded with rubber rings just round the eye pieces. This gas only affected our eyes. I don't think it had any ill-effect through inhaling it. They used to shell us here too with phosphorous shells. These were very pretty to watch exploding and that is about all you can say for them as they would burn a hole in our skin or our uniform wherever they touched you. There must have been some other deadly chemicals in them as well.

Lt Col Warden, seen here in later life, assumed command of the Battalion on 18 July 1917.
Warden Bruce & co

This state of affairs did nothing to help Lieutenant-Colonel Newton's continuing ill-health. Since early July, Lieutenant-Colonel Atkins had rejoined from his training to again serve alongside Newton, but on 5th August he returned to England and on the 12th Newton was re-admitted to hospital and left the Battalion for the last time. Six days later Lieutenant-Colonel Herbert Lawton Warden arrived to take over as the new commanding officer. A keen golfer and motoring enthusiast, Warden's peace-time occupation had been as a partner of the Hagard and Burn-Murdoch practice of solicitors in the Edinburgh Supreme Courts. A member of the Royal Scots' Volunteer and Territorial forces from 1901 to 1912, Warden was thirty-seven years old when war broke out. Married with two young daughters, he might have been excused a lack of enthusiasm for participating in the conflict. Instead, Warden immediately founded the Edinburgh Military Training Association in 1914 and volunteered to rejoin the Royal Scots. Serving with the 16th Battalion, as a Major and second-in-command, he was then promoted in 1916 and posted to command the 27th Battalion, Northumberland Fusiliers where he received a Mention in Despatches. A well-experienced and battle-hardened

Men of the Wandsworth Battalion at the entrance to a trench near Villers-Plouich, summer 1917.
Mrs P. Hucker

Lt James in the ruins of Villers-Plouich, summer 1917.
Mrs P. Hucker

officer, Warden was a sound replacement for Newton, but the Battalion's first action under his command was to prove inauspicious.

On the night of 21 August a patrol led by Second Lieutenant Rose was surprised and heavily bombed by the enemy in Fifteen Ravine. Rose himself was wounded, along with eight others, and one man was killed. In the desperate scramble back to their own lines, Lance-Corporal Cartwright stood out amongst the East Surreys for his great courage in helping the wounded, though Sergeant Sutcliffe, badly hit in one knee, had to be left behind. When this news reached the 13th Battalion's trenches, Lieutenant Victor Scott twice organised search parties to look for the missing Sergeant, accompanying them himself and remaining in No Man's Land for several hours. The award of a Military Cross recognised Scott's bravery and his citation recorded that he had shown 'a complete disregard of danger, as well as initiative and resource.'[33] For the same action, Lance-Corporal Cartwright received a Military Medal for his 'great courage and enterprise' in helping the wounded regain the Battalion's positions. It was later learned that Sergeant Sutcliffe had been taken prisoner.

While out of the line and billetted in the village of Fins, the men were witness to an aerial drama when a German aircraft attacked a British observation balloon. Private Bonsey described the scene vividly:

> *He came over the line flying very high, and then swooped down on this balloon firing at it all the time until they had managed to set it alight. Then our two men jumped out of the basket and came to ground with parachutes. They were not hurt. Well, after this we saw several of our balloons brought down like this, but afterwards our people got more artful, so they equipped our balloons with a machine gun. So one day Jerry came over again to put this one down too but not quite so easy this time. Our chaps up in the balloon got their machine gun ready and fired a few shots into them for a change and it was not long before the German aeroplane nose dived and fell to ground. The plane caught fire and burnt out, also burning the two German airmen. We did laugh to see this bit of sport. We all ran over to where it fell to ground to see if we could scrounge any souvenirs. No doubt this was a big surprise for*

The spectacle of a shot down German aircraft was clearly recalled by Private Bonsey.
Mrs P. Hucker

these German airmen as they had previously shot down several of our
balloons.

The village of Fins provided a number of facilities for the troops, including a cinema and a field hospital, the latter consisting of a number of huts erected in the grounds of an old French farm and remembered by those treated there on account of the very good food provision and proper beds. But other than in the hospital, basic provisions were in short supply at this time. Private Bonsey was one of those responsible for the Battalion's water supplies and he was later to recall how scarce this vital commodity became in the summer of 1917:

> *They only had a quart of water per man per day so they could not afford to lose much of their rations and in some parts of the line they didn't get that as it was difficult to find good water. I mean fit for drinking. Perhaps we would be walking all day to get a load of water that was at all fit to drink. I remember water was so scare in one part of the line that we had to guard our water with fixed bayonets so as to reserve the water as far as possible. The chaps kept asking for water but we dare not let them have it, only their ration which was then only one pint per day. It seemed very hard to have to refuse them but that was our orders, and on active service orders have to be obeyed. Us watermen had to account for every pint of water that went out of these carts at this time as it was impossible to find around here for miles. The officer would see that they went up the line full up, and each cart held one hundred and ten gallons, and this had to be issued out in pints and no more, so it was as bad for us as it was for the battalion. As luck would have it we never stayed up at this part of the line for long, so we were not sorry for that part of it... bread was very scarce at times out there, as many as twenty to one loaf, and sometimes none at all. Some days then we would have to fall back on our hard biscuits. At times we had a bigger bread ration, perhaps about six to one loaf.*

For the remainder of August and all of September the 13th Battalion alternated between front-line trench duty and regular patrolling in the Villers-Plouich and Beaucamp sectors, and acted as brigade reserve in Gouzeaucourt Wood and Dessart Wood. Total strength by the end of September was only 19 officers and some 480 other ranks, but the casualty rate slowed as this section of the Western Front settled down into something approaching calm. Some of the enemy took advantage of the lull to surrender, walking in from No Man's Land, hands held high and announcing in good English "Good morning Surreys, we are glad you have captured us so that we can have a rest". The Battalion's only action of note came on 30 September when five men were

The fine summer weather was an inducement to bathing parties. Mrs P. Hucker

The Germans had also made use of the village of Fins for entertainment. D. Goubet

The Picture Palace at Fins, later recaptured by the Germans. D. Goubet

Captain Tom Hucker visiting the 120th Trench Mortar Battery. Mrs P. Hucker

wounded by fire from enemy aeroplanes. The 40th Division was then relieved by the 20th Division and moved back to rest in the Arras area. For the 13th Battalion this involved marching to a camp at Heudicourt and from the 6 to 9 October the East Surreys were taken by lorry and train to Berneville, five miles from Arras. Private Bonsey maintained his detailed chronicle:

Lt Deacon pictured near Villers-Plouich in the summer of 1917.
Mrs P. Hucker

Well, after we left this part of the line we made our way up to Péronne. This was another lively hole. We came into this about a month after some of our chaps had captured it. As the firing line was some four miles farther on towards Bapaume we billeted in this village for a couple of weeks before we went up the line, so they got us to clear the roads of bricks and blown-down houses while we were having a rest. It was some job in places as we could not see where a road had been as at some places it was covered over with tons of bricks and earth owing to the recent heavy artillery bombardments, and some places there would be large shell holes, but we found where one road used to run through the town so they could see we had made a start. I think the Canadian troops took this town. We stayed around here for three or four weeks, going up the line in different sectors. It was here that I saw the first American troops, a few of their engineers. They were working on a light railway that had been laid down along the side of the road. Our engineers used to run these light gauge railways up wherever possible. They were a big help in getting supplies up the line. A little motor engine would pull the trucks along, about two or three trucks at the most, but they used to take a few tons of stuff at a time. There were several of these light railways out there. These few Yankee troops was all I saw of them, although there was supposed to be a few divisions of them at the bases.

Normal training was undertaken until the 29th, followed by a march to Lucheux, a few miles north-east of Doullens. This area consisted of a junction of valleys with thickly wooded slopes and here the Battalion commenced specialised exercises to master wood fighting, a welcome relief after months of trench warfare in open ground. Training was also given in techniques for attacking villages and strongpoints and speculation grew that offensive action was soon bound to follow. Sure enough the Battalion moved on to Courcelles-le-Comte in mid-

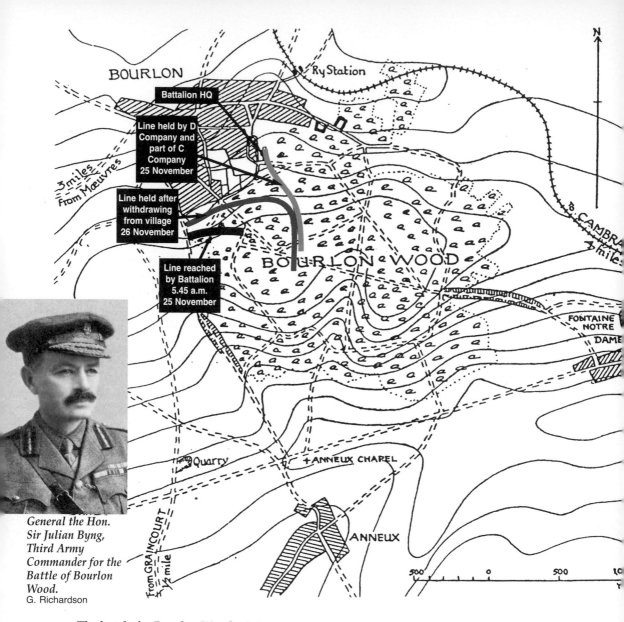

Map labels:
BOURLON
Ry Station
N
Battalion HQ
Line held by D Company and part of C Company 25 November
Line held after withdrawing from village 26 November
Line reached by Battalion 5.45 a.m. 25 November
3 miles From Mœuvres
CAMBRAI 3 miles
BOURLON WOOD
FONTAINE NOTRE DAME
Quarry
ANNEUX CHAPEL
ANNEUX
from GRAINCOURT ½ mile
500 0 500 1000

General the Hon. Sir Julian Byng, Third Army Commander for the Battle of Bourlon Wood.
G. Richardson

The battle for Bourlon Wood, 1917. Author

November where orders of readiness for action were received. On the 19th the men marched to Beaulencourt, south-east of Bapaume and it was there, on the morning of the 20th, that the unmistakable sounds of a massive attack reached them from the north-east, the direction of Cambrai. There was little doubt that this new inferno was to be the Battalion's next destination.

Chapter 5

BOURLON WOOD

By late 1917 it was clear that success was no nearer than at the beginning of the much trumpeted 'Year of Victory'. Consequently, after more than three years of largely static and wasteful warfare, the Allies had planned an offensive which would not only be different, but would also prove to be one of the most notable battles of the First World War. The objective was to smash through the Germans' Hindenburg Line and capture the vital French city of Cambrai.

The attack's major difference was to be in the use of tanks. First committed to action in small numbers at Flers on the Somme over a year earlier, the machines had been much improved by late 1917 and the Tanks Corps of Brigadier-General Hugh Elles had managed to build up an impressive strength of 381 for the Cambrai offensive. These were delivered by special train to Bray sur Somme where infantry were sent to perfect tactics with the machines. Though still clumsy and awkward, the latest tanks had proved themselves able to surmount parapets and cross trenches, provided they were not too

Hindenburg Line defences were designed to channel attackers into killing zones.

A section of the Hindenburg Line with tank obstacles.

wide or too high. They also now carried fascines, bundles of brushwood, on their hulls for dropping into trenches and use as crude bridges for the following infantry.

A second innovation for the assault on Cambrai was that the attack was to commence without the usual preliminary artillery barrage. Instead, the tanks would be responsible for flattening the enemy's barbed wire defences and for providing close-support fire for the infantry. The artillery could therefore wait for the tank attack to begin and then provide covering fire for the infantry and counter-battery fire against the Germans' own guns. In this latter role the British gunners were also to implement new methods of sound-ranging and flash-spotting. The resultant 'predicted' barrage, rather than an indiscriminate area bombardment, was to prove far more accurate and efficient in silencing the enemy's guns. Equally importantly, the new techniques would add to the element of surprise when the attack was launched. Some 1,000 guns were therefore gradually and secretly brought up to the front, carefully concealed and ranged in on predetermined targets.

The British plan for the battle involved General Byng's Third Army attacking on a front from Gonnelieu on the right to Havrincourt Wood on the left. The 40th[34] was one of two divisions held in reserve while the main force consisted of the entire strength of the Tanks Corps along with five full Divisions, namely the 12th, 20th, 6th, 51st and

Tanks with large bundles of brushwood, fascines, for overcoming the Hindenburg line (see opposite).

General von der Marwitz

62nd, plus the 36th in part. A large force of cavalry would also be at hand to exploit the expected break through. On the right flank of the attack the St Quentin canal had to be crossed and in the centre the village of Flesquières was to be seized. North of Flesquières another critical objective was Bourlon Wood, sited on relatively modest high ground, yet able to dominate the western approaches to Cambrai itself.

At 6.20 a.m. 20 November 1917 the attack began. The German 2nd Army of General von der Marwitz was caught by surprise and on the first day a six mile wide breakthrough was smashed through the Hindenburg Line to the south-west of Cambrai. The British had succeeded in bringing their tanks up undetected and the Germans fell back in confusion and terror as waves of the mechanical monsters bore down on them. This was, warfare of a kind previously unseen on the Western Front – rapid and apparently decisive. In England reports of the successful break-out were received with wild optimism and many even dared think the war's end might not now be too distant. The government was only too ready to accept, at long last, one of Field Marshal Haig's promised victories and on 23 November, church bells were rung throughout Britain to mark the 'victory'.

And yet, at the very moment when the Borough of Wandsworth's own bells pealed joyously, its men were waiting to be thrown into a battle which was showing every sign of turning into defeat.

The orders which committed the 13th

Battalion to the already-raging conflict were issued shortly before midnight 22/23 November. These were that the 40th Division, brought out of reserve, would join the 51st and 36th Divisions in making a renewed push forward in order to gain a line running from the high ground north-east of Fontaine-Notre-Dame to the railway line north of Bourlon Wood, on to Quarry Wood and ultimately to Inchy. The 51st Highland Division had already suffered critical delays in advancing beyond the vital village of Flesquières when General Harper, the Division's commanding officer, inexplicably switched tactics from those stipulated. Elsewhere the British infantry had poured, in narrow files, through the gaps that the tanks had torn in the barbed wire. Harper, however, ordered his Highlanders to advance in line abreast and they were soon caught up and delayed by the remaining wire defences. Consequently, the tanks in this sector pressed on without infantry support and paid the price when the well dug-in enemy picked them off in Flesquières. The Scots' attack had therefore ground to a halt as early as 21st November, but by the 23rd the 51st Division's remaining battalions were reorganised to push ahead on the right flank, aiming to capture their next objective, the village of Fontaine-Notre-Dame.

On the left flank of the offensive the 36th Ulster Division had fared little better in attempts to capture Moeuvres, but like the 51st, was still in reasonable condition to regroup for another assault. In the centre, however, the 62nd Division was exhausted after the initial attack on Bourlon village was repulsed with heavy losses. The 40th Division, fresh and still at more or less full strength, was ordered up to take the 62nd's place in the centre of the 51st and 36th Divisions. The 40th's 121 Brigade, under Brigadier-General Campbell, was given the task of storming and capturing the village, while Brigadier-General Crozier (who had replaced Brigadier-General Cunliffe-Owen) was to make a simultaneous attack on Bourlon Wood with his 119 Brigade. For the moment the 120 Brigade of Brigadier-General Drummond Willoughby, including the 13th East Surreys, was to be held in reserve at Havrincourt.

Therefore, 120 Brigade was the last brigade of the 40th Division to enter the battle area, being a day's march behind the others. It was on 19 November that the first definite orders were received as to participation in the attack and there was much speculation as to what part the 13th Battalion would play. An hour's notice to move had been given and all superfluous kit was dumped while everyone stood by in high spirits.

On the morning of 21 November it was still raining, but the bleak conditions were enlivened when the first groups of German prisoners were seen trudging morosely back along the road to Bapaume. By midday 120 Brigade was again moving forward and on 23 November, at dawn, they crossed the Canal du Nord. By now the men were somewhat disgruntled at the extent of their march to the front, especially as the roads were a foot deep in mud, but Brigadier-General Drummond Willoughby arrived with news of the state of the battle and there was considerable excitement, especially when tanks began to gather nearby for another advance. At last the Brigade reached its position of reserve, in the newly-captured Hindenburg Support Line between Graincourt and Havrincourt. There, the 13th Battalion made a lucky find. In an abandoned German dugout extensive supplies of preserved meat and hundreds of cases of aerated water were discovered. Every man, issued with two tins of beef and two bottles of 'fizz', was therefore able to have a decent lunch while watching the battle raging on the slopes of Bourlon Wood in the distance. The spectacle was not overly encouraging, being characterised by constant explosions in the wood and shrapnel bursts above it.

With both 119 and 121 Infantry Brigades fully committed to the battle raging around Bourlon, it was not long before the 40th Division had to call on its reserves of 120 Brigade. During the afternoon of the 23rd the Wandsworth men again waited as first the 14th Argyll and Sutherland Highlanders marched off, followed by the 11th King's Own Royal Lancaster Regiment. Only the East Surreys and the 14th Battalion, Highland Light Infantry remained uncommitted and this was further reduced when, in the evening, the Highlanders were called up to reinforce 121 Brigade.

On the 24th the 13th Battalion moved further up to a spot some three quarters of a mile south-west of Graincourt. This village housed the headquarters of 121 Brigade and shortly after 9 p.m. the same evening, Lieutenant-Colonel Warden was ordered there for orders. By this time the 40th Division's front had become seriously disrupted. The 12th Suffolks had withdrawn from Bourlon and were holding some trenches just south of it. The village itself was still held by strong pockets of Germans, but just to the north one company of the 14th Highland Light Infantry was holding out on the railway line. To their left there was nothing but Germans, for the 36th Ulster Division had been unable to push forward. On their right 119 Brigade was still struggling in the wood.

On arrival at the headquarters Warden was told of the beleaguered company of Highlanders who had earlier pushed through Bourlon village and were occupying the railway station, a stretch of the railway line and a trench line just north of the village. He also learned that 119 Brigade was reported to be holding the north-eastern edge of Bourlon Wood. Warden's orders were to clear the western portion of Bourlon of any enemy and to then continue through the village in order to extend, to the left, the forward line already formed by the 14th Highland Light Infantry. To help in clearing the village it was planned that tanks should assist if available, but there was to be no artillery barrage.

For the rest of that night Warden personally reconnoitred the southern edge of Bourlon village in order to plan the 13th Battalion's advance. Doubling back he then chose an assembly point in a sunken road leading towards the village. This road ran north from an old quarry and there, about midnight, Warden joined the commanding officers of the 12th Battalion, Suffolk Regiment and the 20th Battalion, Middlesex Regiment. These two units had their headquarters staff sited in the quarry and advised Warden that they thought it no longer possible to reach the headquarters of the 14th Highland Light Infantry, which were believed to have been somewhere in the southern limits of the village. The generally pessimistic view was that "there were no British troops north of the cross-roads just ahead of the quarry, and that the Highland Light Infantry must have been wiped out."

Warden, however, was not so sure. Even as he consulted with the other units the Germans began to shell the south-western approaches to the wood and Warden instinctively felt this was an attempt to prevent reinforcements reaching the cut-off Scots. He had personally scouted almost as far as the last reported position of the Highlanders' battalion headquarters and he therefore elected to continue with his plan. The shrewd former lawyer decided that his best chance of helping his fellow Scots would be to make his primary objective the securing of the ground north of the village in order to strengthen the front line already held. Making his way back to where he had left the Battalion at Graincourt, Warden came upon his men already moving up in anticipation of his orders. It then took only a few minutes more before all the Battalion's companies were assembled for orders in the sunken road.

Warden explained his scheme to the company commanders and then cautiously led the Battalion forward to the line he had decided upon in front of the village. During the night all the roads south and west of Bourlon Wood had been subjected to a heavy barrage of enemy artillery fire, but the East Surreys suffered only a few casualties. By 6 a.m. the situation was much quieter as they formed up on a three-company front for the attack. The leading platoon of each company was to go straight through the village, still under cover of darkness, in order to join the Highlanders in the trench beyond. The remaining three platoons of each of A, B and C companies were to deal with the enemy parties in the village while D Company was held in reserve on the north-western edge of the wood in order to protect against any enemy flank attack.

Warden had fixed zero hour for 6.15 a.m. The hoped-for tanks had not appeared, but since his orders were not conditional upon their arrival, the advance began as planned.[35] Warden had left his own headquarters personnel in the old quarry with those of the 12th Suffolks and 20th Middlesex while he elected to lead the attack personally. The weather was foul, with driving rain, but the Battalion was in good spirits as it marched towards the gloomy, thickly-timbered, wood. Roughly 600 acres in total, Bourlon Wood stood on a ridge and rose to a maximum height of only 150 feet or so above the Cambrai to Bapaume road. From the road the ground sloped relatively gently upwards to the tree line, the wooded ridge standing out starkly from the surrounding, largely cultivated, fields. It was still dark and therefore difficult to see ahead clearly, but within only a few minutes of the advance starting Warden was proved right in ignoring the earlier cautionary advice he had been given. In a farm house on the edge of the village he came upon the headquarters of the 14th Highland Light Infantry and was able to hand over the message from 121 Brigade to Lieutenant-Colonel Battye, the Highlanders' commanding officer. Quickly, Warden explained the plan for his own advance and Battye readily gave his approval. Very soon after, however, heavy machine-gun fire opened up at 6.30 a.m. from the north, east and south of the house occupied by Battye and his staff. It was obvious that strong enemy parties still held the north-eastern portion of Bourlon Wood and would have to be dislodged. Since there were no signs of an attack from the west flank and with Battye's approval, Warden therefore ordered Captain Jim Hucker's D Company out of reserve and to advance southwards and eastwards through the wood in order to cut off, or deter, any enemy parties

Major-General John Ponsonby, pictured earlier in his career, commanded 40th Division. Author

117

coming up from the south. Today the landscape is very much the same, though firs have largely overtaken the predominance of oaks which closed around the twenty-one-year-old officer and his men as they entered the wood by one of the many tracks which criss-crossed the ridge.James Hucker, 'Jim' to most, was one of the two brothers from Allfarthing Lane, Wandsworth, who had been among the first to volunteer for the 13th East Surreys. Formerly a bank clerk with Coutts and Co. in the Strand, he had joined the Inns of Court Officer Training Corps (OTC) before being commissioned into the Wandsworth Battalion. Promoted to D Company commander after the Villers-Plouich attack, where he had also earned a Mention in Despatches, this young man was soon to earn further recognition of his courage.

In addition to the massive trees of Bourlon Wood, there was also thick undergrowth which made any progress off the paths and tracks extremely difficult. Yet as Hucker and D Company struggled on, Warden learned that C Company, led by Captain Burton, had made no better progress through the right of the village. He therefore managed to withdraw most of these men and ordered them into a position stretching from Battye's headquarters south-eastwards along a path in the wood. They were also to attempt to make contact with any friendly troops holding a line through the right of the wood. These two companies, C and D, of the 13th Battalion, aided by the headquarters personnel and reserve company of the 14th Highland Light Infantry, then succeeded in repelling an attack by groups of the enemy who approached from the south, i.e. from the rear of the British line. Captain Alexander Burton, originally from the 14th Highland Light Infantry, but attached to the 13th East Surreys since July, was particularly to the fore in this engagement and though earlier thwarted from forcing a way through the village, he now efficiently organised the defence line through the wood. A grateful Lieutenant-Colonel Warden was later to acknowledge: 'He held that ridge against all comers.'

Despite Burton's success in pushing the enemy back, tragedy struck at 7.15 a.m. just as the heat of the engagement was diminishing. Slipping out of the headquarters house to check a Lewis gun post, Lieutenant-Colonel Battye was caught by a burst of enemy machine-gun fire and hit in the chest. Staggering back into the house, he gasped to Warden that he had been hit, a bullet had gone through his chest and he collapsed on the floor. The Highlanders' medical officer gave immediate treatment, but Battye was dead within minutes. As the senior officer remaining, Warden at once took command of the remaining elements of both battalions.

At 7.45 a.m. orders were received addressed to Battye and stipulating the capture of the railway line north of the village, the objective which Warden had been given to understand was already held by the 14th Highland Light Infantry. Unhelpfully, the 13th Battalion also received orders from their divisional commander, which showed that Brigadier-General Ponsonby had little idea of the current situation.[36] His brusque note read:

> O.C. E Surrey Regt
> 1. *You will push forward at once and gain touch with Col. Battye. If necessary you will fight your way through the village at the east end and reach the trench in front, this is most urgent and will be carried out without delay. Touch must be gained with H.L.I. [Highland Light Infantry] forthwith.*
> 2. *Col. Battye has orders to occupy railway in 7.1.c & d by 9 a.m. 12 tanks should now be in the village BOURLON for this purpose. If necessary 2 tanks may be detached to assist in clearing village.*
> 3. *Act at once and gain touch without further delay.*
> *John Ponsonby*
> *BG*
> *7.20 a.m.*
> *25 Nov 17*

Battye, of course, was dead even before this message was penned and the rest of Ponsonby's appreciation of the position was equally out-of-touch, especially with regard to the supposed availability of tanks. It was unclear as to exactly where the Highlanders' forward troops were, but in the light of the orders received, it clearly fell to the 13th East Surreys to see what could be done. The Battalion's A and B Companies were still closely engaged in fierce fighting in the village and Warden therefore considered whether any element of his other two companies, or of the reserve company of Highland Light Infantry, could be spared to push on to the railway line. By this time, however, it was obvious that the enemy still held the village in great strength. Warden decided that sufficient troops could not be spared for any further operations through the village, if the high spur in Bourlon Wood itself were to be held. Instead, the immediate priority was to join up the Battalion's line in the wood with the still-to-be-found 119 Brigade to the east. But at 7.50 a.m. this plan had to be abandoned when the enemy again suddenly attacked in force from the east, heading for the spur in the wood and, just beyond, Warden's headquarters. The building serving as such was in reality ahead of the British line, but as the enemy was not able to shell the house, Warden had decided to make it a strongpoint. It held a commanding position and could be fortified more quickly than a position could be dug in the wood. Firing positions had swiftly been made on the eastern and southern sides of the building and the 13th Battalion's snipers were posted in the upper part of the house to fire through gaps in the tiles. The enemy attack was thus met by rifle and Lewis gun fire, both from C and D Companies in the wood and from the headquarters house. At 8.45 a.m. the Germans at last withdrew with considerable losses.

During the remainder of the day of the 25th several enemy parties reconnoitring the spur in the wood were dispersed by fire and the headquarters house was further strengthened. Several efforts were also made to push through the village, two platoons of the East Surreys' D Company being ordered at 10.40 a.m. to support an attack through the left of the village. They found, however, that it was impossible to make any progress or to contact the front line where Lieutenant Lanham and the leading platoon of A Company were believed to have reached the railway. The two D Company platoons, along with small parties of the attacking companies who had been driven back, were instead used to establish an outpost line to guard the spur and north-western edge of the wood. To add to the confusion a message arrived from Captain Linge, commanding B Company, reporting that he had been cut off from the rest of his men and was sheltering with Captain Burton and five others in the sunken road just outside the village.

Warden was now uneasy about his left flank being unprotected and so, for reassurance, at 12.50 p.m. he sent a written message by runner to the quarry headquarters of the 12th Suffolks and 20th Middlesex. He asked for a joint report of their positions and of those of the 11th King's Own Royal Lancaster Regiment, whose commanding officer was also based in the quarry. No reply was received to this message, but better news came from the Battalion's eastern flank when, in the early afternoon, contact was finally made with the 12th South Wales Borderers of the previously unlocated 119 Brigade. From their officer sent to brief him, Warden learned that the front line held by 119 Brigade ran in an arc through the wood, from the eastern edge to just right of his own positions. An enemy strongpoint in the middle of the wood had stopped 119 Brigade's advance and Warden therefore repositioned his men to join up with their newly-found colleagues on the right by continuing their outpost line along a couple of roads leading back into the wood. This line was defended in depth and dug

An aerial view of Bourlon Wood after the battle. G. Richardson

in with entrenching tools. Orders were also given for small patrols to try to capture the enemy machine guns which were keeping up almost continuous fire on the East Surreys' headquarters and on the spur in the wood. Finally, in writing, Warden gave the command that the new line was to be held at all costs.

At about 3.00 p.m. the officer in charge of a party of the 14th Argyll and Sutherland Highlanders, who were also sited in Bourlon Wood, arrived to tell Warden that the Hussars on his right had withdrawn. With his right flank consequently left open to attack, the officer had come to seek instructions from the East Surreys, but he could only be given a general picture of the prevailing confusion and uncertainty. In these circumstances Warden could do no more than ask the Argyll and Sutherlands to bend their right flank southwards and try to hold on.

Later in the day a much more positive caller arrived when Second Lieutenant Henderson of the 121st Trench Mortar Battery reached the 13th Battalion's positions with two mortars. Quickly Warden provided a carrying party to bring up ammunition from the old quarry and the mortars then went into action dispersing enemy parties and firing at

The shattered remains of Bourlon village. G. Richardson

houses which were seen to be occupied by machine-gunners and snipers. They immediately made an appreciable difference in subduing the enemy's fire.

Shortly before dusk the Germans began to use their deadly *minenwerfer* heavy mortars (known as 'Minnies' to the British troops), but it was already too dark to enable them to range on the 13th Battalion's positions. Warden therefore decided that it was safe to remain in the house for another night and in addition to the outpost line behind his headquarters, he established a series of posts in front. Enemy snipers had been busy all day from houses and trees and from the reports he received from the attacking companies, Warden realised that the village was still held much too strongly by the enemy to justify committing his men to another assault.

As darkness fell on the evening of 25 November, the 13th Battalion finally received a message, timed at 2.40 p.m. earlier that day, stating the 40th Division was being relieved that night. Tanks were being ordered up, though it was not known how many or when they would arrive. These would be used to cover the withdrawal of those 14th Highland Light Infantry troops still thought to be north of the village near the railway and any other men still fighting in Bourlon itself.

Completion of the withdrawal was to be reported as early as possible to Brigade Headquarters and upon that report being received, relief would begin.

Again the tanks failed to arrive. At 8.30 a.m. on the 26th Warden sent a written message and a small party to find the machines, but they met with no success. At 10.40 a.m. Brigade was consequently informed by runner that the withdrawal could not be carried out, as the tanks had not appeared. Enemy aeroplanes were flying low over the village and wood and further orders were urgently requested. This message to 121 Brigade headquarters was delivered by relay runner to Graincourt, but the headquarters had been replaced there by 187 Brigade and the 13th Battalion's signalling officer had to continue back to Havrincourt to explain the situation.

During the day of the 26th several efforts were made to reach the cut-off troops north of the village with rations and water, but all attempts failed in the face of strong enemy forces, which were showing signs of preparing to counter-attack. To make matters even worse, in the afternoon the Germans at last found the range of the Battalion's headquarters house with their *minenwerfer*. Second Lieutenant Henderson again kept his two Stokes Mortars in continuous action until all available ammunition had been used, but the house, although reinforced, was not strong enough to resist the enemy's return bombardment. As casualties mounted there was no alternative but to move, though it was impossible to do so in daylight due to the intense rifle and machine-gun fire.

As darkness fell, the withdrawal of the Battalion Headquarters' personnel of both the 13th East Surreys and 14th Highland Light Infantry began. The men slipped back to the outpost line in parties of three and the operation was completed without loss. Battalion Headquarters were then re-established in a dugout in the western edge of the wood, just behind the outpost line. At the new location two more parallel trenches were dug, facing north and extending across the wood within the 13th Battalion's sector. Warden still expected an enemy attack that night and this seemed all the more likely when, at about 7 p.m., a heavy barrage of artillery and machine-gun fire rained down on the outpost line and the men working to complete the two new trench lines. An SOS signal was sent up by the 11th Battalion, King's Own Royal Lancaster Regiment on the left flank and the immediate and effective response that this brought from Allied artillery thankfully soon deterred the Germans' fire. At about 7.40 p.m. the enemy sent up several signal rockets of their own and shortly afterwards their barrage ceased.

During the remainder of the evening it was learned that relief units had arrived and at 9.30 p.m. a message was sent to Brigade stating that, except for three companies of the 14th Highland Light Infantry believed to still be north of the village, Warden's force was in a position to be relieved. At about 10.30 p.m. the Adjutant of the 2/4th Battalion, York and Lancaster Regiment reached Warden to inform him of a proposed attack by the 62nd Division the next day. This officer had orders to guide the 13th Battalion men out of the area so they would not get in the way of the preliminary barrage, but Warden decided he could take his men out only if the York and Lancaster officer accepted responsibility for maintaining the outpost line that night. The newcomer was not in a position to do so and Warden therefore arranged that he would continue to hold the line until 5.30 a.m. the next morning. For the remainder of the night the Battalion stood-to in the outpost line and new trenches, but apart from light shelling and machine-gun fire, the expected enemy activity failed to materialise.

After an uneasy night Warden assembled all remaining troops of the East Surreys and the Highland Light Infantry in and around his headquarters dugout between 5.30 and 6.00 a.m. on the 27th. The 62nd Division's attack went in at 6.20 a.m. and after the fresh troops had passed, Warden began to withdraw his command in small parties of ten, each led by an officer or senior NCO. This withdrawal, conducted under heavy artillery and machine-gun fire, led back to the Hindenburg Support Line, which the 13th Battalion had previously occupied. Routes had been carefully chosen in advance and as a result casualties during the withdrawal were light.

Sadly, the same could not be said of the overall picture. After just two days in action, the 13th Battalion found itself back at the Hindenburg Support Line with only the comforting thought that their progress in the attack on Bourlon had been further than that achieved by the units on either flank. Only a handful of men were taken prisoner by the Germans in this bitterly fought action, but among those captured were Lieutenant Harker, the former *Wandsworth Borough News* reporter, and Lieutenant Lanham, both officers having been wounded. The Battalion's headquarters and front-line strength had been twenty-one officers and 602 men when the battle began. At its conclusion, total casualties numbered 229 and of these no trace was ever found of sixty-six of the eighty men who were killed, including the popular Captain William Lowe.[37] One of those injured was VC-holder Corporal Foster, who received a bullet through his right wrist. Foster, promoted to Sergeant, had returned to his unit after three months' leave in England celebrating his award and although he was offered a staff job at base, he had declined, saying that he wanted to stay with his comrades in the Battalion. His wound, however, now took him out of the fighting and eventually led to his medical discharge from the Army in 1918. But good prospects awaited. Shortly before his wounding, Wandsworth Council's Officers and Servants Committee had voted, on 9 November 1917, to offer their hero a promotion post back in the Council's direct employment as a Dusting Inspector. This was back-dated to the date of the notification of Tiny's VC, 27 June 1917, and further benefits were bestowed by a Council ruling that his pension rights were to be made continuous back to April 1909.

On 28 November 1917 the 13th Battalion marched out of the Hindenburg Line and was then taken by lorry and bus to Blairville, five miles south-west of Arras. A welcome rest was enjoyed while the next day was spent refitting, but on 30 November orders were suddenly received for the Battalion to be ready to move at two hours notice. The enemy had begun a counter-attack.

Despite the early Allied successes in advancing on Cambrai, the Germans had clearly recovered quickly from their initial shock. Von der Marwitz had gathered sixteen fresh divisions and, determined to win back what had been lost, surged on to the offensive before the British could fully consolidate their new positions. Within a week the Germans had retaken most of the territory lost and in some areas also advanced up to three miles deep into the original British line. For three grim weeks the 13th Battalion, weakened but still very much needed, found itself back in front-line positions at Fontaine-les-Croisilles. Severe winter conditions added to the ordeal with heavy snow falls which, freezing on the trench duck boards, made progress extremely difficult. Later, when a thaw came, the sides of the trenches invariably collapsed and in many cases it was difficult to keep the water down, even with constant pumping. A widespread outbreak of trench foot was the inevitable result. While there was only one degree of frost back in Wandsworth and Battersea that winter, there were fifteen degrees around Arras and Cambrai. Boots, once taken off, froze solid in just a few minutes, as too did hot tea and food. To add to this misery the Germans made liberal use of gas shelling. Over just three days, from 12 to 14 December, Captain Jim Hucker (hit by shrapnel in both legs and a foot), Captain L. I. Deacon, Lieutenant Rutherford and fifty-one

The 40th Division added an acorn to their divisional badge to mark their sacrifice at Bourlon Wood. A. Clyro

men were wounded, many from the effects of gas, and two men were killed.

When the fighting eventually petered out in December, each side had suffered about 40,000 casualties. 4,000 were in the 40th Division alone which, in a captured enemy document, was optimistically listed as 'annihilated'. While this was an exaggeration, the Division had suffered grievously and would henceforth add an acorn to its divisional emblem of a cockerel in order to signify its bloody struggle among the oaks of Bourlon. Sadly, it was the fate of most of the 13th Battalion's dead to be buried in unmarked graves. Those few who were mortally wounded and sent back were properly recorded, but the remainder fell in and around the wood, which was soon back in enemy hands.

There the Germans had little time or inclination to observe formalities in disposing of the dead from the battle. Many of the corpses were unceremoniously and hurriedly buried with no details being recorded. There also exists a report from local sources that many of the corpses were crudely cremated, saving much effort in what was still an exposed front-line area. Second Lieutenant Wheatcroft, a former amateur international and professional footballer attached from the 5th Battalion, was one of the very few who was properly buried close to where he fell. In the small British military cemetery at Anneux, on the site of the ruined chapel where Lieutenant-Colonel Warden rendezvoused with his men on the morning of 25 November, Wheatcroft is remembered with the epitaph:

'One who never turned his back but marched breast forward.'

By way of reward for the many examples of great individual bravery displayed at Bourlon, fifteen men of the Battalion were decorated with the Military Medal, including a posthumous award to Private Albert Bance. Three Distinguished Conduct Medals were won, Sergeant Bennett also receiving a bar to his existing DCM. Five officers were gazetted for the Military Cross, including Captain Jim Hucker[38] and Lieutenant George Beaumont. The latter had been a Civil Servant in the War Trade Department and, along with two close friends, had enlisted in the ranks of the London Scottish early in the war. He had joined this regiment in France in November 1915, serving in a Lewis gun section and was wounded at Gommecourt the following March. He returned to France in September 1916 and was subsequently commissioned into the 13th East Surreys. After his award of the Military Cross, Beaumont's Company commander, Captain Alexander Burton, wrote a congratulatory note to his subaltern's mother:

Captain George Hucker after receiving his Military Cross at Buckingham Palace.
Mrs D. Hucker

B.E.F.
1.1.18

Dear Mrs Beaumont

I feel I really must write to you tonight and confirm the news which George has already given you I dare say.

I am so pleased he has been awarded the Military Cross for his excellent work during the recent operations. It's a great honour to my company indeed. My only regret is that, having been promoted to Captain, he was given comand of another company. I miss him very much indeed, for we are great friends. He is a slendid chap always so bright and cheery about everything. He is a very fine offficer too – one that can always be depended on. Whenever I used to want a reliable officer to do a job, I'm afraid George was always the one picked for it – not always very pleasant for him of course.

He tells me he intends to be visiting Scotland when the war finishes – to wear a kilt, as he says. I am just hoping we may be able to get our next leave together, and he might have a run up to Edinburgh

127

*with me. You are very fortunate indeed, Mrs Beaumont, to have such a
son.Well, I must wish you a very Happy New Year, and hope you may
soon see your M.C. son again.*

    With very kind regards
    Yours very sincerely
    A.B. Burton

Perhaps most deservedly, in view of his presence in the thick of the
fighting throughout, Lieutenant-Colonel Warden received the
Distinguished Service Order. His citation read:

    *For conspicuous gallantry and devotion to duty. He took command
of the advanced troops in an attack, and maintained his headquarters in
a forward position under heavy fire. He drove off three enemy counter-
attacks, and handled his reserve with such skill as to be able to keep in
touch with three companies of another battalion, which were under his
command. He showed splendid initiative and skill.*

Chapter 6

THE KAISER'S BATTLE

The end of December 1917 found the 13th East Surreys moving a few miles south into a different sector of the front line near Bullecourt. A position known as Horseshoe Redoubt was held there, with reserve periods spent at No. 8 Camp, by the village of Mory, where good entertainment was available, as recalled by Private Bonsey:

We spent a week here in this camp so that the chaps could get cleaned up a bit and have a rest. In this camp there was a large hut used as Divisional Canteen so that we could buy little things that we wanted. These divisional canteens were always an attraction as it seemed nice to be able to get little odd things such as writing paper and envelopes, biscuits, chocolates, fags and tobacco, although we always had plenty of baccy. In this hut, too, there was a divisional concert party one night and it was the best concert party ever I saw in France, as of course it was rare that any troops got so far back from the line to be able to stay there for a few days like our battalion did. I expect this place was about

A leading 'lady' of the Gamecocks.
Author

The 40th Division's touring theatre company.
Author

129

ten miles behind the line. The actors were all amateur players taken from the different regiments in this 40th Division, and one pair of singers I remember were the McGormac Bros, that still used to give turns on the London music halls soon after the war, and all the others were equally as good. It was a first class concert party. They were attached to Divisional Headquarters. They used to go round to our different battalions in the division. There was one little Welsh chap among them that could sing very well, him having a tenor voice. I have forgotten his name now. It sounded well in this large hut. He was from the Welsh Bantams. The chorus of one of his songs took very well amongst the chaps. It ran something like this:

"We are all British boys, young ones and all
All British boys and plucky though we may be small.
Standing by our guns, ever staunch and true.
But if there's a rantum
The gallant little Batam
Will help pull old England through."'

The Battalion's next move was to the town of Suzanne where, at the extreme southern end of the British line, they relieved French units who had been accommodated in a former French-administered camp for German prisoners of war. The site was still surrounded by barbed wire and the billets, if they could be called that, were partly underground, being a square hole in the ground with a roof of mud or grass. Each hole, accessed by three or four rough steps, had to hold six sleeping soldiers and conditions were so woeful that no-one used the shelters during the day, preferring the cold, yet fresh, open air. But the underground holes were the only option, the town was completely ruined, with not a single building inhabitable and huge rats ran about everywhere.

Fortunately, the Battalion's stay in the former POW camp was only four days before it was ordered up the line again, to support positions at Combles. Frontline duty was then in the aptly-named Death Valley, a desolate and shell-shattered place where no grass, hedges or trees were to be found. The weather and enemy gas shelling continued as severely as before, but some satisfaction was gleaned on Boxing Day when the Battalion's snipers were again successful in picking off a number of Germans. On 2 January 1918 another move was made to the Noreuil sector, six miles north-east of Bapaume and here at last the dreaded gas shelling stopped. Only an occasional artillery barrage troubled the front-line trenches and with the bad weather still present, patrolling and raids were kept to a minimum.

For over a month the Battalion shivered in the trenches or reserve positions, miserable but thankful for the relative respite. On 10th February welcome news of relief arrived at last and the East Surreys found themselves bussed back from Armagh Camp to No. 3 Camp at Hendecourt, south of Arras, as the 40th Division moved into GHQ reserve. There, reinforcements caught up with the battered survivors of Bourlon Wood, nine officers and 192 other ranks being posted in from D and part of C Companies of the 7th Battalion, East Surrey Regiment. The 7th Battalion was one of the victims of a reorganisation of the British Army which involved brigades now having only three, rather than four, battalions. This led to many battalions, the 7th East Surreys included, being disbanded and for a short time this gave anxiety over the future of the 13th Battalion. Fortunately, the Wandsworth unit's concerns proved ill-founded. Though they had to leave 120 Brigade which had been their parent formation since February 1916, the 13th East Surreys remained within the 40th Division and were transferred on 16 February to 119 Brigade of Brigadier-General Frank Crozier, joining the 21st Battalion, Middlesex Regiment and the 18th Battalion, Welsh Regiment. Crozier was a strict disciplinarian who was renowned for rejecting subordinates who did not fit his ideal. In addition, he possessed something of a fixation about cowardice or retreat in the face of the enemy and he was happy to back his views up with executions in the field. He was later to describe[39] with some relish how, during 119 Brigade's part in the battle for Bourlon Wood, several of his own men who turned and ran were shot down by Lewis gun and an officer's revolver. Happily, there is no evidence that anyone of the 13th Battalion fell foul of their new brigade commander to such an extreme extent, though it would seem Lieutenant-Colonel Warden did not enjoy a good relationship with his new superior.

Brigadier-General Frank Crozier, a strict disciplinarian who attracted controversy.
G. Richardson

Another result of the reorganisation saw a familiar face return to the 13th East Surreys when Lieutenant George Head reported for duty on the day the Battalion joined 119 Brigade. Head, one of the Wandsworth officers who had brought the Battalion to France in June, 1916, had been serving with the 120th Trench Mortar Battery since early 1917. In addition to Lieutenant Head, only Captain Linge, Captain Beecroft, Lieutenant Corben and Lieutenant G. E. Deacon remained of the original thirty-four officers.

The change of brigade formation called for more training which lasted for the remainder of February and early March and the only incident of note came with news of the Battalion's transport and supply details which had remained at Armagh Camp. A nightly bombing campaign on the camp by enemy aircraft had shaken the men, but while considerable damage was caused almost everywhere, the 13th Battalion men suffered no casualties and even the transport managed to avoid the bombs. Perhaps, after all, fortunes were on the rise again.

Yet, in the higher echelons of the British Army, plans were already being drawn up to commit the 13th East Surreys to another test of their resolve. The Allied High Command was well aware that the enemy was planning a great spring offensive. This, which the Germans were to call the Kaiser's Battle, aimed to break the long stalemate of the Western Front and force victory before the newly-arrived American armies could make a difference to the balance of power in France and Flanders.

Among the units brought to readiness immediately behind the front line of the British VI Corps south of Arras was the 40th Division, brought up from GHQ Reserve. On 12 March the 13th East Surreys moved up with 119 Brigade to Mercatel and were held there in readiness awaiting the German offensive, code-named 'St Michael'. Despite the known imminence of the attack, the men had the opportunity to play the finals of the battalion football competition and battalion orders of 20 March stated that the 40th Division's theatre company, 'The Gamecocks', would be performing in the theatre near Northumberland Camp at 6 p.m. the following evening. The show was destined not to go on.

At 5 a.m. on 21 March the massive German assault broke along a fifty mile front. Although the offensive had been anticipated by the

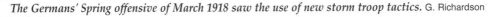
The Germans' Spring offensive of March 1918 saw the use of new storm troop tactics. G. Richardson

On 21 March the massive German assault broke along a fifty mile front. Taylor Library

Allies, the Germans nevertheless managed to secure an element of surprise by delivering a short, but extremely intense, bombardment of the front line, while the rear areas were heavily shelled with gas. The main enemy attacks on the front line were then led by highly-trained groups of storm troops. Armed with machine guns and light mortars, they kept up the attack's momentum by by-passing any stubborn British posts and leaving them to be dealt with by the bulk of the

German infantry. In the face of such determined new tactics, and comparatively weakened by many inexperienced and hurriedly-trained new recruits, the British front lines broke in disarray.

Almost immediately Major-General Ponsonby, commanding officer of the 40th Division, was ordered to occupy a defensive line running from just north of Vaulx-Vraucourt to the south-eastern edge of St Léger Wood. Along this line the Wandsworth Battalion was ordered to a position south of Judas Farm, less than a mile west of St Léger, which it reached at 7 a.m. on the 22nd. St Léger itself was still held by units of the 34th Division, but the British were gradually pushed out of the village during the day. As these troops retreated, the 13th Battalion behind them was also ordered back and on 23 March occupied Ervillers to the south-west. Here the Battalion learned that the advancing Germans were reported to be in the village of Mory, only a mile and a half to the east. Lieutenant-Colonel Warden at once ordered Captain Crowther's B Company to reconnoitre towards Mory, while Captain King and A Company formed a defensive line on the eastern edge of Ervillers, covering the line of approach from Mory. C and D Companies, along with Battalion Headquarters, moved a little further south to occupy and hold the village of Béhagnies.

Captain Crowther's advance towards Mory was not encouraging. Approaching the village, his company came under heavy fire from high ground to the north of the road and he was forced to turn back to Ervillers. There, Crowther was informed Mory was now known to be held by a strong enemy force and that further action by B Company alone would be suicidal. Instead, the Middlesex Regiment's 21st Battalion was ordered to attack the enemy-held high ground to the north and only then did B Company again venture out onto the Mory road. Its task, in support of the Middlesex unit, was to seize the crest north of the Ervillers-Mory road from which they had earlier come under fire. At 11 a.m. the company's attack went in, but a withering fire was poured down on the East Surreys and only a few men of No. 5 platoon managed to reach within twenty yards of the summit before they were cut down. The remainder of the company went to ground eighty yards below their objective and although any movement

attracted instant fire, Private Bark courageously went forward to retrieve a Lewis gun, the crew of which had been killed.

In the meantime Lieutenant-Colonel Warden had received further intelligence at Battalion Headquarters. Contrary to earlier reports it was now suggested that the enemy in Mory, though employing numerous snipers and machine guns, did not have any great strength in numbers. The 40th Division's official history clearly states that, upon receiving this new intelligence, it was Warden himself who suggested counter-attacking into the village. Brigadier General Crozier in his autobiography,[40] however, was later to claim Warden was reluctant to advance, that instead it was Crozier's own idea to do so and he had to threaten Warden with removal from command. It is difficult to reconcile Crozier's account of the situation with the eventual outcome whereby Warden was decorated for his part in this action.

Whatever the truth of the matter, Warden pushed the remainder of the Battalion towards Mory in support of his pinned-down B

A composite battalion moves up to help stem the German advance. Taylor Library

Company. But it could only be a limited counter-attack, into the teeth of an advancing and much numerically greater enemy force, and the East Surreys' flanks were at best unsure. Led by Captain Norman's C Company, the reinforcing elements nevertheless moved up to B Company's position and re-grouped in order to renew the attack.

The Battalion's fresh advance against Mory was timed to start at 2.30 p.m., but Captain Crowther's watch had stopped and it was not until 2.35 p.m. that B Company actually began to move forward by sections, leap-frogging forwards towards Mory and supported by Captain Norman's C Company. Lieutenant Allason and the Battalion's snipers also worked their way forward in pairs and kept down enemy fire from the village. During their advance B and C Companies were still exposed to enemy machine-gun fire from the high ground to their left and suffered many losses. Little effective cover was available, but with casualties rising rapidly the Regimental Aid Post had to be set up in a shallow trench alongside the Mory-Ervillers road. The stretcher bearers displayed total devotion to their task while their officer, Lieutenant Berney, had to attend to the numerous wounded under heavy fire. Berney was a young doctor from the American Army's medical service who had only been attached to the 13th Battalion since January.[41] No-one would have guessed at his inexperience under fire as he crouched over the wounded and, although hit no less than three times by enemy machine-gun bullets, he refused to leave his charges. Both company commanders, Captains Crowther and Norman, were among the many wounded and soon C Company was being led by CSM Reed and B Company by Sergeant Dooley after the last remaining company officer, Second Lieutenant Simmonds, also fell wounded.

Lieutenant-Colonel Warden, realising the attack's momentum was in danger of foundering, now committed his last remaining company to the attack. It was a crucial decision and was made at exactly the right moment. D Company moved rapidly forward along the spur to the south of Mory and succeeded in reaching the western end of the village just in time to meet and reinforce B and C companies there. D Company's officers quickly reorganised the three parties and a final push was made into the village at about 5.30 p.m. This time success was total and the East Surreys swept rapidly through the village, inflicting heavy losses on the Germans who remained. Emerging on the eastern side of Mory, the Battalion established a line just beyond the outskirts of the village, protected on their left flank by the 21st Battalion, Middlesex Regiment who had succeeded in capturing the troublesome high ground north-west of the village.

For the Battalion, the attack on Mory had proved to be another bitter struggle, but had nevertheless been a welcome, if temporary, victory. As well as many enemy dead and wounded, the East Surreys were responsible for taking large numbers of prisoners who were sent back to the rear as darkness fell. But in the gathering gloom, British troops on high ground to the south of the village spotted small groups of the enemy attempting to infiltrate back into Mory. As these Germans slipped around the 13th Battalion's advanced line on the village's outskirts, the enemy also opened up with heavy machine-gun fire. In the distance a strong force of the enemy could also be seen assembling, evidently preparing for a powerful thrust against the Battalion's exposed front. It was clearly only a matter of time before the enemy attack began and, reluctantly, the 13th Battalion was ordered back through the ruins of the hard-won village. A new defensive line just to the west of Mory was feverishly prepared. As the men dug in for all they were worth, the enemy launched their attack from the far side of the village, not having realised that the 13th Battalion had slipped away before them. Charging forward, the Germans were surprised to find the British seemingly gone and the enemy poured through the village until they were pulled up short on the western outskirts. There, Lewis gun and concentrated rifle fire from the 13th Battalion awaited them and the Germans were forced to halt. Among the Lewis gunners Private Geary particularly distinguished himself after bravely working his gun up to a forward position. From there he kept up a highly effective fire against the enemy and when the order to retire was given, Geary continued to man his position and covered the Battalion's withdrawal with bursts of Lewis gun fire. In a final personal act of defiance against the advancing Germans he then pushed forward alone to a small trench previously occupied by the enemy and silenced several snipers. Geary's gallant conduct was later considered to have materially affected the course of the battle and was recognized by the award of a well-earned DCM.

With the Germans temporarily repulsed, the East Surreys rapidly dug trenches in preparation for the next enemy advance. The Wandsworth Battalion was now on the extreme right flank of VI Corps of Third Army, forming the boundary with IV Corps on the British Army's front line. In the darkness and confusion there was every possibility the enemy might exploit this boundary between the two Corps at the point where communications between different divisions could suffer. Accordingly, from the high ground where units of the 41st

Division had watched the 13th Battalion's grim struggle, a patrol was sent down to attempt to make contact with the Wandsworth unit. The patrol's officer, Lieutenant Frank Matthews, went forward at some risk and eventually arrived at the 13th Battalion's positions, to be warmly greeted. For Matthews's unit on the hill was none other than the 12th (Bermondsey) Battalion of the East Surreys. Unaware that their immediate neighbours in VI Corps were the 13th Battalion, their regimental and Metropolitan Borough brothers-in-arms, the 12th Battalion were serving with the 41st Division's 122 Brigade. They had been placed on the extreme left flank of their IV Corps front and had been positioned to fill a number of dangerous gaps which had opened up when another division's troops retired to Favreuil.

While this contact between the two London Borough battalions was hurriedly welcomed, the anticipated German attack commenced. For two hours the valley of the Sensée River between Ervillers and Mory became the scene of bitter and confused fighting. Sadly, news of the Wandsworth Battalion's proximity never reached the 12th East Surreys. Making his way back to the Bermondsey Battalion, Lieutenant Matthews spotted and set off in pursuit of an enemy scout, but was shot down when he ran into a party of advancing Germans. He died of his wounds shortly afterwards and has no known grave.

Eventually the enemy's attack was driven off. Lieutenant-Colonel Warden quickly took over command of the remaining troops of 119 Brigade and regrouped. On his left flank contact was successfully made with 4 Guards Brigade, but on the right, communication with the East Surreys of the 12th Battalion could not be reopened.

Warden's aim was for his brigade, and that of the Guards, to hold the Ervillers-Mory road for as long as possible. But another German advance down the Sensée valley was expected at any time and Warden appreciated that, in such circumstances, retreat was his only option. As dawn broke on the 24th it could be seen that Warden's fears were well-founded. A large enemy force was spotted gathering around Mory, clearly with the intention of another push towards Ervillers along the very road held by the 13th East Surreys and their comrades of 119 Brigade. Quickly, Warden arranged that the Guards of 4 Brigade on his left flank would hold their fire until his own 119 Brigade opened up.

The arrangement agreed, the British apprehensively awaited the inevitable. They did not have long to wait. Soon after dawn the enemy advanced out of Mory, keeping to the south side of the Ervillers-Mory road. The Guards watched them pass and advance up to the outskirts of Ervillers. Suddenly a devasting fire opened up from the hidden Vickers guns of 119 Brigade which had been lying in wait, Warden and the 13th East Surreys amongst them. Almost instantaneously the Guards also opened up and the Germans found themselves trapped in the narrow valley under a murderous cross fire. By the time the enemy managed to withdraw back towards Mory they had again suffered heavy losses.

For the remainder of that day the 13th East Surreys maintained their brigade line on the eastern outskirts of Ervillers. Another enemy attack, supported by a close-range heavy artillery bombardment, was thrown back, but at 4 p.m. came the news Lieutenant-Colonel Warden had feared. Neighbouring positions had fallen under the Germans' persistent attacks and a strong enemy force was reported moving up the St Léger valley. This advance would soon threaten the two British brigades from their rear and accordingly the 4th Guards quickly pulled back to the Arras road north of Ervillers. 119 Brigade likewise withdrew, staying in touch with the right flank of the Guards and extending their own left flank into the outskirts of Ervillers from the north. Here the Wandsworth Battalion took up a position in the village and spent an anxious night in anticipation of further enemy assaults.

All next day, 25 March, the Germans were unable to advance further in the face of the spirited resistence of the East Surreys and it was not until the 26th that the enemy eventually forced their way into Ervillers.[42] Falling back to the north the 13th Battalion fought a successful rearguard action in order to cover the withdrawal of the remainder of 119 Brigade, but confusion reigned, particularly in the ranks where the average soldier, such as Private Bonsey, did not have even the scant briefings of the officers:

> It was impossible to stop them. Our officers told us to keep cool and to give the Germans time to come in front of our guns and things would be alright. But they came up too fast for our guns to stop them. They came over as thick as ever they could walk, rows and rows of them, one behind the other. Our guns could not put them down fast enough as their gaps filled up as soon as two or three of their chaps got knocked out. We thought there was no end to them, and so they came on through us, taking lots of our chaps prisoners of war, and of course all the dead and wounded, and we must have had good few casualties here. When the Germans got us out of our trenches they came after us with their armoured cars and cavalry. We were so cut up and disorganised that we didn't know what to do. We lost something like four to five hundred men here and what few there was left of us had to fight a rear-guard action for a few miles. We still had our CO and two more officers with us. We could not make a stand anywhere. He drove us back the whole fifteen miles he had retreated from. The roads were all blocked with our

'When the Germans got us out of our trenches they came after us with their armoured cars and cavalry.'

retiring transport and ammunition columns. The enemy was also shelling these main roads with his long range artillery. He made us run this time alright, for a little while anyway. When troops get disorganised like this it is a serious matter as all the different regiments get all mixed up, no proper officers or NCOs, so you see what a mess it is. Nobody knows anything as in this rear-guard fighting it is practically every man for himself, that means look after yourself.

We had two or three days of this fighting. It was a plight to be in, seeing all our headquarters staffs retiring as best they could over fields and in the roads. The farther back we went, the more disorder we ran into. Our mounted military police were galloping about trying to straighten the transports and different ammunition columns out of the mess, and they actually had their revolvers in use too on our own men. This was something unusual. It was the only time I have ever seen this

sort of thing happen, and I doubt if any of the other chaps had.

We were all mixed up, we did not know where to go, not even for our rations. We must have left tons of stores and equipment, as well as tons of foodstuff for the horses and mules, as we had not time for anything. It was a pretty stiff job to look after oneself just then.

The withdrawal ultimately led beyond Hamelincourt and as far as Bucquoy, north-west of Bapaume. From Bucquoy the Battalion marched a further three miles north on the 27th and occupied an entrenched position close to the Bois d'Adinfer. For a while it seemed the Battalion might again find itself in the thick of the fighting, but early on 28 March orders came to move out of the front line to Sombrin, twelve miles to the south-west of

Germans rifling through captured British stores.

The village of Ervillers.

Arras. The next day another march was made to Houvelin, south of La Comté, where the Battalion moved into billets for a well-earned rest.

Without doubt the attack on Mory and the defence of Ervillers had been another epic chapter in the history of the 13th East Surreys. And although Private Bonsey had feared heavy losses in the fighting, in reality the Battalion had been relatively fortunate in terms of casualties. The casualty list for the month of March 1918, almost all of which came from the Mory/Ervillers engagements, was 18 killed, 148 wounded and 52 missing. Among these was thirty-five-years-old Lieutenant Mallett, recently arrived from the 5th East Surreys, but appropriately for the 13th Battalion, a local man who lived in Atkins Road, Clapham Park. Married with one daughter, Mallett had been in the Territorial forces for ten years prior to the war and the death of this experienced officer was keenly felt. As had been the case at Bourlon Wood, most of those killed in action or missing were left in territory captured by the Germans and proper identification and burial of the dead was consequently rare. Mallett, along with twenty-eight other members of the Battalion, is listed on the Arras Memorial to those with no known grave. For others among the casualties, death and burial were plainly recorded. Lance-Corporal Percy Herbert Sellers, born in Clapham, was a typical case with an added element of tragedy. Sellers had been wounded, for the second time in his service with the East Surreys, in the recent fighting. Evacuated from the front line, he was taken to the large base hospital on the coast at Etaples, close to Le Touquet. There, despite some of the best care that the Army's doctors could provide, Sellers succumbed to his wounds on 8th April 1918 and was buried in the extensive military cemetery adjoining the hospital. He had only married in July of the previous year while home on leave and his young widow, Maud, was never to remarry. Three months after her husband's death, however, she gained a lasting reminder when their son, Herbert, was born.[43] For Maud Sellers and the other young widows and grieving sweethearts, the sacrifice had been far too great, yet the 13th Battalion could take some comfort from the thanks of their divisional General:

> To All Ranks of the 40th Division.
> I wish to thank the Division, one and all, for their splendid courage and behaviour. You know what the Commander-in-Chief and your Corps Commander think of you, and I can only say you have done your duty like British soldiers always do.
> We shall, no doubt, be called upon again to fight for all we are worth.
> We in the 40th Division, I know, will be ready again, and I feel very proud to be the Divisional Commander of such a splendid body of men that you have proved to be. I thank you all from the bottom of my heart and whatever may happen I feel complete confidence in the ultimate result with soldiers of your spirit and bravery under my command.
> JOHN PONSONBY,
> MAJOR-GENERAL, COMMANDING 40TH DIVISION
> 28/3/18

Though numerous, the Battalion's losses were nevertheless quickly made up and by the end of March the 13th East Surreys could still call upon a strength of some 800 men. Thus, while operations had ultimately ended in retreat, the Battalion's achievements, along with those of 119 Brigade and the 40th Division in general, had been crucial in slowing the enemy's offensive.

On 30 March the 40th Division was visited by the King, who was fulsome in his appreciation of the Division's performance. General the Hon. Sir Julian Byng, Third Army Commander, also congratulated the Division saying:

> By their devotion and courage they have broken up overwhelming attacks and prevented the enemy from gaining...a decisive victory.

In the 40th Division's own report on the fighting of 21-26 March,

Lieutenant-Colonel Warden's attack on Mory was specifically praised and for this he was awarded a second Distinguished Service Order. In addition, the Wandsworth Battalion's men received no less than seven Military Cross, four Distinguished Conduct Medal and three Military Medal awards for the operations. Among those decorated was the young Medical Officer, Lieutenant Berney who, despite his wounds, had survived to become the first American of the First World War to be awarded Britain's Military Cross. Another medic who had distinguished himself was Private Warman, a twenty-year-old stretcher bearer from Alston Road, Lower Tooting. Warman brought in no less than thirty wounded men under heavy enemy fire and at the end of the day carried Lance-Corporal Castle, a badly wounded comrade, several miles back to a dressing station. For his courage, Warman was among those decorated with the DCM.[44] Lieutenant-Colonel Warden also noted the Battalion's transport had performed well under considerable artillery and machine-gun fire in order to bring up supplies of ammunition and bombs. Particular mention was made of Sergeant Holmes, Corporal Bull and Private Burrell for their gallantry and Captain Beecroft was one of those awarded the Military Cross.

Chapter 7

DISASTER

The 13th East Surreys, together with the rest of the 40th Division, were now ordered to move into the valley of the River Lys, an area some twenty miles north-east of their billets at Houvelin. On 1 April 1918 the Battalion therefore marched to Barlin and entrained there for Neuf Berquin. The next day the men continued to le Nouveau Monde, near Estaires, where they were billeted as Divisional Reserve. This was a pleasant spot, where the fields, trees and hedges remained untouched by the war and where most of the French civilian population still lived, despite the battalion's officers warning them that Intelligence reported an enemy attack to be imminent.

On 6 April the Battalion then moved up to the XV Corps front-line positions in order to relieve the 14th Battalion, Highland Light Infantry in the Fleurbaix sector. A and C Companies held the forward trenches at Foray Post and Croix Maréchal, while B and D Companies formed their support. As a defensive position, the front now occupied was far from ideal. The troops had their backs to the River Lys which, though sluggish, was unfordable. A much better position would clearly have been to hold the northern bank of the river and to use the Lys itself as the defensive line. Due to the siting of the remainder of the front, however, this was not possible and the position was further compounded by the network of deep irrigation ditches in the area which were able to serve as covered ways for an advancing enemy. Due to the river and the irrigation ditches, it was impossible to dig proper defensive positions in the water-laden and marshy ground. Breastworks were the most that the men could use for cover, these being mounds of earth piled up in front of shallow, scraped-out trenches.

Another cause for concern was that the Battalion, like the 40th Division in general, was still not up to maximum efficiency for the trials ahead. Some replacement drafts had been picked up during the journey north and more continued to arrive during the taking over of the new front, yet this only served to temporarily increase the handicap by resulting in a high proportion of unknown and untried

New arrivals to the Western Front – Portugese troops. Taylor Library

officers and men, including many 18-year-olds who, in theory, were ineligible for overseas service. But all these worries paled into insignificance when the Wandsworth Battalion found its right flank to be held by the 2nd Portuguese Division.

Though long-standing historical allies of the British, the Portuguese had only belatedly entered the war in March 1916 and it was not until February 1917 that two infantry divisions, forming the *Corpo Expedicionário Português*, had reached their operational zone within the thirty-five mile front of First Army. The Portuguese sector never exceeded twelve miles, but the newcomers were always under strength and were viewed with some suspicion by their British neighbours as having no great taste for the war. Certainly, the conditions on the Western Front must have been a great shock after the benevolent climate of Portugal. Nor would morale have been helped by news from home where President Sidónio Pais had declared himself against participation in the war and had even been accused of being sympathetic to the German cause. Unsettled by the political turmoil back home, and considerably less battle-hardened than the British, the Portuguese troops were reported to suffer from low morale and the East Surreys were not reassured by the little they saw and heard of their allies.

The British High Command were no less wary of the abilities of the Portuguese and because of the indications of an imminent German attack, it had been planned to pull them out of the front line on 9 April. Unfortunately, the Germans too had recognized this weak link. They had raided the Portuguese trenches with a bombing party and had taken a number of prisoners from whom they had undoubtedly extracted further useful intelligence. Consequently, and as it turned out fortuitously, the Germans planned to attack in the early morning of 9 April while the Portuguese, were still holding the line and were looking forward to moving into reserve positions.

For the first few days of April the front had been relatively quiet, with only intermittent gas shelling by the enemy. Intelligence and reconnaissance reports had warned the 40th Division's commander that the Germans were any day expected to reopen their great Spring offensive by an attack, code-named 'St George', in the Lys valley, but on the night of 8/9 April a thick mist settled on the front and all seemed quiet. Patrols from both the 18th Welsh and 13th East Surreys were sent out and worked down the enemy trenches known as 'Necklace' and 'Nephew'. No enemy troops were met and most of the patrols were safely back in the British lines by 3 a.m.

At 4.15 a.m. on the 9th, however, a great barrage opened up and the whole front of the 40th Division was subjected to an intense bombardment of high explosive and gas shells. Every single inch of ground seemed to receive its own enemy shell, the explosions being only partially masked by the fog which somehow also seemed to amplify the awful cacophony of sound. The roar and screech of shells was constant, coupled with the crack of branches and trees being toppled. The air itself seemed to grow hot as it became filled with the thick and acrid black smoke of explosions. The cowering men were continually spattered with falling earth and as huge shell craters appeared all around them, it appeared impossible to be missed. It was by far the worst bombardment that anyone could remember. Man after man was hit and as the stretcher bearers rushed to help the wounded, they too fell victim to the unceasing deluge of hot metal. An NCO ran among those still alive and called for men to replace the dead and wounded stretcher bearers. It was an unenviable task for those who answered the call, yet Private Bonsey was one of those who

Inexperienced Portuguese troops were to bring disaster to the 13th East Surreys. Author

did, struggling to find the wounded men in the fog and mud, but guided by their moans, shouts and screams:

> I remember we had just taken one poor fellow to the dressing station which was a covered-in shelter with galvanised iron and covered over with earth. This little place, lucky enough dodged all these shells somehow, he had one of his legs nearly severed right through the thigh. When we picked him up he was laying back on his leg, I suppose that was the way he had fallen when he was hit. I have thought of that chap many a time, wondering how he fared.

The 2nd Portuguese Division had 4, 5, and 6 Brigades in the front line with just 3 Brigade in reserve. All its units were weak and its front-line sector was too long for just one division. When they were hit by elements of the Germans' 42nd, 35th, 8th, 81st, 10th Ersatz, 1st Bavarian Reserve, and 16th Divisions, they almost immediately broke. British reinforcements, including a cyclist battalion, were sent forward to try to help 3 Portuguese Brigade form a line and stem the breakthrough, but as soon as remnants of the other three Portuguese brigades fell back through the 3rd, it too gave way, appropriating the bicycles of the reinforcing British battalion to aid their flight.[45]

Shortly after 5 a.m. word reached the 13th East Surreys of the Portuguese fleeing from their trenches on the right. It was not known until later, but the Portuguese (disparagingly known as the "Pork and Beans") had been unprepared for the attack, many allegedly having their equipment and even their boots off. But they paid dearly for their premature flight. Their uniforms were a medium bluish grey, with a similarly-coloured heavy winter overcoat, and were therefore not dissimilar to the German feldgrau or field grey. Due to the thick fog and the colour and unfamiliar foreign cut of the uniforms worn by the soldiers running at them out of the gloom, D Company of the neighbouring 18th Battalion, Welsh Regiment mistook the Portuguese for the German attackers. D Company's commanding officer subsequently reported his men had "killed hundreds."

Soon after, news arrived that the Germans had overwhelmed the front trenches to the right of the 40th Division and Brigadier-General Crozier was organising a counter attack by 119 Brigade to drive them out. But by 6 a.m. total confusion reigned and the thick mist only added to the difficulty in determining what was happening. Shells burst all around and the presence of gas meant that respirators had to be continually worn, further restricting visibility. The enemy had clearly targeted the neighbouring sector of the front held by the inexperienced Portuguese and the German 6th Army poured through the breach before swinging round onto 119 Brigade's positions. First in their path, the 18th Welsh fought stoutly, but were virtually annihilated. By 8.30 a.m. the Germans had swung northwards towards Fleurbaix itself and the enemy's 32nd Division, supported by the 11th Reserve Division, hit the 13th Battalion from the rear and right flank, the support trenches being the first to be attacked at about 9 a.m. Positions were rapidly switched to try to face the attack from the south, but in no time at all the Battalion found itself under fire from three sides. Major West, deputising for Lieutenant-Colonel Warden who had been admitted to hospital on 6 April suffering from fatigue, quickly found himself in an unenviable position. The enemy was breaking through everywhere and the Wandsworth Battalion's position was cut off on both flanks from any hope of assistance. Only a few minutes after 9 a.m. a wounded Company Sergeant-Major of the East Surreys reached the headquarters of the neighbouring 20th Middlesex with the dramatic news that the advancing enemy was only minutes away. A telephone message was immediately sent to brigade headquarters with this information, but it was to be the last communication received from the 13th Battalion. For a while the East Surreys fought on where they stood, but they were facing in two directions and both artillery and machine-gun support had been forced to withdraw. As the enemy swiftly completed their encirclement of the East Surreys, Major West realised the hopelessness of the situation and gave the order "every man for himself". Most of the men rose from their positions with their hands raised in surrender, a few tried to make a run for it, but the majority of these were shot down by the advancing Germans. Private Bonsey had the decision of whether to flee or surrender made for him:

> I remember a German officer rushing up to me and pointing a revolver at my head and his batman tearing my equipment off and making me put my rifle down. It was good for me that he didn't pull the trigger of his revolver.

The captured men were made to lie on the ground until the Germans were ready to shepherd them away. When the order to move was given, the Wandsworth men suffered the indignity of having to carry their own machine guns (without ammunition) that had been captured by the enemy. They were led out through the German trenches, still unable on account of the fog to see what was happening or where they were going. The German positions proved no better than the British, the trenches being half full of water and

mud so that it took a full hour before they emerged from the rear of the German lines, some three hundred yards from a busy junction where three roads met. While they paused to take up an extra burden of carrying some of the German wounded further back, they watched as every form of enemy transport moved forward, including pontoon bridges to ford the River Lys. Suddenly, a great roaring noise was heard, louder than any normal shell and causing the POWs to throw themselves flat into the mud. It was as well they did so for immediately before them a massive shell, fired from a British 12-inch naval battery some nine miles away beyond Estaires, burst exactly in the middle of the choked road junction. The resultant hole was large enough to take a bus and shreds of German vehicles, men and horses were scattered far and wide. Even though some three hundred yards away from the point of impact, the captured men had a narrow escape as a red hot piece of shrapnel scythed into the group. It cut Major West from elbow to wrist with an ugly, gaping wound, but a considerate German immediately took him back into the German trenches to have it dressed at an aid post. While the others waited, still under close guard, for West to return, they had a grandstand view from the shelter of a German trench as the British naval gunners continued to put a huge shell into the road every few minutes.

Of great amusement to the watching British was the spectacle of the German cooks emerging after each explosion and dashing forward to hack large slices off the dead horses for their portable field kitchens - the first direct evidence seen that the enemy was very short of food. The entertainment was cut short, however, when Major West returned and the men were again moved on towards the rear. German troops accosted them for souvenirs, but as the men had already been made to empty their pockets immediately after capture, the pickings were slim. Frustrated, the Germans started pulling the warmly-lined sleeveless leather jackets off the East Surreys who, thinking ahead to the long cold nights of captivity, were none too pleased.

While the first captives were being marched away, some of the 13th Battalion's isolated strongpoints had managed to hold out until the

British prisoners of war captured in the March offensives being marched to the railhead for transportation to camps in Gemany.

afternoon, but as ammunition ran out these pockets of men also either surrendered or attempted to slip back through the German lines towards Sailly-sur-la-Lys. Other remaining troops of 119 Brigade had already been forced to cross the River Lys and they then held the northern bank defending the bridges, both permanent and temporary, which were still in place. From 2.15 p.m. onwards bridge demolitions began as the enemy approached the river. Some of the last troops to cross the bridge at around 3.30 p.m. at Sailly were the survivors of the 13th East Surreys and the 18th Welsh, led by Lieutenant-Colonel Brown of the latter battalion. Together with a hundred or so reinforcements these men made their way along the northern bank of the river to Bac Saint-Maur. While other units manned forward positions on the south bank of the Lys, Brigadier-General Crozier placed his survivors in a second line on the north bank of the river and awaited the arrival of the advancing Germans.

Sure enough, the enemy soon appeared in the form of the 10th Ersatz Division and quickly captured a line of houses on the southern bank. From the cover of the houses, artillery and machine guns pounded the exposed British positions just across the river and made further retirement inevitable. Taking swift advantage the Germans forded the river and 119 Brigade fell back again, firstly to Croix du Bac and then, by 6 p.m., to Le Petit Mortier where it was finally relieved. There, numbering only about fifty men in total, the 13th Battalion's survivors were held in reserve and remained under the command of Lieutenant-Colonel Brown. Later the same day they were joined by the Battalion's support details who, together with the transport, had marched up from La Couronne led by Second Lieutenants Wilks and Rowland.

'With our backs to the wall... each one of us must fight on to the end.'
Field Marshal Sir Douglas Haig.

In just a couple of hours the Wandsworth Battalion had been destroyed as a fighting unit. In this it was not alone, since the entire 119 Brigade was now down to the strength of a single battalion. Nevertheless, 119 had to continue fighting in the face of the enemy's continuing offensive. With the 13th Battalion's survivors and rear echelon troops in its midst, the Brigade took up positions on 10th April to the north of le Doulieu and le Verrier. The situation looked extremely grim for the Allies and on 11 April, Field Marshal Sir Douglas Haig issued his famous order that:

> *There is no other course open to us but to fight it out. Every position must be held to the last man. There must be no retirement. With our backs to the wall and believing in the justness of our cause, each one of us must fight on to the end.*

That same day three enemy attacks were driven off until a local counter-attack by the 31st Division at last eased the pressure. Early on 12 April 119 Brigade was relieved, withdrew northwards and in the afternoon dug in before the village of Strazeele. The next day the Brigade again pulled back to Hondeghem, near Hazebrouck, where the survivors joined up with the Battalion's transport and Lieutenant-Colonel Warden resumed command after his stay in hospital. After a hot meal the 13th Battalion's meagre strength marched off to billets in Staple.

Following the successful defensive action at Mory and Ervillers only two weeks before, surrender came as a bitter contrast for the battalion, with crippling losses. The regimental history records only twelve officers and men killed, with a further eighty-one wounded. But closer scrutiny of casualty lists, while confirming eighty-one wounded, suggests six officers and some sixty-seven other ranks were killed. Of the remainder, eleven officers[46] (including Major West and Battalion Adjutant Captain Ainger) and around 377 other ranks were captured. Another of the Battalion's popular officers attached from the 14th Highland Light Infantry, Captain Alexander Burton, was among those killed, Lieutenant-Colonel Warden later describing him as: '...one of the finest men I ever met; a splendid fellow, a great athlete and a leader who was absolutely loved by his men'.

Also lost was Burton's friend and former platoon officer, Captain George Beaumont. It had previously been Burton who had written to Beaumont's mother when the then Lieutenant had won his Military Cross at Bourlon Wood. Now it was a clearly-emotional Warden who had the unenviable task of informing Beaumont's mother of her son's death in action:

13th Battn
East Surrey Regt
B.E.F.
18.4.18.

Dear Mrs Beaumont
With a very heavy heart I write to tell you the sad news of the death in action of your son Capt. George Beaumont. We look over trenches in the north after having been in the severe fighting south, and we were all looking forward to a quiet time. Personally I was so worn out that I was sent off for a week to sleep and the battalion went in under Major West, who, with your son and the other Company commanders, were fresh as they had not been in the preceding affair. The second day they were in, the Huns started this fierce attack, up here, and broke through the

Portuguese on our right and surrounded our Battalion with the result we have got only four officers and about sixty men. It is very terrible!

I am told that Capt.Beaumont was wounded in several places, but was quite cheery and that later he died of wounds. You may take it that his body is buried near Fleurbaix, a village a few miles south-west of Armentières. Some of the men (now evacuated to England wounded) told me how courageously your son fought, as indeed I well knew he would and he died a brave soldier fighting to the end.

I have given you the details as far as I know them, because I can understand your wish to have them. You might possibly see some of our men in No. 3 General Hospital Wandsworth, who can give you more information.

I am very much distressed about Capt. Beaumont's death. He was not only a splendid officer, who knew his work well, and had the hearts of all his men, but he was indeed a 'white man' whom to know was indeed a pleasure. And so, I mourn your son as an officer and as a friend and I sympathise deeply with you and your family in your loss. But I hope that when the first sharpness of your grief has passed, you may have comfort and even pride in the reflection that your boy was enabled to be of the bravest and was faithful always even to the supreme sacrifice.

Believe me
Yours very sincerely
H.J.Warden

Again, the ranks of the 'originals' had been depleted. Captain Linge was among those captured, leaving just Captain Beecroft (commanding D Company) and Lieutenants Corben and Head of those officers who had left Wandsworth in 1916. To redress the balance a little, Lieutenant G. E. Deacon was posted to rejoin the Battalion from 3rd Echelon, but the remaining Wandsworth character of the Battalion had been irrevocably shattered.

Captain George Beaumont killed 9 April 1918.
Brotherton Library

Chapter 8

CAPTIVITY

Of the men captured, those who were badly wounded were placed in hospitals for treatment, while of the able-bodied, the officers were sent directly to Germany and the rest, including some of the unfortunate Portuguese, began a march of some twenty miles towards the French city of Lille. The men were tired, dirty and cold and as they passed old ladies came to their doorways to watch, calling out sympathetically, but prevented by the German guards from giving any food – which the men were quick to ask for.

The first night's billets were in a large brewery, disappointingly empty of beer. The food dispensed by the Germans was not encouraging – a basin of thin and watery cabbage stew. The next morning, after being counted but without further food or drink, the men continued their march to Lille. Occasionally, local people managed to throw a piece of bread, but more frequently the escort pushed the French roughly back into their homes.

Eventually, the trek halted at Fort MacDonald[47], a fortress in Lille. The men were again paraded and counted and then packed into one long underground room where there was so little space that turns had

The Germans took care to parade the 13th Battalion prisoners before their press photographers.
G. Richardson

to be taken in standing and sitting. This dungeon-like room soon became almost unbearable with the heat and smell generated by the unwashed soldiers, and was alleviated by only a single barred window, high up at one end of the chamber. For the remainder of that day and the following night the prisoners suffered before they were taken back up to ground level in the early morning for another basin of cabbage soup. For lack of other utensils, most had to have the soup poured into their dirty helmets and then had to drink it as best they could manage, not helped by the broad brim of the helmet. Their meagre fare finished, the men were marched back to their stinking underground room for another twenty four hours. When again brought up from their dungeon, they were led out into the town square of Lille and were made to march round and round while the German press took photographs, to an accompaniment of jeers and catcalls from the guards. Many of the men were now in a very weak state, almost crawling rather than walking and in their dirty and soiled uniforms they presented a pathetic picture. Later, they were shown the photos that appeared in German newspapers under the humiliating caption: 'A fine specimen of British fighting troops'. But for the moment, the captives were beyond caring and close to despair as they were marched back into Fort Macdonald. At least some sort of food awaited them, a three inch square of German rye bread with marmalade. The bread was heavy and dusted with wood pulp since flour was so scarce, the marmalade was in reality a puree of sweet carrots. The next day they learned they were to be taken to a proper POW camp in Germany, but although they were paraded and counted at 5 a.m., it was not until 10 a.m. and after five hours of standing on parade, that they were escorted out of the fort. Another lengthy march took them to a railway siding where they were locked, forty to each wagon, into cattle trucks which had recently been hosed out. With them again went many of the captured Portuguese troops, largely unwelcomed.

A slow, four-day, rail journey took them out of France, across Belgium and into the Westphalia region of Germany, stopping only every twenty four hours for another serving of lukewarm cabbage soup. The floors of the cattle trucks remained so wet that the men sat on or in their helmets, not the most comfortable position, but preferable to the floor. At last they arrived at a German station and from there a final march took them to Dülmen Camp.

Dülmen was a recently-built prisoner of war camp, twenty-two miles south-west of Münster, in Westphalia. Constructed on sandy heathland and in a pine forest, the wooden barrack huts and countryside were not dissimilar, nor the accommodation any worse, than the Battalion's first experience of a British Army camp at Witley in Surrey in 1915. Dülmen, however, was enclosed by a stiff barbed-wire fence nearly three metres high and heavily-armed sentries patrolled inside and outside the wire, backed up by constant vigilance from watchtowers and large arc lamps which floodlit the entire camp at night. Private Bonsey recorded the process on arrival:

> *All the pine trees had been cut down from the centre of this wood and these wooden huts put up. The soil here was very sandy, two or three inches deep with sand. When we first went into this camp we were all taken into a large hut and had our names and numbers taken. They then searched us all again and took what little we had managed to carry in our pockets, such as pocket knives, safety razors and photos. In fact they took everything from us. We only had just our old dirty khaki uniforms that we were captured in. We must have looked a poor dejected party on our arrival. We then had to stop in this hut for forty-*

The camp's main gate. Stadtarchiv Dulmen

eight hours until we were all taken to the bath hut and all had a shower bath. This was alright and seemed refreshing as it was the first wash we had had during these three weeks of captivity. The barbers also came in and clipped off all our hair short. We looked quite bald-headed then. What surprised us here was we had to use sand as soap as the Germans were very short of soap. We found this sand very rough against our bodies. It didn't half scratch, and it was my first experience of washing with sand, and when it came to wipe ourselves dry we found we had to use towels that had been made from paper. They were fine paper twisted round to make towelling and at first sight they looked like real towels but when we came to use them we soon found out a difference. They just pushed the water off, not much good as towelling. But still, I suppose that was the best kind of substitute they could find as they were all substituted, everything, even to their foodstuffs.

The hutted accommodation was decent enough, but what remained in the memories of the men for many years afterwards was the lack of food. Already near to starvation, the prisoners were left in no doubt as to the general shortage of food in Germany when they were introduced to the camp's regimen. Roll call was at 6 a.m. every morning, and took a full hour. Breakfast, a pint of so-called coffee (made of baked chestnuts crushed into flour) followed, and there was still no solid food at lunch which was a pint of thin soup made from cabbage, peas and seeds. Very occasionally, a small piece of potato would be found in the soup and heartily welcomed, for even at dinner at 6 p.m. there was nothing to eat, just another pint of the impoverished 'coffee'. This menu never varied, to the extent that the normal state of all men quickly became ravenous hunger, accompanied by an obsession with finding any supplement to their diet. Within the camp, the only possibilities were from scavenging for vegetable peelings in the rubbish bins and this rapidly became a popular pastime. To counter their prisoners' weakened condition, the Germans pursued a rigorous programme of inoculations and vaccinations, but the British were suspicious that they were being used as guinea pigs and did not thank their captors.

None of the Battalion's officers were held at Dülmen as it was a camp for NCO's and other ranks only. This also meant that, despite the lack of food that so weakened them, the prisoners were eligible for working parties and Private Bonsey was among those who were swiftly disabused of the notion that there might be a correlation between one's past experience of work and the Germans' needs:

They read out a list with all our names on it, and mine was there too. They said I had volunteered for the coal mines, as our little party of

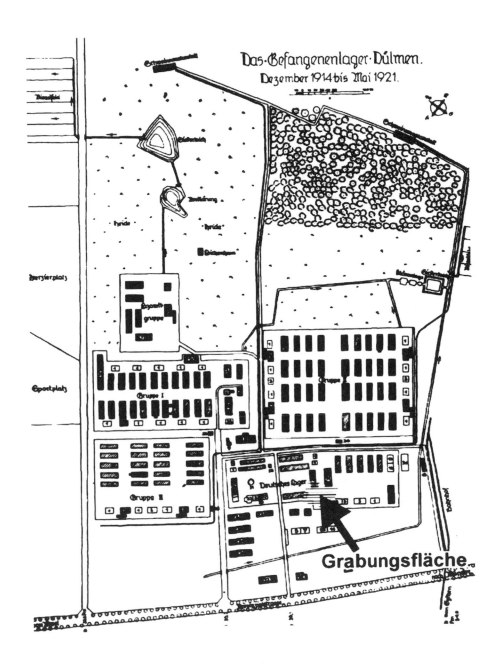

A plan of Dulmen POW camp. Stadtarchiv Dulmen.

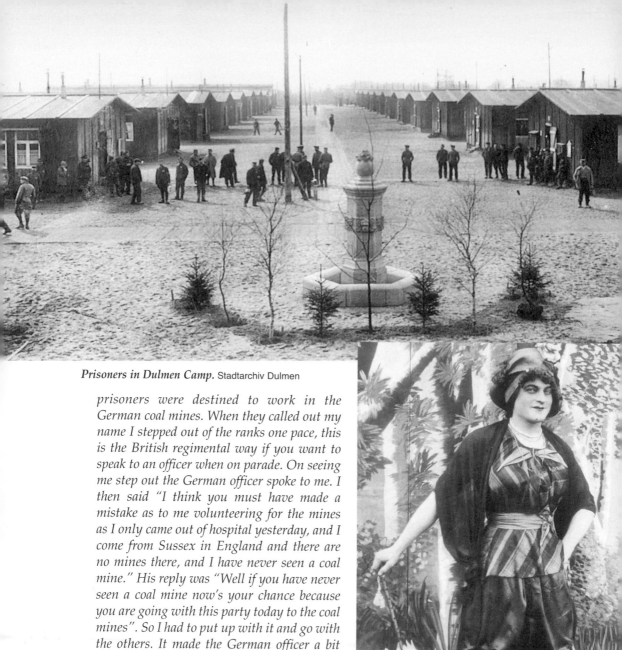

Prisoners in Dulmen Camp. Stadtarchiv Dulmen

prisoners were destined to work in the German coal mines. When they called out my name I stepped out of the ranks one pace, this is the British regimental way if you want to speak to an officer when on parade. On seeing me step out the German officer spoke to me. I then said "I think you must have made a mistake as to me volunteering for the mines as I only came out of hospital yesterday, and I come from Sussex in England and there are no mines there, and I have never seen a coal mine." His reply was "Well if you have never seen a coal mine now's your chance because you are going with this party today to the coal mines". So I had to put up with it and go with the others. It made the German officer a bit wild me butting in like this but I knew I was far too weak to work. So the next morning our little party was on parade again, this time to proceed to the mines at Dortmund near

One of the few entertainments at Dulmen was the camp theatre. Stadtarchiv Dulmen

160

Essen, some thirty miles from this camp. We went down by train. We had three German sentries with us. The one that got in our carriage was a decent chap. He tried to talk with us when the train started and at midday he shared his dinner with us, although they themselves never got much, but what he had he divided between us so we had a mouthful of food that day. He also gave some of us a cigarette which he had in his pocket, so we came off fairly lucky on this journey. It was something like four o'clock when we got to Dortmund, a very large town with several coal mines and blasting furnesses that we could see as we were on our way to our mine.'

While the men taken prisoner settled to the toil and hunger of captivity, the survivors of the Battalion were facing a challenge of a very different, but ultimately equally devastating, kind. On 14 April 1918 the remnants of 119 Brigade, including those of the 13th Battalion, had thankfully left the battle zone for Tilques, via St-Omer. Over the next ten days the 13th Battalion men moved billets from Moulle to Boisdinghem and then on to La Wattine and Nieurlet by the end of the month. On 1 May the Battalion reached Oudezeele, but returned to Nieurlet the following day where Lieutenant G. E. Deacon was promoted to Captain and became the Battalion's Adjutant in place of the captured Captain Ainger. Deacon soon found that there was much to do as several replacement drafts reached the Battalion, but despite the reinforcements it was quickly clear the Battalion faced huge difficulties in recovering from the recent disaster. Many of the new men were young and inexperienced soldiers, fresh from England, and the Battalion no longer possessed the cadre of experienced officers and NCO's necessary to rapidly train the fresh recruits. In the face of these problems it was decided the Battalion should temporarily revert to being a training staff only. Strength had by now grown to some 500 men, but in view of the new orders 447 other ranks were posted out on 5 May to return to base depots at Calais for redirection to other units. Most found themselves posted to the East Surreys' other battalions, many of which were still in the thick of the fighting. One such soldier was Private Herbert Davis, the young library assistant who had been among the first to volunteer for the 13th Battalion. Posted to the 8th East Surreys, he was killed in action on 23 August 1918, the second death among the four serving sons of Wandsworth's Borough Librarian. Those who went to the 1st Battalion also found themselves facing fresh challenges as the Allied armies continued their advances, including the second capture of Villers-Plouich in September, 1918.

The remaining training staff of the 13th Battalion, consisting of

Americans arrive, seen here with their field kitchen. Taylor Library

Americans undergoing training by British officers. Taylor Library

officers and NCOs only, had found themselves subjected to a bewildering sequence of moves and command changes. On 18 May they moved to a camp south-east of Hazebrouck and then to les Trois Rois, near Cassel. On the 29th news reached them of the award of the Military Cross to Captain Daintree, Lieutenant Corben and Second Lieutenants Wilks and Sewell for their conduct at Fleurbaix.

Another move took the staff by train to Rinxent, near Boulogne, on 3 June and from there they marched to Hardinghem, being transferred to 102 Infantry Brigade of the 34th Division. Yet another transfer then took place to 101Brigade at Bayenghem on 11 June, where new orders revealed that a fortnight's training was to be given to two new American infantry units, the 1st and 3rd Battalions of the 310th American Regiment. This proved to be a highly rewarding task as it was clear that the experience and know-how passed on by the 13th Battalion were much appreciated by the untested newcomers. The job was made all the more enjoyable by the British and the Americans establishing many friendships.

On 29 June the staff moved to Boulogne under orders to return to England in order to raise the 13th Battalion to full strength again within the 15th Division. The Channel crossing was made on the 30th and the staff, some fifty-six strong, moved into camp at Mytchett, near Frimley, close to where the Battalion had finished its training before leaving for France two years earlier.

A period of leave was granted and on 16 July the staff reported to Lowestoft in Suffolk where the Battalion was to be brought up to strength. On arrival they found a draft of seventy-four men from the East Surreys' 3rd and 5th Battalions already waiting for them and by the end of the week another 306 recruits had arrived. Training proceeded rapidly throughout late July and August and the final drafts of men and officers arrived. By 31st August full strength was achieved, but a severe blow then fell when the Battalion underwent medical examinations in preparation for a return to the continent. Of a total of 825 men, only 393 were passed as fit enough for overseas service, a damning condemnation that Britain was now clearly 'scraping the bottom of the barrel' in terms of finding manhood for her armies.

For the 13th Battalion this indictment proved its death knell. On 7th September orders arrived from the parent 225 Infantry Brigade that the Battalion was to be disbanded. With almost indecent haste twenty-three officers were posted to France on the 18th of the month, while the other ranks were swiftly transferred to other units. By the 30th only eleven officers and seventy-six other ranks remained, charged with closing accounts and finally disbanding the Battalion. In late October numbers fell further to just Lieutenant-Colonel Warden, his Adjutant and Assistant Adjutant, Quartermaster and nine other ranks. These remaining staff returned to the regimental depot at Kingston-upon-Thames and formally handed over the last of the Battalion records. Warden[48] and the Quartermaster returned to other units in France and the remaining staff were posted to the 3rd (Reserve) Battalion in Scotland. On 3 November 1918, just eight days before the Armistice[49] was signed to end the war, the 13th Battalion formally ceased to exist. Cheated of existence at the very moment of victory, 'Wandsworth's Own' quietly passed into history.

PART THREE

THE 10TH (SERVICE) BATTALION (BATTERSEA), THE QUEEN'S (ROYAL WEST SURREY) REGIMENT

Chapter 9

THE BATTERSEA BOYS

The first recorded mention of Battersea was in the 7th century, when King Caedwalla of Wessex granted the manor of Batrices Ege to Eorienwald, Bishop of London (675-693). During the medieval period the area was mainly laid out as strip fields, long and narrow, for farming and grazing and the area served as a market garden for London for several hundred years. The heart of the original Saxon settlement and the village that developed from it was just south of the river Thames. In 1700, Sir Walter St. John, 3rd Baronet, established the Battersea Charity School to teach twenty poor boys of the parish, much of the curriculum being based on the Bible. By 1859 the school had moved to a new building in Battersea High Street and was known as Sir Walter St. John's School. The parish church of St. Mary was a short distance away on the river bank, off what is now Battersea Church Road. The present building dates from 1775, although a Norman church is believed to have preceded it. Old Battersea House in Vicarage Crescent has a sundial dated 1699 and the house is even older. The parish grew from several distinct areas, surrounded by open land: the original village around what is now Battersea Square; the crossroads that would become known as Clapham Junction; the residential area between Clapham and Wandsworth Commons; and the industrial district of Nine Elms. But by the late 19th Century, the rural elements of the area had largely disappeared under an urban sprawl, accelerated by the construction of railways, factories and workshops, many along the river which still served as a major conduit for the transport of goods and materials. Much of the open land was taken up by four railway companies, who not only laid track, but also had sidings and workshops. The earlier riverside windmills and wharves gave way to new industries, such as Price's Candle Works, opened in 1843, Morgan's Crucible Works, Carton's Glucose Factory, flour mills, breweries and the Nine Elms Gas Works.

With the 1863 opening of Clapham Junction Station (confusingly named, as it is in Battersea, rather than Clapham), the focus of Battersea changed from the riverside to St. John's Hill and St. John's Road, which became the main shopping centre. At its heart was the landmark department store Arding and Hobbs, built in 1910, while cheaper products were available from the street market in Northcote Road. Lavender Hill became the location of public buildings such as the Town Hall, police station and magistrates court and the post office. Entertainment was also provided in the shape of a theatre and a cinema. As well as trains there were horse buses and horse trams, which were later replaced by the electric tram and the motor omnibus. This creeping urbanisation was relieved by the open spaces of Clapham and Wandsworth Commons, but the major attraction near the river was Battersea Park, opened by Queen Victoria in 1858 and in which all sorts of sports facilities and other attractions were available. The park, an oasis of open space alongside the Thames, was designed to relieve the relentless industrialisation of the river bank and still admirably serves today as a classic example of a well-maintained urban park.

The park served, too, to delineate the community of Battersea itself from Nine Elms to the east, the latter having always been the Borough's most industrialised area and displaying little to attract the visitor or to live up to the leafy character suggested by its name. Nine Elms railway works were built by the London and South Western Railway (LSWR) originally near the Vauxhall end of Nine Elms Lane in 1843, but moved to a larger site south of the main line between 1861 and 1865. Between 1843 and 1850, and then from 1862 to 1908 the Nine Elms works were responsible for the construction of more than 800 steam locomotives for the LSWR. Perhaps the other best-known site in Nine Elms was the internationally-known Battersea Dogs Home relocated to Nine Elms from Holloway in 1871 to house the capital's strays and which flourishes to this day.

The advent of the Great War in 1914 was therefore against a backdrop of rapid industrialisation, yet its history as a Surrey village

Battersea Park, 1911. Author

The machine shop in the locomotive works at Nine Elms in the early 1900s. E. W. Fry

Above: Clapham. Junction at the turn of the century.

was recent enough to make the Borough of Battersea, like Wandsworth, look to the county's infantry regiments once the Council's original aim of only raising an artillery battery was discarded. In a move undoubtedly designed to underline the different character and the political rivalry of the two Councils, Battersea ignored the East Surrey Regiment chosen by Wandsworth and instead looked to Surrey's other infantry regiment, The Queen's (Royal West Surrey) Regiment.

The Queen's, as they were more commonly called, were among the most senior regiments of the British Army. Their seniority came from a history dating back to 1661 when, following the restoration of Charles II, The Tangier Regiment of Foot was raised. In 1684 this became The Queen's Regiment and in 1881 The Queen's (Royal West Surrey) Regiment. Unfortunately, no battalion diary remains to detail the very earliest days of Battersea's battalion, but the Army granted it official status on 3 June, 1915 as the 10th (Service) Battalion (Battersea), The Queen's (Royal West Surrey) Regiment. This was immediately followed by the Council's formal approval, at its meeting of 9 June 1915, for the Mayor, Mr T. W. Simmons JP, to organise and initially command an infantry battalion, pending the appointment of a

G. R.

BATTERSEA'S OWN REGULARS.

JOIN NOW.

The Queen's Royal West Surrey Regiment,

Battersea Battalion.

RECRUITING DEPOT:

TOWN HALL, LAVENDER HILL.

Recruitment was initially low despite posters and newspaper advertisements.
South Western Star

permanent commanding officer. The Mayor had already seen his own sons volunteer for the services, but the task now was to find no less than 1,350 men, of whom 1,100 were to be sent on active service as soon as training permitted, while the remainder were to remain as a depot element. Battersea Town Hall's Lower Hall was designated as battalion headquarters and two adjacent small cloakrooms and kitchen were provided for offices and clothing and equipment stores. The official war diary for the 10th Battalion was not commenced until some eleven months after these events, in May 1916 while at Aldershot, so what details can be found of the raising of the unit largely come from local press reports and the minutes of Battersea Council.

Battersea Town Hall, the first recruiting office.
Author

On 23 June 1915 the Mayor was able to hand the new unit over after the hurried appointment of a proper commanding officer, Colonel William Raymond Inglis. It was Inglis's job to raise recruits for the Battalion, though it was recognized that he would not lead his men into battle. Already in his fifties and retired to his home at Rickling Hall, Essex as a Major by 1914, Inglis had last seen active service on the North West Frontier, India, in the Tirah campaign of 1897-98. The son of a General and educated at Eton, he had originally gone out to India with The Queen's Regiment and had completed twenty-one years of soldiering in that regiment, the Connaught Rangers and Norfolk Regiment, before rejoining the Army immediately when war broke out in August 1914. He had initially been promoted to become Inspector of Recruiting for the Army's Eastern Command. But his earlier experience with The Queen's, together with his recent experience of recruitment, was considered to be just the job for raising the new battalion and he was described by the local South Western Star newspaper as 'a splendid commander, a thorough soldier, and a thorough gentleman'.[50]

FREE TICKETS ISSUED To BERLIN, Via Boulogne or Havre, to Adventurous Young Men. [P.T.

The ladies of Battersea handed these tickets out to young men not in uniform. D. Inkster

From June onwards Inglis began to gather and instruct his recruits in the Battersea area. He had been joined by another Regular Army officer as his Adjutant, 45-year-old Lieutenant Alexander Lawrence, a Scot from Macduff, Banffshire, who was formerly Adjutant with the 1st Battalion, Gordon Highlanders. Lawrence had gone to France and Belgium with this unit in August 1914 after previous active service that had included the North West Frontier of India and the Boer War in South Africa. He had been badly wounded at Ypres in November, 1914, but was now considered to be fit enough to help organize Battersea's new unit.

Inglis and Lawrence were helped in their task by no fewer than three Battersea councillors who took commissions in the 10th Queen's. Councillor F. A. Abbott, whip of the Municipal Reform Party and representative of Broomwood ward, had become the first officer gazetted to the Battalion when he was appointed paymaster with the rank of Lieutenant. Abbott's commission was an immediate step towards the Council's wish that all officers, other than the commanding officer and adjutant, should be Battersea men. This was

170

to prove an over-optimistic aim, but Councillor C. W. Owen was also commissioned as recruiting officer in the rank of Captain. Both Abbott and Owen had some previous military experience as past members of the Volunteer Force and in addition, former councillor William Carter, who had given up his seat on the Council, became the Battalion's Quartermaster. Carter had served in a similar capacity as a career soldier with the Dragoons and 13th Hussars and took up his former rank of Honorary Major.

The ladies of Battersea also pledged their support to the recruitment drive and, while they did not go quite so far as to hand out white feathers to young men not in uniform, they did pursue a variation on the theme. This involved the printing of many hundreds of facsimile First Class rail tickets on pink card. The destination boldly printed on the ticket was 'Berlin via Boulogne or Havre' and the holder was cordially invited to join the 10th Battalion on its journey to the German capital. These were then distributed by a committee of ladies to any young men who appeared to be shirking their patriotic duty. Sadly, the local press reported at least one case of a Battersea youth who had been 'worried into suicide by accusations of a lack of patriotism'.

By the end of June, however, only fifty men had come forward to volunteer. The *South Western Star* commented on what it perceived to be a lack of enthusiasm from Battersea Council and noted sourly that, in comparison, 'Wandsworth is like a garrison town.' In truth, it was more a vindication of the Mayor's fears that Battersea had already contributed more than her fair share of men to the war effort, especially in respect of volunteers for the 23rd County of London Regiment, the Territorial unit based in St. John's Hill. The situation was not helped by the Royal Irish Rifles beginning to advertise in Battersea for recruits of Irish origin or connections and another factor may have been the sight of many wounded soldiers coming and going from the local

Pte George Franks was an early young recruit. Ivy Sharp

Bolingbroke Hospital. In an effort to encourage men to join up, the Board Room at Nine Elms Baths was converted into a recruiting office and a number of free lettings at Battersea Town Hall were approved for the Battalion's social events, including a 'Bohemian and Smoking Concert' organised by Captain Owen. In July, use of the small hall at the Council's Latchmere Road Baths was granted for indoor drill purposes while Battersea Park and Clapham Common served as outdoor venues. Yet still, the numbers of recruits only continued to grow slowly. By the end of that month, Wandsworth's battalion had 700 men, but Battersea had only managed to attract the 100 necessary to complete an embryo A Company.

One area where something could be done about numbers was in the complement of officers. While it was the declared wish of the Council that almost all commissions should be gained by local men, this had proved difficult in practice. Instead, officers or potential officers already serving with other units were diverted to the new battalion if they had Battersea links. One such commission was given to the son of Mr L. Inkster, Battersea Council's first Borough Librarian who, like his Wandsworth Council librarian counterpart Mr C. Davis, had seen his sons quickly volunteer for active service. Born in the staff accommodation at Battersea Library in 1891, young Lawrie Inkster had chosen to pursue a career in banking when he left Emanuel School in 1906, working in the West Brompton, Barnes and Clapham branches of the London and South Western Bank. In 1909 he had enlisted in the Territorial Army for five years with the 14th Battalion,

Lt Lawrie Inkster, son of Battersea Council's Borough Librarian. D. Inkster

Early recruits in training. Author

County of London Regiment (London Scottish), transferring to the Reserve in early 1914. Immediately called up on the outbreak of war, Inkster joined the 1st Battalion, London Scottish and sailed for France and Belgium in September 1914. He had fought at Messines where he considered himself lucky to survive and was in more or less constant action until August, 1915, when he returned to England for his officer training. Commissioned as a second lieutenant the following month, Inkster then became an obvious candidate for transfer to the Battersea battalion.

Lawrie Inkster's closest companion in the 10th Queen's was a friend from Emanuel School who had acquired similar military experience. Second Lieutenant William Archer 'Joe' Pope was the son of Mr and Mrs J. W. Pope of Kendrick Avenue, off Nightingale Lane and close to Wandsworth Common. After leaving Emanuel to complete his education at Christ's Hospital School in Sussex, Pope had returned to London to start employment with a firm of shipbrokers in the City. He had enlisted as a rifleman with the Queen Victoria Rifles on the outbreak of war and had soon gone to France with the first contingent of Territorials. After serving in the trenches throughout the winter of 1914 he was wounded in the foot near Ypres, Belgium, in March 1915 and was shipped back to England. While recovering at home he was recommended for and awarded a commission in the Battersea Battalion by Mayor Mr Simmons.

Other local men who were made officers included Second Lieutenant S. J. Ranson, son of Battersea Council's Alderman Ranson; Second Lieutenant H. A Dawson, who had lived in Clapham for some years; and Second Lieutenant A. F. Robson, originally of Stormont Road, Battersea. An assistant Master in mathematics at Sir Walter St John's School, Robson had lived in Battersea all his life and had attended the school himself as a boy before taking a degree at King's College, London. Three years' service in the Universities and Public Schools Officer Training Corps (O.T.C.) gave him a slight advantage over those of his brother junior officers who possessed no military expertise at all. From only slightly further away came Second Lieutenant Shortman of Brixton, a nephew of the Mayor of Woolwich, and Second Lieutenant Raynham of Sutton, who had already served in France with the 6th Battalion of The Queen's.

Second Lieutenants H. Ereckson and Claude Hastings had both attended school in Wimbledon, the latter being a cousin of the Earl of Huntingdon. Another officer with links to the aristocracy was Lieutenant Lawrence Petre, son of the late Hon. Arthur Petre and Lady

Catherine Petre, and grandson of the Earl of Wicklow. Petre was described as having family estates in Essex and being a distinguished athlete and tennis champion. Lieutenant J. Deakin Yates, educated at Rugby and Oxford, was among the few junior officers with any experience of active military service. He had served in the Sharpshooters' Imperial Yeomanry and had seen action with them in the South African War.

Of the company commanders, Captain Mowbray Bessell was a stockbroker from Effingham in Surrey. A keen supporter of the Volunteer movement, he had been a captain for many years before the war in the 3rd Volunteer Battalion of the Royal Fusiliers. On the outbreak of war, and despite then being a thirty-eight-year-old married man, Bessell was quick to volunteer for active service. Required to drop a rank, he was first gazetted as a lieutenant in the East Surrey Regiment, but promoted back to captain before transferring to the 10th Queen's.

Another experienced and unusually-decorated company commander was Captain J. B. Dodge. The son of the Hon. Mrs Lionel Guest, Dodge had already seen action at Gallipoli where he had been wounded in both arms. Still managing to swim ashore to continue his duties, Dodge had received the Distinguished Service Cross, a naval decoration. Joining the newly-arrived officers was Battalion Sergeant-Major Stevens DCM, a long-serving professional soldier who had served with The Queen's Regiment in South Africa.

As these officers joined, one was lost. In October, Lieutenant Abbott, the Battalion's first local officer and former Battersea councillor, suffered a serious injury while being trained in bomb throwing on Clapham Common. This led to an operation at Millbank Hospital which was only partially successful. Although Abbott managed to rejoin the Battalion in March 1916 for light duties, he was clearly unable to go overseas on active service and was therefore transferred to the 12th (Reserve) Battalion of The Queen's Regiment.[51]

In November, Inglis's second in command, Major Talbot Jarvis, liaised with Alderman Ranson in arranging for the first and second

Captain Mowbray Bessell, one of the first company commanders. T. Miles

class baths at Latchmere Road to be covered over. These then served as the Battalion's drill hall and recreation room, just in time for a late surge of recruits. This came in December when a deadline was placed on volunteers being able to sign up for specific units. Henceforth, it was expected that recruits would be placed in any unit that the Army authorities wished. Consequently, the recruiting offices for both the 23rd London Regiment and the 10th Queen's suddenly saw great activity. Battersea Town Hall remained open until 2 and 3 a.m. on a number of nights, yet there was still an overflow that had to be directed down to Clapham Junction and the recruiters for the 3rd Battalion of the 23rd London Regiment.

A boxing tournament was among the social evenings and events which were organised to both help knit the new unit and recruits together and raise funds. In addition to numerous bouts among the new recruits, Sergeant Ernest Barry (also a world sculling champion) gave an exhibition of his own top-class boxing skills. Sergeant Barry was joined in this by Corporal Pat O'Keefe, a middleweight champion. The tournament had been scheduled for the second weekend in January 1916, but was hurriedly brought forward to Tuesday the 4th when news at last arrived that the military authorities were ready to take over responsibility for the Battalion. Orders immediately followed that a move was to be made on Thursday, 6 January 1916, to the Albuhera Barracks at Aldershot in Hampshire. The Army formally expressed its sincere thanks to Battersea Council and the latter agreed that some permanent record of their achievement in raising the Battalion should be displayed in the Town Hall buildings. As the Battalion set off from Battersea, its officers riding at the head of the column, one horse stumbled badly and narrowly escaped a fall. The rider was Major Jarvis, a tall, well-built man who did well to remain in the saddle. With a hearty laugh he called to onlookers lining the route "I wonder if that is an omen!", but many looked uneasy as they thought that the Major's comment was tempting fate.

An interesting loose end was left to be tidied up in London. At Bow Street Magistrates Court on 28 January one Bertram G. Grand appeared, charged with falsely wearing the uniform of an Army Captain about the capital. It transpired that Grand had indeed obtained a commission in the 10th Queen's, but had resigned it some time previously. The only excuse offered by the defendant was 'flattery' and he was fined £20.

With the move to Aldershot came the Battalion's first death when thirty-seven-year-old Private James Shepherd of Battersea died and was buried in Aldershot's military cemetery. The record remains unclear as to whether the cause was disease or accident. At Aldershot, together with the 26th and the 32nd Battalions of the Royal Fusiliers and the 21st Battalion of the King's Royal Rifle Corps, the Battersea unit became part of 124 Brigade within Major-General Sydney Lawford's 41st Division which had originally been formed in May 1915. The Hampshire town was completely given over to the military, but comparative proximity to Battersea enabled some semblance of normal life to continue in the 10th Queen's. In addition to weekend passes being available for a return home, wives and sweethearts were able to come down to see their loved ones. Second Lieutenant Inkster, newly married in February 1916, managed to have his young wife Elsa visit for two days after their wedding and the young couple hosted a dinner party for their best man, Second Lieutenant Pope, and Second Lieutenant Hoggett and Lieutenant Hastings and their wives. Two of the four young officers would be dead within eight months.

Major-General Sydney Lawford.

In a similar process to that encountered by the 13th East Surreys, training continued and the remaining unsuitable or unfit recruits were weeded out. Sadly, one of those whose constitution was not up to the demands was Colonel Inglis himself. His health had already broken down and he was in hospital in Seaford when, in April 1916, he suddenly died, aged only fifty-three. A replacement was swiftly found in the form of Lieutenant-Colonel Richard Oakley, late of the Cameronians (Scottish Rifles), another regular officer who had seen active service on the North West Frontier of India from 1897 to 1898. The new Mayor of Battersea, Mr William J. Moore JP (a former civil servant and accountant), visited Aldershot to both meet Oakley and to attend a parade before King George V.

Finally, already-trained drafts from other units arrived to fill the gaps caused by the weeding-out process and among these last recruits to join was a Carshalton boy, Charlie Young. Charlie had still been under age when he first tried to join the 5th (Territorial) Battalion of the East Surrey Regiment at Sutton just before the war started. He had then made a second attempt after war was declared, reasoning that the Army might now be in greater need of eager young men. This time he went to Croydon to try to join the 1st/4th (Territorial) Battalion of The Queen's (Royal West Surrey) Regiment. As he had hoped, his age was overlooked, but the eyesight of his left eye was deemed inadequate and he was again turned down. Returning home dispirited he had

Lieutenant-Colonel Oakley

almost resigned himself to a civilian life when, a few months later, friends told him that The Queen's Regiment's recruiting office in Sutton was gaining a reputation for accepting almost anyone. Charlie tried again and despite his earlier disappointments was accepted. He took the King's shilling and was given a voucher to travel to the Regimental Depot in Guildford.

By this time it was May 1915 and after just two days at Guildford, Charlie was sent to Chatham for three months' training. In September 1915 he was lucky to be posted to the 3rd (Reserve) Battalion at Sittingbourne in Kent where a camp was maintained for soldiers of The Queen's Regiment who were recuperating after service on the Western Front. Safe for the moment in England, Charlie was called upon for no more than guard duty on bridges, railway lines and the Short's Aeroplane Works. The 1st/4th Battalion, which he had been so keen to join, went overseas in December and straight into the fighting at Gallipoli where it was decimated.

Tiring of the routine, however, Charlie responded when three volunteers were called for to go as Lewis Gunners to France with a new division. He was sent off to Aldershot with his two fellow volunteers, only to find that just twenty-four hours' leave was granted before his new unit, the 10th Queen's, left for France. Charlie was to later recall that he immediately found the Battalion a "good mob of Battersea boys", happy to share everything with the newcomers.

At 9 a.m. on the showery morning of Friday 5 May 1916, the Battalion, led by Lieutenant-Colonel Oakley, left Aldershot in three trains for Southampton. There the men boarded the *Hunscraft* (which, a month later, was to help transport Wandsworth's 13th East Surreys

The French port of Le Havre – for many the first sight of a 'foreign' shore.

to France) and sailed the same evening for Le Havre. Everyone donned a life-jacket before most went below and sat on their packs, suffering from little ventilation as all portholes were kept shut to prevent any light giving away the ship's position. The French port was reached at 6 a.m. on the 6th and the troops marched off over the unfamiliar and uncomfortable cobbled streets in clear, bright weather to No. 1 Rest Camp. Idling about, dozing and eating the three substantial meals provided, were the only requirements of this first day. At dawn on the

Road leading out of Le Havre in summer 1916.

7th the Battalion left Le Havre by train for Steenbecque, south-west of Hazebrouck, and then marched on from there to the area between Strazeele and Outtersteene, west of Bailleul. The normal standard of ten minutes' rest after fifty minutes' march was practised, all marvelling at how numerous small children would appear as if from nowhere every time a stop was made. All demanded a "souvenir" and if refused, many displayed a shocking grasp of English invective and oaths.

The men settled into billets and training efforts were renewed with a grim sense of purpose. On the 30th the Battalion marched to Steenwerck, close to the border and the next day crossed into Belgium to settle into billets in Ploegsteert, invariably referred to by the British troops as 'Plugstreet'. This area was part of the Flanders front and though still relatively quiet, it was here the men saw the first signs of action, damaged and destroyed houses and numerous shell craters. The 10th Queen's was given the job of improving old trenches and as this work was under way the first casualties were suffered when Privates Browett and Youl were wounded by shrapnel from enemy shelling on 1 June 1916. The next day, while still in their reserve area billets, another ten men were similarly wounded.

On the 4th the Battalion commenced its first tour of active duty in the front-line trenches between Ploegsteert and Le Bizet, relieving the

12th (Bermondsey) East Surreys. Private Farr was fortunate to survive a bullet from an alert enemy sniper on the first day, but the Battalion's first fatality was inevitable and this came on 7 June when Private Henry Ireson was killed and seven others were wounded.

These first spells of trench duty were not nearly as bad as many had feared. The trenches, like the weather, were clear and dry. Even when, on their third day in the line, the men experienced their baptism of artillery fire, all they had to do was to lie in the bottom of the trench while the enemy bombardment raged overhead. This was indeed a misleadingly gentle introduction to the front, yet many of the young and inexperienced troops were only too ready to believe that this was the normal course of events. It also gave comfort to many when the most nervous man in the trenches proved to be not one of the young volunteers, but an old soldier sporting Boer War medal ribbons. Yet despite the relative calm there were some whose nerve failed early. An immediate example was made of one such man who was court-martialled for having left the forward trench to take refuge in a reserve trench. After being found guilty and sentenced to Field Punishment Number One, the hapless man was tied to a wagon in disgrace, while the entire Battalion was marched around him.

Charlie Young was himself lucky to avoid a similar fate when, one night on guard duty on the trench parapet, he was startled by the

Trenches between Ploegsteert and Le Bizet.

approach of an officer. The officer accused Charlie of having been asleep and ordered him to report at Stand-down. When Charlie did so he was threatened with court-martial, but the officer must have had his doubts, since the punishment eventually given was the order to pick up all the litter in the trench.

Generally, the food in the trenches was considered good by the largely working-class Battersea boys. Maconochie stew was a favourite, while bread and jam or bread and cheese were the regular stalwarts, supplemented by as much foraging as could be managed in the locality. Perhaps because of such efforts, and in contrast to the earlier warm welcome given by the French population, the local Belgian farmers seemed to resent the British Army's presence instead of being grateful for the Tommies' willingness to fight on their behalf.

Entertainments, for the time being, were home-made, as shown by the following programme, and unidentified critic's comments, of a concert that the Battalion staged:

Progamme of a Concert at Y.M.C.A. Hut on Monday, 22/5/16, under the patronage of Lieut.-Colonel R. Oakley and officers of the Battalion.

1. *Pianoforte Solo, Pte. Davidson* **(very good)**.
2. *Comic Song, Pte. Sonny Davis.*
3. *Song, Corpl. Button.*
4. *Comic Song, Lieut. R. A. Hawes* **(encored)**.
5. *Patter Duo, Ernie and Birnie* **(brought the hut down)**.
6. *Piccolo Solo, Corpl. Burchell.*
7. *At the Piano, Captain D.C. Johnston* **(extra special)**.
8. *Comic Song, L-Corpl. Kimbs* **(very hot stuff)**.
9. *The "Upper Farm Six", D Company* **(wash out)**.
10. *Song, Lieut. L. Inkster.*
11. *Song and Dance, Pte. Defries* **(splendid)**.
12. *Song, Pte. Jimmy Hart.*
13. *Song, Pte. Fitzjohn.*
14. *Song (Comic), Dr. Messenbird.*
15. *Song, Sergt. E. Hartland* **(some artiste)**.
16. *Song, Drummer Wheadon.*
17. *God Save the King, The Whole.*

Stage Manager, Sergt. E. W. Hartland. Pianist, Pte. Davidson.

At home, Battersea and Wandsworth Councils had started funds for comforts, with a matinee performance at the Grand Palace, Clapham

Lieutenant Inkster's Battalion Concert Party first performed in May 1916. D. Inkster

Junction, taking place on 13 May for the 10th Queen's and 23rd London Battalions. A fortnight later donations and subscriptions were formally invited for the Battersea Battalion's fund and the first contributions came from Battersea's Mayor, Mr Moore, and the relatives, wives and friends of the battalion's officers including Mr and Mrs Oakley, Mrs F. E. Johnston, Mrs Andrews, Hon. Mrs Guest, Mrs E. Bessell and Mrs E. Sutherland. The *South Western Star* of 16 June 1916 announced the appeal in its editorial page:

> BATTERSEA BATTALION
> THE MAYOR'S APPEAL
> *The public are again reminded of the appeal of the Mayor, Mr. W. J. Moore, for support for his fund for supplying comforts to the 10th Queen's (Battersea Battalion), which has recently left England. It is hoped that all residents in the borough who can afford to help will do so. The officers' wives are arranging to send regular contributions, so as to be prepared to meet the demands which will be made from time to time on the fund, and, while the Mayor will be grateful to receive donations, he will be very pleased if the residents will follow this example and send a contribution with a promise to repeat it periodically.*
> *There are many things not provided by the authorities which*

10th Queens D Coy officers and NCOs in 1916. S. Page

voluntary help can supply, and which are a real boon to men on active service. The knowledge that friends at home are giving them kindly and practical thought is wonderfully inspiriting, and the physical refreshment and help that well chosen gifts supply are an undoubted asset to the recipients. All contributions will be officially acknowledged from the Town Hall, and the progress of the fund will be frequently reported upon in these columns.

An initial sum of £142 9s 6d was raised from this appeal, but for the moment, supplies of cigarettes seemed to be the only result reaching the troops in the trenches.

Little action of note occurred during the remainder of June, though casualties continued to mount. On the night of the 18th, soon after dinner, Captain Brereton (commanding C company) and Second Lieutenant Hoggett were both caught by a burst of enemy machine-gun fire. Brereton was hit badly in the lungs and was not expected to live, while Hoggett was described as receiving 'a useful one in the shoulder' which would ensure his return to hospital in England. Three other ranks were also wounded and the same night a blustery wind blew an Allied gas shell attack perilously close to the 10th Battalion's lines. By the end of the month a total of six men had been killed or had died of wounds and forty-four had been wounded. The

enemy's snipers also continued to make their deadly presence felt. C Company's Private Dumbleton, of 79 Castle Street, Battersea, was killed on 15 July and on the morning of 26th July Private Albert Wheadon was another unlucky victim. A former plumber's mate of 40 Joubert[52] Street, Battersea and son of Mr Henry W. Wheadon, a long-serving employee of Battersea Council, Albert served as a drummer in the Battalion's band and was a celebrated singer in the concert party. Once in the front line, however, he acted as a stretcher bearer for Lieutenant Sweetman, the Battalion's Medical Officer. The *South Western Star* published the letters received by Wheadon's family:

France. Aug. 8, 1916
Dear Mrs Wheadon
Your son, Dr. A. G. Wheadon, 9908, Queen's, was admitted to this hospital (No. 1 Canadian Casualty Clearing) July 26 at noon, suffering from severe wounds in the head. It was seen at the time that he could not recover. He was irrational, was able to take nourishment, and talked often, but there was no meaning to anything he said. He did not suffer pain. August 1 he became much worse, grew gradually weaker, and just passed away in his sleep this morning at 6.20 a.m.

I hope it will comfort you a little to know that he was given every care and comfort during his illness, that his body has been reverently prepared for burial, and will be buried in the military cemetery in [censored – but Bailleul Communal Cemetery Extension] this afternoon, when our chaplain will hold a service. Any personal effects he may have had will be sent to you.

With sincere sympathy, I am, very truly yours,
Christina E. Cameson (Sister).

Dear Madam
It was with the deepest grief that this evening I learned of the death of your son.

Your son was one of my stretcher bearers for the past six months, and during that time I had many opportunities of forming an opinion of his merits.

He always took a deep interest in his work, was one of my best stretcher bearers and one whom I could always rely on, no matter how difficult or how dangerous the work was.

You have my deepest sympathy and I trust your other boy, who is also a stretcher bearer, and a boy whom I hold in the highest esteem, may be spared and brought back in safety to you when the war is over.

Yours sincerely
T. W. Sweetman (Lt. R.A.M.C.).

Tragically, Lieutenant Sweetman's hopes for the safety of the other Wheadon boy were in vain. Robert Wheadon survived his older brother by less than three months and was killed while serving with the 1st/13th Kensingtons of the London Regiment.

While the Canadian doctors and nurses were assessing Albert Wheadon's wound in the Casualty Clearing Station, over 150 of his comrades were about to face the first major test of the Battalion's resolve. On 17 July volunteers had been requested for a company-strength raid on the enemy's lines. The men's high morale was immediately apparent when several times the required numbers stepped forward. Those selected were sent by motor-bus to the Bailleul area for training over specially-prepared ground. The officers for the operation were Captain Sutherland, Lieutenant Hopkinson and Second Lieutenants Ranson (son of the Battersea councillor), Burgess and Serley, leading 154 other ranks and eight Royal Engineers.

The raid, eventually launched on the night of 26/27 July, soon ran into trouble. From 11 p.m. Allied artillery pounded the enemy's front-line defences until, at midnight, the barrage lifted onto the German reserve trenches and the raiding party moved into action. Even as the volunteers climbed from their trenches, however, retaliatory enemy shelling began to crash down. Men fell all the way out across No Man's Land, including Captain Sutherland, the operation's leader, who was wounded along with Lieutenant Hopkinson and Second Lieutenant Serley.

The enemy's wire had at least been effectively cut by the preliminary bombardment and the raiders, now lead by Second Lieutenant Ranson, had little trouble in making their way through. As they did so they met a group of the enemy, some ten to fifteen strong, emerging from their own trench. The Battersea men immediately threw their bombs and then rushed forward, bayonets to the fore. The Germans may conceivably have been about to surrender after the terrific shelling, but if so, fortune was not on their side. After their own losses across No Man's Land the 10th Queen's were in no mood to pause and only some three or four of the enemy avoided the initial slaughter by jumping back into their trench. Even then they were not safe. Their blood up, the raiders leapt in after them, vaulting over dozens of shattered bodies in the enemy's forward trench which had been almost totally destroyed by the Allied barrage. For the hapless Germans there was no escape as they were ruthlessly chased and despatched by the bayonet.

The Queen's men paused to take stock of their position. Three

dugouts had been discovered and while these were investigated, the trench was blocked on both flanks to prevent the arrival of enemy reinforcements. The dugouts yielded several packs, helmets and a number of important-looking papers which were all snatched up. The next objective was to explore three communications trenches which led back to the enemy's support line. Two of these were found to have been blown in by the shelling and were impassable, but the third was still clear and a party advanced cautiously along it. The support line had almost been reached when the Germans reacted, a hail of bombs and machine-gun fire coming down the trench, felling Sergeant Clarke and making any further advance impossible. At the same time, one of the flanks of the captured front-line trench came under counter-attack and it was clearly time to withdraw before the situation deteriorated further. Again there was no respite across No Man's Land from the enemy shelling. Second Lieutenant Ranson covered himself in glory by bringing in no less than four wounded men before he himself was hit and wounded, leaving Second Lieutenant Burgess as the only untouched officer of the party.

In the comparative safety of their own front-line trenches, the

Lieutenant-Colonel Oakley's sketch of the raid on the enemy's trenches, 26-27 July 1916.
S. Harcourt-Smith

surviving raiders counted their losses. Almost all the casualties had been suffered during the advance and withdrawal across No Man's Land, five men having been killed and thirty-nine wounded, including four of the five officers. A further four men were missing, Clapham-born Sergeant Henry Clarke being one of these and later confirmed as having been killed in the German trench. In the heat of the engagement no enemy prisoners had been taken for interrogation purposes, but a great deal of valuable information came from the material seized in the enemy dugouts. The opposing unit was discovered to have been the 104th Saxon Regiment, supported by a machine-gun company. Personal letters also contained many useful details of internal conditions in Germany.

Today's observer might consider that the loss of forty-nine men killed, wounded or missing for such limited results is difficult to justify. Almost certainly, in the context of today's conflicts, this magnitude of loss would result in the raid being termed a disaster, with blame and recrimination flowing freely among the military, national government, the press and coroner. Yet the commanders of the day in 1916 had nothing but praise for the operation. The Army Commander sent a message with his congratulations 'to all concerned on the successful raid carried out last night which inflicted much loss on the enemy' while Major-General Lawford, commanding the 41st Division, added his 'congratulations on the gallant manner in which they carried out the enterprise.' The Battalion was later to parade before General Lawford (affectionately known as 'Swanky' to his troops) who personally decorated Sergeant G. F. King with the Distinguished Conduct Medal and Privates Phillippe and Crichton with the Military Medal for their bravery in the attack. The latter soldier, Alfred Crichton of Wandsworth Road, had a particularly eventful night. Returning from the enemy's trenches he had come across a wounded British soldier lying in a crater in No Man's Land. Unable to drag him out alone, Crichton elected to stay throughout the night with the wounded man, finding food and water and arranging rescue the next day.

Private Alf Crichton, awarded the Military Medal for his actions in the raid of 26-27 July 1916. A. Crichton.

N.STAR, AUGUST 4, 1916.

BATTERSEA BATTALION IN ACTION.

BRILLIANT WORK.

We have great pleasure in publishing the following letter from the Mayor :—

Dear Sir,—I have received a message from the Front to the following effect :—

"You and all Battersea will be delighted to hear that the Battersea Battalion (the 10th Queen's) has been very highly complimented both by the General Commanding the Division and the Army Commander for gallant work in a small attack they made on the enemy lines."

Yours sincerely,
WM. JAS. MOORE,
Mayor.

Town Hall, Battersea, S.W.
2nd August, 1916.

THE MAYOR'S APPEAL.

The public are again reminded of the appeal of the Mayor, Mr. W. J. Moore, for support for his fund for supplying comforts to the 10th Queen's (Battersea Battalion). It is hoped that all residents in the borough who can afford to help will do so. The officers' wives are arranging to send regular monthly contributions, so as to be prepared to meet the demands which will be made from time to time on the fund, and, while the Mayor will be grateful to receive donations, he will be very pleased if the residents will follow this example and send a contribution with a promise to repeat it periodically.

There are many things not provided by the authorities which voluntary help can supply, and which are a real boon to men on active service. The knowledge that friends at home are giving them kindly and practical thought is wonderfully inspiriting, and the physical refreshment and help that well chosen gifts supply are an undoubted asset to the recipients. All contributions will be officially acknowledged from the Town Hall, and the progress of the fund will be frequently reported upon in these columns.

The fund has now the benefit of an inviting collecting box affixed prominently at the side of the main entrance to the Municipal Buildings on Lavender Hill. "You know what our lads are doing for you" the passer-by is told with all the forcefulness of red printer's ink. "What are you doing for them?" No one is asked for anything out of the way. Handsome donations would not be rejected of course, but what pleases the Committee best of all is the promise of a steady inflow of subscriptions, small or large, at regular intervals. If they know what their income is likely to be they can spend with better judgment on behalf of the gallant lads of the 10th Queen's.

N.

The raid was mentioned in the South Western Star, 4 August 1916.

Chapter 10

DEVIL'S WOOD

The first three weeks of August saw a combination of trench duties, which included hazardous night-time dashes across No Man's Land to leave bundles of English newspapers in the German lines, and reserve spells in billets at Soyer and Notteboom. The Germans retaliated by dropping English-language propaganda leaflets from aeroplanes. On the 23rd the Battalion entrained for Pont-Rémy and from there marched on to Buigny l'Abbé. Several days' training was undertaken here, learning attack techniques and practising wood fighting. All the signs pointed to preparations for a major action and sure enough, the Battalion marched to Longpré on 7 September to take a train south to the Somme front where a bitter Allied offensive had been under way since 1 July. Training continued in bivouac camps in the Dernancourt and Méaulte areas, south of Albert, until the night of 13/14 September when 124 Brigade moved up to the Pommiers Redoubt in the front line. The countryside here had been churned up by heavy shelling in earlier actions and the resultant landscape was like a scene from Hell. Bodies hung from the few trees that remained and the situation worsened when eventually the Battalion moved up at night through the shattered remains of Delville Wood[53], on the north-eastern outskirts of the village of Longueval. The promised guide did not materialise and despite an almost full moon, the 10th Queen's soon became lost and found themselves going round in circles. Everywhere was the terrible stench of death from the recent fighting and the men continually tripped and fell over parts of corpses which stuck out of the ground. Eventually, at 2.30 a.m. on the 14th, the men reached the front-line trenches on the northern edge of the wood and late that afternoon orders were issued for an attack the next day.

The Battalion found itself on the extreme right of 124 Brigade's line, with its four companies distributed C, D, A and B, from left to right respectively. The 41st Division had been called up to take the place of one of the divisions which had suffered badly in the continuous fighting since July and was now, with the 14th Division to its right and the New Zealand Division to its left, part of XV Corps commanded by

Delville Wood. 'Everywhere was the terrible stench of death.' Taylor Library

General Horne. In the plan of battle for 15 September the 41st and 14th Divisions were to take the ground east and north of Delville Wood, while the New Zealanders had the village of Flers as their objective. Other divisions on the left of XV Corps were to attack Courcelette and Martinpuich and clear High Wood, while units on the right were to move against Lesboeufs and Morval, capture Bouleaux Wood and hold a defensive flank.

In preparation for the attack 124 Brigade was formed up with the 10th Queen's on the right and the 21st King's Royal Rifle Corps on the left of the front line, distributed in depth in eight waves in Brown Trench and No Man's Land. Two battalions (the 26th and 32nd) of the Royal Fusiliers were in support in four waves in and between Green Trench and Inner Trench. The Brigade had four objectives: the first being the enemy line 800 yards south of Flers (Switch Trench) from the junction with Cocoa Lane to junction with Coffee Lane; the second was the German line running south-east on the south-western and southern sides of Flers (Flers Trench); the third was the village of Flers

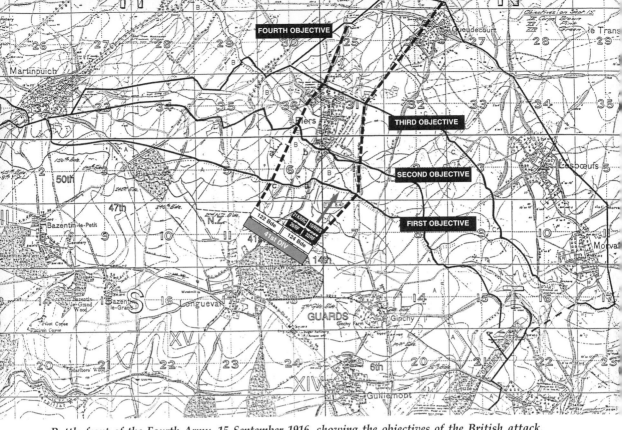

FOURTH OBJECTIVE

THIRD OBJECTIVE

SECOND OBJECTIVE

FIRST OBJECTIVE

Battle front of the Fourth Army, 15 September 1916, showing the objectives of the British attack. Position and direction of advance of 124 Brigade and specifically the 10th Battalion The Queen's (Royal West Surrey) Regiment.

and a line described as crossroads-northern edge of Flers-road junction; and the fourth objective had no description, merely being a line marked on the map issued to the troops.

The Brigade attacked at 6.20 a.m. on the 15th, the leading wave in extended order and those following in shallow columns. Two tanks[54], never seen before and which the men then called caterpillars or landships, came up in support and within half an hour the first objective, Switch Trench, was captured. Leaving small parties of men

Female tank during the advance of Flers. Taylor Library

to consolidate and construct a strong-point, the remainder pushed on and the second objectives, Flers Trench and Flers Avenue, were taken after heavy fighting by 8.50 a.m. All seemed to be going well, but the enemy's fire gradually intensified and it was not long before both the 10th Queen's and the 21st King's Royal Rifle Corps found themselves pinned down in a corn field on a slight rise before the much-ruined village of Flers. The two battalions' commanding officers, joined by a Major from Brigade headquarters, held a hurried conference and agreed that a final push should be made without delay. As they prepared to move forward again, heavy enemy machine-gun fire found them and Lieutenant-Colonel the Earl Feversham of the 21st K.R.R.C. fell back dead. Lieutenant-Colonel Oakley immediately took command of all the scattered men around him and succeeded in signalling a message to an aeroplane of the Royal Flying Corps which appeared overhead. This news of the battle did not reach brigade headquarters until just after 10 a.m., Oakley reporting that some 200 men of all battalions had reached a certain map point. They were in touch with scattered parties of the 14th Division on the right, but could see nothing of 122 Brigade on the left. Ten minutes later, however, it was reported that 122 Brigade was apparently retiring and that Oakley's grouped remnants of the 124 Brigade might have to do likewise as they were now being heavily shelled again.

Fortunately the fight then died down a little and therefore, about mid-day, Oakley ordered only a limited withdrawal to the line of the second objective. There, and in various places between the second and third objectives, Oakley assembled and reorganised the bulk of the Brigade. This was none too soon as at 3.20 p.m. Brigade Headquarters called for a renewed advance on the village of Flers and the line of cross roads-northern edge of Flers-road junction. Reports as to the general situation and progress of the attack were not clear, but word reached Brigade that the enemy was counter-attacking and the situation looked grim. It was not until 7 p.m., when Lieutenant-Colonel Oakley returned wounded, that it was confirmed that the survivors of the 10th Battalion and the Brigade's other

units had managed to take and hold the third objective, the village of Flers itself. Major Jarvis, the Battalion's second in command, had taken over and was ordered to hang on. A pilot of the Royal Flying Corps reported that he had watched a tank slowly making its way up the main street of Flers, followed by a body of troops. These were subsequently realised to have been the survivors grouped together by Oakley and Jarvis, joined by men from 122 Brigade.

On the morning of the 16th the Battersea battalion was released from its forward positions and moved back to Switch Trench which had been the previous day's first objective. Still there was no respite. In addition to heavy shelling, the enemy launched two counter-attacks during the day which threatened to overwhelm the new British lines, but on each occasion the Germans were eventually repulsed. On the 17th enemy artillery continued to pound the Battalion, but at last it was ordered back into support in Green and Brown Trenches. It was only then that the true scale of the bloody cost was realised. A total of 335 men were dead, missing or wounded and only some fifty men were led back to the Flers Switch trenches by Major Jarvis.

The 10th Queen's, after only its first battalion-strength action, had been savagely decimated. Of the officers, Captain Alexander Lawrence (the Adjutant), Captain Mowbray Bessell and Second Lieutenants Henry Mance, Frank Baker and Robert Javes were killed or died later. Lawrence and Bessell, who had done so much with the late Colonel

Approaches to the ruined village of Flers.

A tank in Flers village. A. Dupont

Inglis to form the Battalion, were particularly sad losses. Despite his severe wounds from the first battle of Ypres in 1914, Lawrence had recovered sufficiently to return to the Front with the 10th Queen's, only to be killed in his new unit's first major engagement. The *South Western Star* wrote of him: 'He had the professional soldier's contempt for inefficiency and softness, yet at heart he was the kindest of men.'

Of Bessell, Lieutenant-Colonel Oakley wrote:

> *You know how much we all loved him, and personally I feel I have lost a real and dear friend; never was there a more loyal and hardworking officer. I can't tell you what I and all the regiment owe him. He loved his Company and was always working for them, and it was through him that they were able to do what they did last Friday, and go through everything with the greatest dash and in a manner unsurpassed by any regiment in the British Army.*

The wounded included Oakley,[55] Captains Johnston, Hayley Bell, Dodge and Robson, Lieutenant Sweetman (the Medical Officer), and Second Lieutenants Berrangé, Heath, Savereux, Scott, Cox, Hawes and Cashel. Among the NCOs killed was Sergeant Charles Barrington of 51 Castle Street, Battersea, son of Battersea Council's Councillor Barrington who had done much to help form the Battalion. Lieutenant-Colonel Oakley, in writing of the losses to Battersea's Mayor, revealed that Barrington had been recommended for both a gallantry award and a commission:

> *I am very sorry to hear of the death of Sergeant Barrington – the best all get taken. He was one of the best N.C.O.'s we had in*

Lieutenant Mance kia 15th September 1915 at Flers. No known grave, commemorated on the Thiepval Memorial.
D. Inkster

German prisoners after the fighting around Flers. Taylor Library

the Regiment. Sergeant Barrington had done so well and gallantly that I sent in his name after our raid, but he got nothing, and I fear his father will get nothing, as they will not grant any posthumous honour except a V.C.

Will you tell his father how deeply grieved I am to hear the news, and tell him how highly we all thought of his son. His name had gone forward for a commission, as I daresay his father knew.

On 19 September the Battalion's surviving strength, commanded by Major Jarvis, moved back to the Dernancourt area where it remained for the rest of the month, frequently in pouring rain. Battalion Headquarters were established above the morbidly-named Death Valley, overlooking Mametz Wood and it was here that much-needed reinforcements reached the 10th Queen's early in October. A large draft came from the Surrey Yeomanry, the peace-time Territorial regiment of mounted troops which had its headquarters in King's Avenue, Clapham Park. The 1/1st Battalion had been split up into its three constituent cavalry squadrons in late 1914 and attached to three different divisions proceeding abroad. Of these, C Squadron had served in Egypt before returning to France in 1916. Their horses were taken from them and all were posted as infantry reinforcements, over 100 reaching the 10th Queen's where they had some consolation in finding themselves among many others from south-west London. Another large contingent was led by Major Roland Gwynne and came from the 2/1st Sussex Yeomanry, a reserve battalion which had been raised in Brighton in September, 1914 in order to replace the 1/1st battalion when the latter was called overseas. Typical of the newcomers from Sussex was Private George Osborne who had enlisted in Brighton at the very beginning of the war, only to spend two years on home defence and training duties. He then became part of an advance party of a draft of men ordered to leave the battalion and sail for France to be sent to under-strength infantry units. As in the case of the Surrey Yeomanry, horses had to be left behind when Gwynne's party sailed from Folkestone with an escort of two destroyers. On arrival in France, they were given just two weeks' training at Etaples on the coast before being rushed forward to plug the holes smashed in other battalions by the continuing Somme offensive. To add insult to injury, the Surrey and Sussex Yeomanry men who were posted to infantry battalions lost their coveted rank title of Trooper, and became ordinary Privates instead. George Osborne was to suffer this when, on 4 October 1916, he arrived at his new unit, the 10th Queen's, in a camp area which was generally about six inches deep in mud, apart from the numerous shell holes which could hold two or three feet of water. The latter were regularly increased in number by enemy shelling which was still able to reach this rear position. Lieutenant Alfred Eaves, a former pupil of Sir Walter St John's School in Battersea, was unlucky to be caught by this the previous day. Formerly in the Brigade's Trench Mortar Battery, Eaves had been transferred into the 10th Battalion to help fill the vacant officer positions. A brother officer wrote to his widow, Cordelia:

I feel his loss myself very greatly. He was at the time of his death in charge of his company. The company was digging in under heavy shell fire. I did not actually see him fall, but I understand his death was a gallant one. He was urging on the men to dig hard for cover, and, regardless of danger to himself, was supervising their work, when a shell burst just over his head and mortally

Private George Osborne, one of a draft from the Sussex Yeomanry to make up for losses at Flers.
G. S. Osborne

Lieutenant Alfred Eaves, a former pupil of Sir Walter St John's School, Battersea, kia 3rd October 1916.
D. Inkster

wounded him. I need not say how very deeply mourned he is by his brother officers.

On 6 October, Private Osborne and some of the other new arrivals had a taste of how bitter the recent fighting had been when they were in a party sent back up to Delville Wood to bury the dead, both British and German, from the September battle. The dreadful task and shattered landscape were bad enough, but the Germans also persisted with deadly shrapnel shelling and for a while there was a good chance that the burial party would join their charges. The grim wood was finally left behind when the Battalion returned to the trenches north of Flers between the 7 and 9 October.

During this move back up the line, twenty-four-year-old William "Joe" Pope, newly promoted to Captain, was hit and seriously wounded. He was evacuated to the 36th Casualty Clearing Station where, three days after his wounding, he was well enough to dictate a cheery note home to his parents in Kendrick Avenue. The next day, however, before the letter had been sent, he suddenly worsened and died. Lieutenant-Colonel Oakley, while at home recovering from his own wounds, wrote to the young officer's parents:

'It is a great blow to me and the Regiment, for officers like him are few and far between nowadays. A better officer in every way never wore the King's uniform. He has always been the greatest help to me – hardworking, clever, trustworthy and beloved by officers and men.

Pope's replacement was Second Lieutenant Claude Hine. Like Pope, Hine was twenty-four years old and also from the Wandsworth Common area, in Bolingbroke Grove. He too had sound previous military experience, having enlisted in the Honourable Artillery Company in August 1914 and having later obtained a commission with the 2nd Queen's. Despite his front-line background, Hine lasted just nine days before also being killed and he was buried in the same

Captain Joe Pope, seen on the far right, leading a column of the 10th Queen's.
Tony Webster collection

Heilly Station cemetery as Pope.

On its return to the front line on the 7th, the Battalion was immediately thrown into action in support of a fresh attack on the enemy's positions by the two battalions of the Royal Fusiliers. A and D Companies were to the fore in Gird Trench with B and C in Factory Trench. Soon after the attack began D Company received orders to move up to assist the front battalions and B and C Companies also advanced up to Gird Support. This operation was of the kind the troops hated most – a daylight attack against a dug-in enemy waiting for them. Starting shortly after 1 p.m., the initial climb from the trenches and the slow, walking advance in line abreast initially went well. But lines of dead Fusiliers ahead showed where the advancing British came within sight and range of the German machine gunners, sweeping back and forth with deadly effect. Those who succeeded in avoiding the streams of bullets went to ground in shell holes, digging with picks and shovels to scrape shallow trenches in the chalky soil. At about 2 p.m. Major Jarvis was wounded, but it was not until night fell that he could be sent down to the dressing station.[56] Again, communications became very difficult and all sorts of rumours came back from the front, the most dramatic being that D Company had been completely wiped out. Messages took as long as five hours to get back to Brigade Headquarters and critical movement orders were in some cases only received hours after they had been issued. This situation inevitably required a great deal of initiative on the part of the front-line officers who eventually received the orders. Lieutenant Leslie Andrews, only recently promoted and made Adjutant, took command of the Battalion until the arrival on the morning of the 8th of Major Clarke, a temporary replacement C.O. from the Royal Fusiliers. Following Clarke's arrival the 10th Queen's were withdrawn and pulled back via Mametz to Bécordel, east of Albert. For the moment, the men were able to enjoy sights that many had not seen for several months: fields with grass, trees with leaves and barns housing cows instead of being crowded with sheltering troops.

But the Battalion had again suffered heavily. In particular it had not been far from the truth when it was rumoured that D Company had been wiped out. From a reduced strength of some 100 men, eighty-four were killed or wounded and a further seven were missing.

196

Chapter 11

RETURN TO FLANDERS

After their trial on the Somme the 10th Queen's again found themselves on the move, first to Buire and Airaines and then back to the Flanders front, to le Thieushouck and on to the area around La Clytte [De Klijte]. Life again settled to a routine of trench duties in the Ridge Wood sector, interspersed with training and working parties, and these duties were to see the Battalion through the remainder of the year.

Casualties lessened to a trickle, but the weather was now as much an enemy as the Germans. Severe frosts began in November and any water or stream turned to ice up to eighteen inches thick. Shaving water and hot tea froze quickly and every piece of wood, including floorboards from the reserve area camp's nissen huts, was swiftly burned for heat. Rats, made desperate by the cold in their hunt for food, became ever-more bold and at night would nibble at exposed hands or noses and tug on men's hair. If this were not bad enough, the enemy's snipers were also particularly active in the sector. An officer was wounded early in November and on the 10th, a clear moonlit night proved the downfall of a Royal Fusilier from the adjacent battalion who was shot through the head while on a working party. The Fusiliers received further attention from the enemy when a minor raid was launched on them on the night of the 14th. The attack was beaten off without loss, while the Germans left one dead behind in the British trench which they had succeeded in entering. To counter the enemy's efforts, aggressive patrols in No Man's Land again became the order of the day, but the 10th Queen's lost Second Lieutenants Ernest Woodward killed on the 24th and David Jacques, just nineteen years old, on 1 December. In these miserable conditions, it came as no surprise when a forlorn German soldier stumbled out of the thick fog which ushered in December and gratefully surrendered.

The fog did not last, but was replaced by driving rain which, while it only served to worsen trench life, did nevertheless offer an additional measure of safety since the continuing poor visibility at least hampered the enemy snipers. The Battalion's first Christmas abroad was greeted with heavy snow falls and a pause in operations while further reinforcements (including another seventy men from the

Sussex Yeomanry) joined at La Clytte. One young replacement officer was Second Lieutenant James Parkes who had originally gone out to France in early 1916 as a Private in the Artists Rifles. He had only got as far as Saint Omer, however, when he contracted a serious illness through drinking contaminated water. Some three months' hospitalisation followed back in England, after which he took up a commission in The Queen's. A first posting brought only a brief stay with the 3rd Queen's, the draft-finding battalion based at Sittingbourne in Kent. Parkes was then quickly sent out to the Battersea Battalion via the notorious holding and training camp, the 'Bull Ring' at Etaples near Le Touquet. On reaching the 10th Queen's he was pleasantly surprised to find that his allocated Company had an even number of officers, all of whom shared one batman between two officers. With no-one wanting to share a batman among three, Parkes was permitted a batman all to himself, to be chosen from his own platoon. The newcomer wisely left this choice to Sergeant King, his platoon Sergeant and a former postman, stipulating only that someone not in the first flush of youth might benefit from the lighter duties. Parkes was to recall:

> *My Sergeant chose well, and Johnson, a man about twice my age, became so kindly and efficient a batman that everyone from the second in command downwards tried unsuccessfully to steal him from me. I gave Johnson a list of the supplies I wanted always to be in my kit when we went up the line. Thereafter I did not have to worry. They were always there. When we first met I gave him only one instruction. I said to him: "My job is to look after the men. Your job is to look after me." I hope I did my job as well as he did.*

Second Lieutent James Parkes, formerly of the Artists' Rifles.
Brotherton Library

Parkes was to gain a reputation as the Battalion's unofficial war artist. He had already had to learn how to sketch accurately for his former duties as a scout in the Artists' Rifles. He managed to continue his art as a hobby with the 10th Queen's, sketching and painting the towns, villages and trenches of Flanders. While this was strictly contrary to Army regulations, Parkes found that the Military Police were normally sympathetic enough to turn a blind eye if he sought permission in advance.[57]

The 10th Queen's remained in the Ridge Wood area for the first two months of 1917, only notably being disturbed on 5 January when battalion headquarters were shelled. Six men were killed and fourteen wounded. Captain Burgess, acting Adjutant while Captain Andrews was home on leave, was among the latter when he 'escaped death by

Second Lieutenant Parkes's sketch of the old front line, Ravine Wood near Hill 60.
Brotherton Library

one second.' The remainder of January was only characterised by the atrocious weather and trench conditions, one man's diary for the 7th noting 'stream rose up to knees during night'. The conditions were not helped by the Germans who, on higher ground facing the Battersea Battalion, had a habit of pumping water out of their trenches and consequently into the positions of the 10th Queen's. Much of the trench line therefore collapsed, necessitating crawling behind low earthworks or, at worst, simply dashing across completely exposed sections of swampy ground. Occasional walks into the old town of Ypres were possible, but there was little else to lighten Tommy's mood.

On 3 February Lieutenant-Colonel Oakley, recovered from his wounds and awarded the Distinguished Service Order (DSO), returned in time to oversee preparations and training for an important daylight raid on the enemy's trenches in the Hollandscheschuur Salient, near Vierstraat. The object of the raid was to take prisoners, inflict losses on the enemy and destroy his dugouts, defences and material. The operation was to involve the Battalion's entire available fighting strength with seventeen officers and 525 men taking part, along with a section of Royal Engineers and a party from a tunnelling company. The raid was judged to be of great importance, being only the second undertaken by a whole battalion in the sector, and was to be led by Major Gwynne, now the 10th Battalion's second in command, supported by Captain Andrews, again promoted.

Training for the operation began on the 17th in reserve positions and detailed orders for the raid finally arrived on 24 February. The Battalion moved up to its assembly position and the raid was launched in the late afternoon. After less than half an hour the first and second objectives were captured, along with scores of prisoners who were swiftly passed back. By 6.30 p.m. the enemy's retaliatory shelling had become intense, but was dealt with by the British artillery. Messages from the forward companies reported that all enemy dugouts around the second objective had been destroyed and the German troops manning them had been killed or captured. Of four enemy machine guns discovered in concrete emplacements, one had been captured and sent back and three destroyed. Within an hour and a half of the 'off', the raiders were back in their lines with all objectives achieved and fifty-five German prisoners, including one officer.

The operation, staged in daylight and in large numbers, had entailed great risk and consequently, praise for its success was swift to arrive. Messages of congratulations were sent by the Commander-in-Chief and even HRH The Prince of Wales. General Plumer, commanding Second Army, called at Murrumbridge Camp on the 27th to personally express his appreciation and thanks. But successful or not, the raid had not been without considerable loss. Within just ninety minutes twenty-eight men had been killed or fatally wounded, ninety-three were wounded and a further eleven men were missing. Captain Edwin Bird, a twenty-four-year-old company commander from Brixton, was among the dead. Yet losses of 24%, even in such a short space of time, were nevertheless still acceptable to the British High Command of the time. Among those decorated on 1 April by Major-General Lawford in the market square at Steenvoorde was the wounded Major Gwynne who received a well-earned Distinguished Service Order (DSO) for:

> Conspicuous gallantry and judgment in commissioning and carrying out a daylight raid with his battalion. His personal example of courage and coolness was of great value throughout the operation. He personally went over to the enemy lines and supervised.

Also decorated was Lieutenant Lawrence Inkster, son of Battersea Council's Borough Librarian. The citation for his Military Cross (MC) read:

> For conspicuous gallantry and devotion to duty. During a raid on the enemy's trenches he handled his company with marked ability and

ro Lieut Lawrence Inkster

10th Queens.

I wish to place on record my appreciation of *your Courage & Skill in leading your Company during a Battalion raid on the enemy's trenches in Vierstraat, 24 Feb 1917.*

Major General.
Comdg. 41st Division.

NOTE—It does not follow that your name will be submitted to higher authority.

General Lawford's congratulations to Inkster. D. Inkster.

A Comforts Fund was maintained by Battersea Council throughout the war to support the Battalion.
Author

SAINT GEORGE'S ENGLAND'S DAY.

Saturday, 21st April, 1917.

Borough of Battersea.

Proceeds to the

BATTERSEA BATTALION COMFORTS FUND
and the
BATTERSEA VOLUNTARY
WAR WORKERS' ASSOCIATION.

The Battalion are fighting in France and have already distinguished themselves on several occasions.

The Association are working hard to supply comforts to the soldiers, and crutches, bandages, &c., for the wounded in every country where the war rages.

FUNDS ARE LOW—BUY A FLAG.

carried out the task allotted to him with conspicuous success. He subsequently reorganized the defence of the front line.

Sergeant-Major Thomas Baker, whose family had lived at 15 Theatre Street, Battersea, before moving to Tooting, was awarded the Distinguished Conduct Medal. Leading a bombing party, Baker brought back no fewer than twenty-five enemy prisoners despite being wounded. His DCM medal was eventually presented by the Mayor of Battersea in July 1918, when Baker returned to England for officer training.

After this major raid the 10th Battalion was allowed a measure of safety while holding the front line around Ridge Wood. The weather remained testing, with snow blizzards well into April, but the enemy in the opposing trenches remained relatively quiet from March through to May and the British were happy to reciprocate. The enemy in the air, however, was still notably active, regularly attacking British observation balloons and always ready to swoop on any unguarded activity of the troops, even at night. One such occasion was on 7 April when, around midnight, a party of men from D Company were returning from unloading a train. Above, a keen-eyed German flyer spotted the group and the next moment a stream of bullets spat out of the night sky as the enemy machine roared low over the ground. Diving for cover too late, the party was caught in the open and one man was killed with another wounded.

Fortunately, such dangers when out of the line were relatively infrequent. Evenings were generally free and many men took advantage of the cafés and estaminets in nearby Poperinghe (affectionately known as 'Pop' by the troops), Reninghelst or Steenvoorde. It was during this time that news had broken of the United States' entry into the war on 6th April 1917. This was

201

Lieutenant Inkster's Senior NCOs of B Company, 10th Queen's. D. Inkster

welcome, though surprising, news as President Wilson had appeared so determined to keep his country out of the European conflict and the average British soldier had come to expect that the Americans could not be relied upon to help. Now, there might be a little more light at the end of the tunnel and it would only be a matter of time before strong reinforcements crossed the Atlantic.

In the meantime, the Battalion was not seriously engaged again until, in early June 1917, it was called upon to take part in the Flanders offensive known as the Battle of Messines. Orders on 24 May had announced that the Second Army was to be prepared to assume the offensive soon after the end of the month. The front of the attack occupied by X Corps (in which the 41st Division was now serving) was to be from Dieppendaal Beek to the high ground known as Observatory Ridge, south-east of Ypres [Ieper]. On the Corps's front the 41st Division was to be on the right, the 47th in the centre and the 23rd on the left. Within the 41st Division 124 Brigade was placed on the right for the first stage of the attack. Extensive training took place in the reserve areas immediately behind the front from where, ominously, the troops noted that many more civilians had recently been evacuated. Companies were sent, two at a time, to view a large-scale model of Messines Ridge and the land over which they would soon be expected to storm. All the enemy positions which had been spotted, right down to individual machine-gun posts and even the lines of barbed wire, were faithfully reproduced on the model and pointed out to the troops.

Such detailed preparation was one of the trademarks of General Plumer, Second Army commander, who was rightly one of the most popular British military leaders of the First World War due to the concern he invariably displayed for his men. He was always anxious to keep casualties to a minimum by careful and methodical planning and consequently, in preparation for the attack on the Messines ridge, Plumer's engineers had been tunnelling under the enemy's positions since August 1915. From Hill 60 in the north to St Yves in the south the tunnellers eventually completed the

General Plumer, commanding Second Army. G. Richardson

task of siting a series of nineteen huge mines containing nearly a million pounds of high explosive. In addition to the mines, Plumer

The men were sent to study a model made for the Messines attack. G. Richardson

had assembled over 2,000 artillery guns and 144,000 tons of ammunition. The preliminary bombardment had begun on 21 May, supported by 300 aircraft of the Royal Flying Corps. By the morning of 7 June, three and a half million shells had rained down on the enemy's positions. The 10th Queen's were to find themselves uncomfortably close to some of these lethal preparations.

124 Brigade was to advance on a three-battalion front with the 10th Queen's on the right. All units assembled in their designated positions on the night of 6 June, and despite the mood of tense expectation, most of the men managed to catch at least a couple of hours' sleep. While his

men rested, Lieutenant-Colonel Oakley had taken advantage of the nearly-full moon to have a number of gaps dug out of the front-line trench parapet. By so doing he hoped that his leading assault companies might be able to go over the top without being silhouetted against the skyline and seen by the enemy. Shortly before zero hour the men climbed out to wait in No Man's Land, some choosing to calmly walk over the skyline despite Oakley's concerns and efforts. Almost certainly the enemy spotted these movements, but apart from a few desultory shells over on the left, the Germans were not able to summon any substantial response before zero hour for the main Allied assault.

When the mines were triggered, commencing at 3.10 a.m. on the 7th, the effect was truly devastating, the massive explosions being so loud that they were heard across the Channel in England. The Battalion discovered that the nearest mine, at St Eloi [Sint-Elooi], was little more than a hundred yards away and the men watched in amazement as the enemy's concrete dugouts were blown sky-high by the explosions. Taking advantage of this mayhem and the supporting artillery barrage which now screamed overhead with unerring accuracy, the Battalion picked itself up from the still-shaking ground. Despite some difficulty in keeping to the right direction, the men advanced rapidly and suffered only a few casualties in the early stages while the Germans reeled in shock. Capture of the German front line

One of the huge mines such as exploded at Messines, June 1917.
G. Richardson

SNIPER'S BARN ST ELOI

Second Lieutenant Parkes found time to sketch a feature, Sniper's barn, at St Eloi.
Brotherton Library

presented little difficulty and soon the 10th Battalion was formed up on the Red Line in Oaten Wood, to the south-east of St Eloi village. A further advance was then made to the Black Line which was the Battalion's final objective and there the men dug in and remained for the rest of the day of the 7th. One officer of the Battalion with an unusual story to tell of that day was Second Lieutenant Parkes. Although his platoon was in the first attacking wave at zero hour, Parkes himself had been given duties with Battalion Headquarters and was therefore left to sleep in the early hours of 7 June. It is an indication of how severe his fatigue was that, almost incredibly, he managed to slumber right through the massive mine detonations, screaming artillery barrages and general noise of the erupting battle. He woke at his normal time of 6.45 a.m. and eventually went forward to the captured positions at around 11 a.m. He would never forget the smells of death and destruction that day, but many years later would reflect how, in the absence of orders to advance further or use any form of local initiative, the Battalion just sat in the German positions that were their ultimate objective, and waited. With the Germans so obviously in utter disarray, there was the feeling expressed by one participant that 'we could have walked through to Berlin that day.' On the 8th the Battalion was relieved and moved back to Ridge Wood, having suffered only seven killed, thirty-six wounded and fourteen missing from the 626 men who went into action. The only officer lost had been Second Lieutenant Seeds, from Streatham, on the 6th, while preparing for the attack. Undoubtedly, the initial onslaught had been successful, as indeed was the entire battle which ended on 14 June with all objectives either reached or surpassed. Even so, the British

German bunkers such as this one could withstand all but direct hits and mines.   G. Richardson

suffered over 24,000 casualties to take an area only ten miles wide by four miles deep.

As June drew to a close, the Battalion moved to the Meteren training area and remained there for more than a fortnight in order to receive reinforcement drafts of 158 NCOs and men. It then moved to the Westoutre [Westouter] area and finally back to La Clytte. Here the

Present-day remains of a German pillbox on Messines ridge. Author

weather was very changeable, with cold nights and the start of occasional heavy rains which were to have a dire effect on the next major offensive planned by the British. General Plumer's Second Army, fresh from its triumphs at Messines Ridge, was now to take part in the first phase of the Third Battle of Ypres, though Second Army's role was to be a subsidiary one, restricted to capturing La Basse Ville [Basseville] on the right and the village of Hollebeke on the left. Secondary objectives were then to clear the ground north of the bend of the Ypres-Comines Canal and east of Battle Wood.

The Third Battle of Ypres was to become a nightmare for the Allied troops and one of the bloodiest battles in history. The offensive began on 31 July 1917, and coincided with the start of a month of heavy rains. The countryside around Ypres, already pounded into a shattered mess after weeks of artillery bombardment, turned into a vast quagmire of water-filled pools which sucked even able-bodied men to their deaths. In particular, conditions around Passchendaele [Passendale], north-east of Ypres, were atrocious and the horrifying losses there led to the village's name becoming synonymous with the battle and the very worst of warfare. Fortunately the 10th Battalion's sector of the front was spared the most awful conditions, but an outbreak of dysentry added to the misery of the men in the terrible weather. The water-logged ground conditions made it impossible to dig latrine trenches and the alternative of a biscuit tin or two soon led to disease. The same impossibility of digging into the ground also meant there were only shell holes for cover, both from the elements and from the German shelling.

The Battalion, now commanded by freshly-promoted Lieutenant-Colonel Gwynne DSO,[58] was ordered to move from Bluff Tunnels on the morning of 1 August and to advance to the Red Line. B and C Companies were to lead off shortly after 3 a.m. and mop up any remaining enemy positions between the Red and Blue Lines. At 4.30 a.m. the remaining two companies were to pass through in order to capture and hold Green Line which was the spur of a hill.

The operation got off to a disastrous start. Only a single guide had been provided for the entire Battalion, despite the fact that no officer or man had been over the ground. But even this guide lost his way and as a result the leading company arrived at the Red Line at 4.30 a.m., way behind the planned 3.10 a.m. 'off'. To make matters worse, the rear of the column was heavily shelled and A Company suffered heavily. Its commander was Captain Henry Willders-Lewis, a twenty-one-year-old from Anerley, near Croydon. A keen cricketer, Willders-

Private Sam Froment, of Swavesey, Cambs., the Battalion's demon cricket bowler (seated on ground, right), kia 6th July 1917. P. Curme

Lewis had left university in London to enlist in the ranks of the Universities and Public Schools battalion, the 16th Battalion of the Middlesex Regiment. He had served in France from November 1915 before being commissioned in September 1916 and posted to the 10th Queen's. As enemy shells rained down, this experienced soldier's luck finally ran out as he was first injured and then killed outright. The rest of A Company became badly disorganised under the heavy barrage and suffered many wounded, to the extent that only fifty men under Second Lieutenant Parkes eventually reached Battle Wood. Casualties were worse due to the Germans using deadly mustard gas shells while many men had removed their gas masks to see better in the gloom and confusion.

By 4.40 a.m. Lieutenant-Colonel Gwynne had realised that the creeping Allied barrage which had been promised to cover his advance would now be of little help. He therefore went forward alone into No Man's Land to see whether it were possible to attack without the barrage, but he was hit twice in the thigh by enemy heavy machine-gun bullets. Gwynne found himself in a dire situation. His men were unsure of his exact position out in front of them, but with dawn on the way, the Germans were as likely to spot him at first light. With a severed artery, it was even questionable whether Gwynne could last until dawn without bleeding to death. His thigh bone had shattered into twelve pieces, making movement impossible, but inspiration suddenly came to him. As mutedly as possible, Gwynne began blowing his whistle and luck was with him thanks to the acute hearing of Lieutenant Lawrie Inkster back in the trenches. Correctly guessing that the whistling came from his missing commanding officer, Inkster quickly assembled a party of stretcher bearers and a runner and led them out into the darkness. Sure enough, the search party soon came across Gwynne and despite the danger of attracting further enemy fire, managed to hoist him onto a stretcher and struggled back to the trench line.[59] In a letter home, Inkster scarcely mentioned his heroic deed, saying simply 'I am glad I was able to look after him and get him away. He was very nice to me when I saw him off.'

Clearly, movement over certain sectors of the front was impossible due to the heavy machine-gun fire from a number of dugouts. At 7 a.m. the Battalion therefore dug in: C Company in shell holes and dugouts along the eastern side of the railway embankment;[60] B and D Companies along the embankment's western side; and A Company in Battle Wood. At about 1.30 p.m. Major Leslie Andrews, who had come to France with the Battalion as a lowly Second Lieutenant, took command in place of the wounded Lieutenant-Colonel Gwynne, but any further action became an impossibility as the weather worsened.

The 10th Queen's positions near Battle Wood, Third Ypres, still visible today.   Author

Light drizzle turned to heavy rain which, by late afternoon, was torrential. The ground, torn up by the Allied artillery bombardment, quickly became a quagmire and visibility worsened under the leaden sky. Under this cover the Germans made a half-hearted attempt to counter-attack, but were beaten off by machine-gun fire and artillery support. At 11 p.m. the 10th Queen's were relieved from the front line.

2 August proved to be a relatively quiet day spent in the support trenches, but on the night of the 3rd the Battalion went back to the front line. It took over a sector of some 600 yards of outpost line, an area covered by rifle and machine-gun fire from the railway embankment above. The Battalion's arrival was marked by the appearance of two Germans who had lost their way and proved perfectly happy to surrender to a welcoming Captain Berrangé.

During the 4th the line was heavily shelled while the Germans counter-attacked into Hollebeke. The Battalion's positions on the right were temporarily breached, but the enemy was driven out again. There was persistent fighting all through the 5th and until the night of the 6th when the 10th Queen's were relieved and went back to rear camp. They had again suffered badly. Captain Willders-Lewis and

Captain Henry Charles Willders-Lewis kia at Hollebeke, Third Ypres, 31 July 1917.
Author

twenty-seven men had been killed while Lieutenant-Colonel Gwynne, Second Lieutenants Wilson and Wills and 130 other ranks were wounded. Five men were reported missing. For Second Lieutenant Parkes, the only officer left alive or apparently unwounded in A Company, a belated shock awaited. Without realising, he had inhaled mustard gas during the enemy's bombardment of Battle Wood on the 31st. This only became known some days later when he suddenly went blind while on parade at the reserve camp. He once again found himself in hospital back in England and though his sight returned, he was never again fit enough to return to the Front and spent the remainder of the war in reserve battalions of The Queen's, appropriately running a training school for anti-gas measures.[61]

Major Andrews's temporary command of the Battalion ceased on the 7th when Major Frank Hayley Bell was promoted Lieutenant-Colonel and took over. Hayley Bell had been one of the Battalion's company commanders wounded at Flers, but who had now recovered from his wounds and returned to active

Temporary blinded as victims. Taylor Library

service in time to lead the Battalion to the le Thieushoek area where it moved into a tented camp in a large open field. Brigade baths and the de-lousing machine were among the site's attractions, together with peaceful rural scenery and one or two small village shops dotted among the farms. Yet it was here, in the supposed safety of a rear area, that tragedy again struck.

The tents of three companies had been crowded into as small an area as possible owing to the need to save some of the field for cultivation by the local farmers. During the day of 18 August a German aeroplane had already overflown the camp, but had done nothing and the significance of what had undoubtedly been a reconnaissance flight had therefore been overlooked. The same night, when a second enemy aeroplane was heard approaching the site at 9.45 p.m., there seemed no reason to expect any different outcome. Rather than concern, most of the men were only moved by curiosity and turned their faces skywards to watch the intruder's approach through a hail of anti-aircraft fire.

The troops had enjoyed a big evening meal as extra rations were available due to the recent losses. Many had then enjoyed a visit to the local estaminet and were in a merry mood as they prepared for bed. At the very moment that the camp bugler was playing what proved to be his own personal 'Last Post', the German aeroplane droned directly overhead and dropped a stick of bombs across the fields. Just one bomb found the 10th Queen's as it fell straight into the middle of camp. The three companies of the Battalion who were camped together in restricted space suffered most as their tents, despite sandbag protection, were shredded by the blast. No fewer than 107 casualties resulted, including thirty-eight men who were killed outright. These were buried the next day in a single mass grave in a corner of the field, along with four men from other units.[62] A further seven men of the Battalion later died of their wounds.

A visit by Field Marshal Sir Douglas Haig on the last day of the month was hoped to raise spirits after this disaster, the Commander in Chief finding the 10th Queen's in billets in the village of Martinslaers. Here, some of the men were lodged at a farm where 124 Brigade's

Lt-Col. Roland Gwynne DSO.
S. Harcourt-Smith

famous wartime cartoonist, Captain Bruce Bairnsfather, was to draw a number of his sketches. Indeed, one particular barn used as a billet was clearly recognisable in one of Bairnsfather's popular 'Old Bill' sketches. There was little time for humour, however, as the Battalion was then again called to the front to join the next phase of the Third Battle of Ypres. The weather had by now improved and the ground was drying fast to help the eight-mile front of attack from the Ypres-Staden railway north of Langemarck to the Ypres-Comines canal north of Hollebeke.

The orders for this offensive, known as the Battle of the Menin Road, involved the 124 and 122 Brigades being on the right and left respectively of the 41st Division's front, with the 123 in reserve. Each of the forward brigades was to present a line of two battalions, and in 124 Brigade the 10th Queen's and the 21st King's Royal Rifle Corps were to be the attacking battalions for the first stage of the attack. On 18 September the Battalion returned to the Ridge Wood area near Dickebusche [Dikkebus] and spent the night in tents. The next day the

Second Lieutenant Caleb Henry Adams kia 20th September 1917 at Third Ypres. Author

men were issued with bombs, extra ammunition and two days' rations before marching into trenches below the ridge known as Tower Hamlets, a strong enemy position just south of the Menin Road.

The whole area of the offensive had been subjected to an intense bombardment for several days prior to the advance and a thick mist helped the troops move to their assembly positions undetected on the night of 19/20 September. A rum issue was made to raise spirits and the men then moved out into No Man's Land, still under cover of darkness, but shortly before dawn. It was a quiet, cold night and as the first hint of light came, white tapes could be made out, put in place to guide the advance. Bayonets were fixed and at 5.40 a.m. the Battalion moved forward at walking pace, one officer managing to note that, incongruously, there was still patchy grass in this otherwise devastated landscape. Just a few seconds later the Allied artillery crashed out behind them and the Battalion broke into a run as the shells rushed overhead. The barrage rolled on ahead of them, but in the reflected light of their supporting artillery, the 10th Queen's had only covered 50 yards when they began to attract enemy shelling and were then caught, still in close formation, by two enemy machine guns. The accurate fire proved devastating, especially among the leading officers where Major Leslie Andrews MC and Lieutenant Gordon Webb, both among the Battalion's original complement, were killed instantly, together with Second Lieutenant Adams.[63] Lieutenant Inkster was also put out of action by a bullet wound to his right shoulder.

124 Brigade's other battalions had suffered similarly and for a while it seemed as if retreat might be the most prudent step. But at a crucial moment, the Brigadier came up in person from his headquarters. In his shirt sleeves and carrying a machine gun, he rallied the mixed-up remnants of all battalions and urged them on. In spite of the losses and inevitable confusion, Second Lieutenants Hare and Toombs, together with Sergeant Busby,[64] marshalled several men of the 10th Queen's and managed to work round the enemy gun positions, silencing and subsequently capturing them. The Brigade then pushed on and though still exposed to heavy machine-gun fire, reached both the first and second objectives, finding the German trenches full of dead and dying from both sides. At about 8.30 a.m. the next morning the reserve force, 123 Brigade, came up to complete the attack, crossing the valley of the Basseville Beek and storming up the slope of Tower Hamlets.

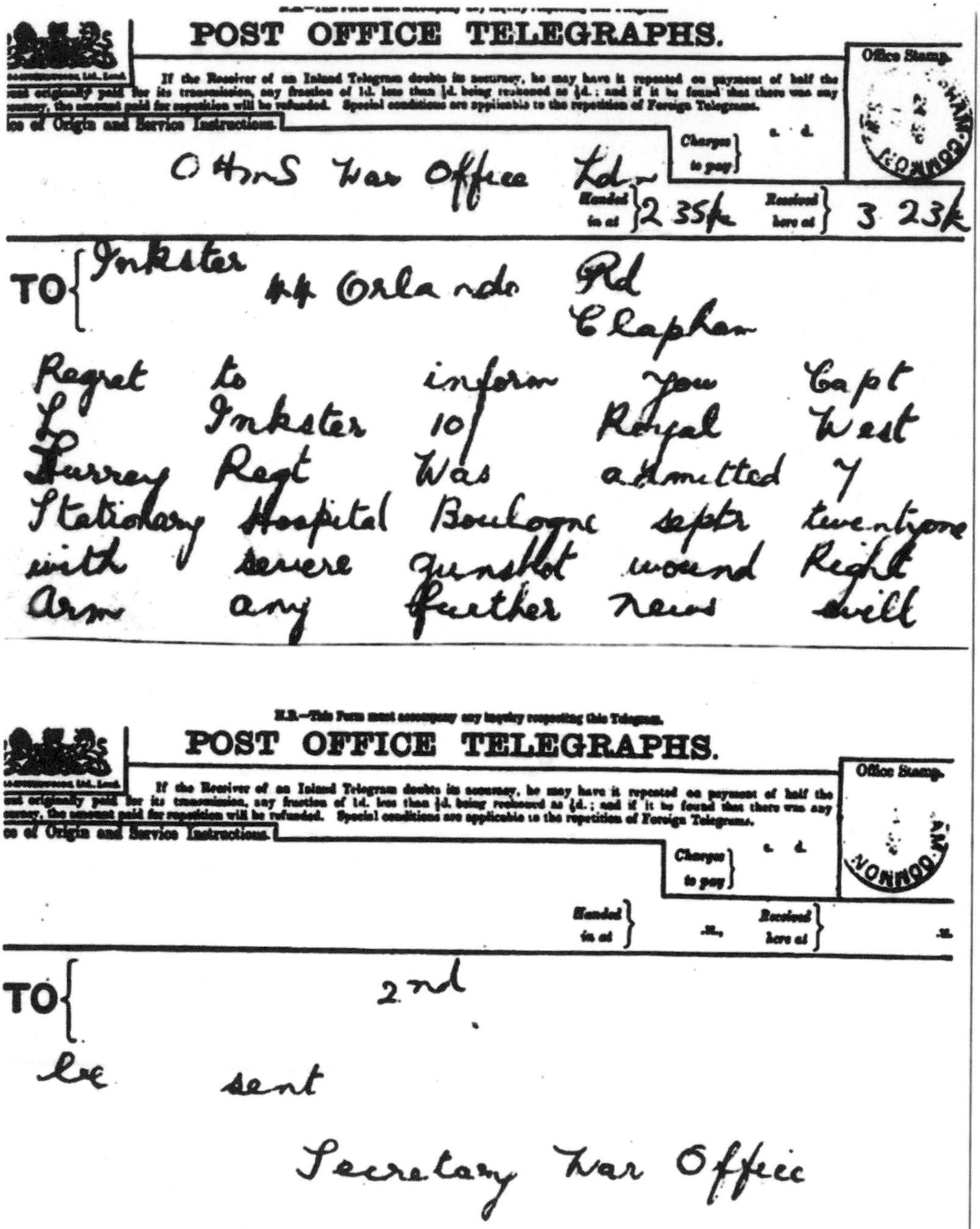

POST OFFICE TELEGRAPHS.

If the Receiver of an Inland Telegram doubts its accuracy, he may have it repeated on payment of half the amount originally paid for its transmission, any fraction of 1d. less than ½d. being reckoned as ½d.; and if it be found that there was any inaccuracy, the amount paid for repetition will be refunded. Special conditions are applicable to the repetition of Foreign Telegrams.

Office Stamp.

Office of Origin and Service Instructions.

O H M S War Office Ld

Charges to pay s. d.

Handed in at 2 35p Received here at 3 23p

TO Inkster 44 Orlando Rd Clapham

Regret to inform you Capt L Inkster 10/ Royal West Surrey Regt was admitted 7 Stationary Hospital Boulogne septr twentyone with severe gunshot wound Right Arm any further news will

N.B.—This Form must accompany any inquiry respecting this Telegram.

POST OFFICE TELEGRAPHS.

If the Receiver of an Inland Telegram doubts its accuracy, he may have it repeated on payment of half the amount originally paid for its transmission, any fraction of 1d. less than ½d. being reckoned as ½d.; and if it be found that there was any inaccuracy, the amount paid for repetition will be refunded. Special conditions are applicable to the repetition of Foreign Telegrams.

Office Stamp.

Office of Origin and Service Instructions.

Charges to pay s. d.

Handed in at .m. Received here at .m.

TO 2nd

be sent

Secretary War Office

The telegram that families dreaded – news of a loved one killed or wounded. Lt Inkster recovered. D. Inkster

Both 123 and 124 Brigades again suffered from machine guns east of Bodmin Copse and found they could progress no further once on the plateau of the Tower Hamlets ridge. In spite of repeated enemy counter-attacks, the evening of 20 September found the Battalion well established in its new positions and only short of its final objective beyond the ridge, though for the next two days there was stiff fighting to hold the new line.

Intermittent shelling on the morning of the 21st steadily increased during the afternoon until, at 7 p.m., the Germans attacked, only to be thrown back with heavy losses. Matters were no better on the 22nd, when shelling and snipers made communications and re-supply of food and water very difficult. Some of these enemy snipers had been left behind when the Germans were pushed back. With little hope of eventual escape, they nevertheless continued their deadly trade, attracting a mixture of hatred and admiration from the men of the Battersea Battalion who were their targets. The 10th Queen's were relieved at night between the 22nd and 24th, and were eventually withdrawn to the rear at Ghyvelde where the rest of the month was spent dodging frequent enemy air raids while reorganising, clearing up and receiving drafts of reinforcements. The majority of the latter came from the dismounted 1/1st Surrey Yeomanry (six officers and 121 men) and the 2/5th Buffs.

Second Lieutenant Busby won a Military Medal at Third Ypres in September 1917. D. Inkster

In October 1917 the Battalion moved to hold an outpost line among the North Sea coast dunes. Author

On 25 September General Plumer wrote the following letter to Major-General Lawford, commanding the 41st Division:

My dear Lawford.

The 41st Division are shortly to leave the Second Army for a time and before they go, I should like to express to you and to ask you to convey to the Commander and Staffs in the Division my appreciation of the excellent service they have rendered during the period they have been in this Army.

They have taken a prominent and very creditable part in all the offensive operations in which we have been engaged and their work on the defensive has been equally satisfactory. Throughout the whole period the discipline has been excellent and all ranks have maintained a fine fighting spirit.

I hope at some future time the Division may again be in the Second Army and wherever they may be I wish you and all the best of luck.

Yours sincerely
(signed) HERBERT PLUMER

Clearly, the High Command had fresh plans for the 10th Queen's, but in the interim yet another sector of the Western Front beckoned. Moving north westwards in early October the 10th Battalion's destination proved to be the very limit of the front line on the North Sea coast, close to La Panne, just inside Belgium but close to the French border. Here, coastal defence duties were interspaced with extensive training in support positions. The area was very quiet and fortunately so, as the sand dunes gave only poor defensive cover and it was almost impossible to dig trenches that would hold up for any length of time. The opposing armies, however, generally seemed content to leave one another alone for the present and as a consequence no casualties were suffered during this period.

Chapter 12

ITALIAN INTERLUDE

In his letter to Major-General Lawford, Plumer had hinted at a change of scenery for the 41st Division and this duly came when, after three weeks on and around the coastal sector of the French/Belgian border, orders were received to prepare to move to the Italian front. The 41st was one of five British divisions to be transferred from the Western Front to support the Italian Army against the Germans and Austrians facing them in the north of the country. In October and November 1917 the Italians had suffered badly at the Battle of Caporetto and though the enemy had not exploited this success, the British were concerned that the abilities of the Italians were now highly suspect and needed bolstering by experienced troops from the Western Front. The move was also to reunite General Plumer with the 41st Division much sooner than he had anticipated, for Plumer was appointed commander of British forces in Italy.

For the 10th Queen's the orders to leave the Western Front also came as something of a surprise as the Battalion had been expecting to return to the Somme. The reinforcement drafts had restored the Battalion's fighting strength, including a new second in command, Major Eric Thesiger from the Surrey Yeomanry. Shortly after his arrival, however, Thesiger was attached to the King's Royal Rifle Corps and his place taken by Major Bonser, another new arrival. Inevitably, the latest reinforcements again watered down the Battersea flavour of the unit, less than 200 men of the original unit now surviving:

COMPOSITION OF THE 10TH QUEEN'S, NOVEMBER 1917

Original Battersea Battalion	196
Sussex Yeomanry	88
Army Ordnance Corps draft	42
Surrey Yeomanry	129
2nd/5th Battalion The Queen's	155
2nd/5th Battalion The Buffs	105
Drafts from eight other Queen' s battalions	216
Total	**931**

On 4 November the Battalion marched down from the coast to Wormhout and a few days later to Esquelbecq, from where the troop trains departed on the 11th and 12th. On the journey south local French people made a great fuss of the men at every stop and spirits remained high as the trains slowly wound their way down through France, via Paris, Lyons and Marseilles. By the time they reached the large naval port of Toulon, hundreds of the men were perched on the carriage roofs, enjoying the mild weather and their first view of the bright blue Mediterranean. Continuing along the Riviera, through Cannes and past Monte Carlo, everyone marvelled at the beautiful scenery. At the Italian border an electric locomotive took over and the overhead cables brought an end to troops enjoying the view from the carriage tops. The train wound its way through the suburbs of the large city of Genoa [Genova] where the Tommies marvelled at the apartment blocks, some five or six storeys high, which seemed to house thousands of people. At last, on arrival at Mantua [Mántova] on 16 and 17 November, the troops detrained to find a military band waiting to accompany their march to billets at Gazzoldo. The purpose of the band was not, however, purely ceremonial. Its main purpose was to help cheer the men on a forced march which immediately had to be made to form a defensive line between Vicenza and Grisignano. Only iron rations of bully beef, hard biscuits and the like were

British troops arrive in Italy. Taylor Library

provided and no more than twenty-nine officers, plus the Medical Officer,[65] were permitted. Twelve officers were consequently returned to the base area.

Starting on the 19th the Battalion began its great march across the beautiful Italian landscape. The route was largely cross-country, keeping to minor roads, and represented one of a series of parallel routes followed by the 41st and 23rd Divisions towards the front. The thinking behind this organisation was that, in the event of a further enemy advance, the advancing Allied units could be quickly deployed into a broad defensive line. So it was that to the south, the 23rd Division's battalions set out on the main Padua [Pádova] road, while the 41st Division enjoyed the scenic, but less well-maintained, secondary roads. These routes meandered through numerous villages and the local people, often forewarned by the approaching strains of Keep the Home Fires Burning or Take me back to Dear Old Blighty, invariably stopped to wave and cheer their newly-arrived Allies. The weather, even in November, was glorious by day with clear blue skies and a welcoming sun. Nights were cold, to the extent that the road would still be icy and slippery when the Battalion set out early each morning at 5.30 a.m., trying to make the most of the fresh, chill air which was much preferred for long-distance marching. The sun would come up gradually, burning off the mists which shrouded the countryside and bathing the men in a warmth so different from the conditions back in France and Belgium. In the far distance, snow-capped mountains could be seen easily as there was little haze in the clear atmosphere until the afternoon, when the heat would become oppressive. Frequent halts were necessary to relieve aching limbs, but despite the rigours of the march itself, covering up to twenty miles a day, most men soaked up their surroundings with enjoyment. For the moment, the war seemed a very long way off.

The advance continued via Tórmine, Tarmassia, Sabbioni, Zovencedo, Montegalda, Ársego, and Resana. On the 28th Generals Plumer and Lawford watched the Battersea battalion march past and on the 29th, Fossalunga was reached at the end of a trek of 120 miles. The 10th Queen's had left Gazzoldo with a strength of 962 all ranks and completed the march with exactly 900. Of the sixty-two men who did not arrive, thirty were passed as unfit for service and of the remaining thirty-two, many were men who had returned to the Battalion from employment at base camps and who had no recent experience of marching or carrying heavy packs. Despite the drop-outs, discipline and general bearing were reported to have been excellent throughout the march, and in addition to their Italian band, the Battalion's Drums, which had been organised only a fortnight before leaving Flanders, did much to help to keep up morale along the way. The health of the Battalion was also noted to have been of a high standard and only one man had reported sick.

On arrival at Fossalunga, the Battalion found it difficult to acquire decent billets as four squadrons of the Italian Air Force were already established there. The town was on a rear defence line created in anticipation of a possible enemy breakthrough on the front line which was still some twelve miles away. Bedraggled and dispirited Italian Army units were also now met, still recovering from the retreat after Caporetto, but the front was presently quiet and on 1 December, The Queen's moved up to Volpago by a very poor road which earned the wry comment 'Roman road-making unduly praised' in the Battalion's diary. Here the 41st Division relieved the Italian 1st Division and the 10th Queen's were held as brigade reserve, undergoing specialist training in what was expected to be the novelty of 'open warfare'. In

The nearby village of Nervesa had already suffered heavily from enemy artillery fire. Author

the meantime the other battalions of 124 Brigade moved into a sector of the front line which covered the bank of the Piave River for some 3,500 yards north of the village of Nervesa. Despite the calm there was still occasional enemy artillery fire directed towards the Battalion's positions, killing Second Lieutenant Henry Phillips and mortally wounding Private Sydney King in an advanced position near the church of Sovilla. Buried in the military cemetery of Giavera, where the Battalion settled for Christmas and the New Year, Phillips and King were to be the 10th Queen's only fatalities in Italy, although another two men were wounded on the same occasion.

The Battalion continued to marvel at the contrast with the way war was waged in France and Flanders. Here, the front had a feeling of stability, despite the enemy being just across the river. The 41st Division was on the right of the 23rd and facing them were the German 12th Division and the Austrian 13th Division. The latter had something of a reputation for a 'live and let live' approach to the war, settling in to a mid-day siesta for a couple of hours to match the habits of the Italians who had previously opposed them. With the advent of the British, the Austrians were soon replaced by the German 11th Division.

Yet even against the supposedly more blood-thirsty Germans, the Battalion experienced only slight losses and inconvenience from the enemy's artillery fire and aircraft. On 26 December a large force of German Gotha bombers, escorted by numerous scouts (the original term for fighter aircraft), had attempted a raid, but were turned back by the volume of anti-aircraft fire which the British threw up at them. For the enemy, it was another lesson learned after the departure of the Italians. In early January 1918 the 10th Queen's again moved into reserve positions, this time in the adjacent Montello sector, the main British defensive position. Il Montello is a seven-mile long, bean-shaped 'island' of hills up to 800 feet high above the Treviso plain where the River Piave widens and forms a double loop. The area was already rich in history and was once covered with forests which provided the Republic of Venice with the timber to build her ships. The Montello's northern and eastern slopes lead down to the Piave and its heights gave a commanding view of the enemy's positions on the river's opposite bank.

At last the Battalion entered the line itself, a stretch of a little over two miles in length along the Piave. On the right and centre of this sector the Battalion's posts were sited in the side of a cliff face, which gave a magnificent view of river and distant mountains. On the left,

British positions on Il Montello above the Piave. E. Forlan

Austrian prisoners under Italian guard. E. Forlan

caves and trenches were manned, cut into the banks of the river and boasting all the normal 'refinements' of fire-steps, bays and dugouts. Here eight days were spent in very cold weather conditions. Snow had fallen and the tracks leading to the various posts were covered in ice, making the work of the ration and fuel-carrying parties extremely difficult and dangerous. Fortunately there were no casualties in this period for, had there been, evacuation would have been impossible. The general discomfort was heightened by day-time movement being highly dangerous owing to enemy observation, and the river, which rose from one to two feet each night, proved quite unfordable by patrols owing to the strong current. There was little to do as the sector was generally quiet, but the men could enviously see Venice in the distance, still lit up at night.

There was nevertheless a good deal of shelling of the front by the enemy, who could also be heard at night busily constructing new strong-points. It was therefore with some relief that the Battalion moved back to a training area near Altivole for the latter half of January, marching there via Montebelluna. All was quiet in this rear position except for the visit of an enemy aeroplane on the 31st which bombed Altivole. Civilian losses from this action consisted of one donkey killed, while the British Army lost four horses belonging to the Royal Fusiliers. Despite the absence of human casualties from enemy action, no less than eighty men were admitted to hospital through sickness in January.

In February the Battalion made several moves, marching on the 7th to Crespano at the foot of Monte Grappa, on the 17th to Riese, and next day to Biadene, where the men's billets were bombed by enemy aircraft, fortunately again without any injury to the troops. The weather then improved, descriptions of 'warm' to 'very warm' being found in diaries of the time. Even the evenings were no longer cool and for a while the troops looked forward to enjoying an early Spring in this beautiful area of Italy. It was not to be. On the afternoon of the 23rd, orders were given to be ready to move at two hours' notice and it was thought this was in response to the heavy firing coming from the left of the Battalion's positions. The next day the 10th Queen's were indeed on the move, but marched south-westwards away from the front, via Riese, Piox, Ramon, Castelfranco and Camposampiero, crossing the Brenta river on the 26th near Límena, north of Padua. This was almost the exact reverse of the route which the Battalion had taken to reach the battle lines and while at Límena the unwelcome news was received that the 41st Division was indeed to return to the Western

Front. Entrainment for France could be expected in the very near future.

The necessity for this switch back to France was an urgent one. The Allies were in no doubt that a new German offensive in France and Belgium was now very close and in mid February proposals were accepted to bring reinforcements from the Italian front. Sir Douglas Haig was asked if would prefer four Italian divisions or two British and he promptly chose the latter. The 41st Division was therefore ordered to return as quickly as possible, along with General Plumer who was replaced by Lord Cavan as commander of the British forces remaining in Italy. The 5th Division was to follow a month later.

The 10th Queen's marched on from Límena on 1 March and the same afternoon reached the little station of Poiana di Granfoin on the main line between Padua and Vicenza. Here the men immediately boarded the two trains which waited and set off for France. The weather had worsened and progress was slow, though two hot meals a day were enjoyed from the Battalion's cookers which had been set up on open trucks.

Chapter 13

WESTERN FRONT AGAIN

The route taken was via Genoa, Savona, Nice, Marseilles, Dijon and Paris until, after five weary days, Mondicourt was reached on the evening of Wednesday the 6th. It was the dreaded Somme again. After detraining, the men marched on to a farm near Sus St-Léger. Intensive training was again the order of the day and this continued until the 20th when instructions were received to entrain the next day for Senlis in the Acheux area north-west of Albert.

It was here that re-organisation of 124 Brigade into a three battalion (rather than four battalion) formation took place. The 32nd Battalion, Royal Fusiliers was disbanded, leaving the 10th Queen's, the 26th Royal Fusiliers and the 20th Durham Light Infantry. Upon the demise of the 32nd Royal Fusiliers, Lieutenant-Colonel W. Clark DSO of that battalion was transferred on 20 March to command the 10th Queen's, replacing Lieutenant-Colonel Hayley Bell who, it would seem, was now judged a little too old for the rigours of a front-line command.[66] The Battalion left Saulty by train at 5.30 a.m. 21 March and learned en route that the long-expected German offensive, the 'Kaiser's Battle',

German advance in March 1918 – some stormtroopers are carrying captured Lewis guns. Taylor Library

had been launched. Many places far behind the front were now under enemy gun-fire and the 41st Division was consequently re-routed to Achiet-le-Grand, north-west of Bapaume. The 10th Queen's arrived there at 1.30 a.m. on the 22nd and marched on to Camp 13 east of Favreuil. After a welcome issue of hot tea the Battalion immediately moved out and dug in to the north-east of the village of Beugnâtre, holding the road to Vaulx-Vraucourt. This position was maintained all day in the face of moderate shelling which caused half a dozen casualties, but only minor probing attacks were made by the enemy on the front line. Around midnight orders were received to relieve the 20th Durham Light Infantry who were supposedly to the right of the 10th Battalion's positions, but it was soon discovered that the Durhams were, in fact, to the left and the 1st/7th Cheshires to the right. Ominously, there appeared to be no British units at all ahead of them, and the only deterrent to an enemy advance were two belts of old wire and a few barricades.

The night of the 22nd/23rd was quiet, but about 8 a.m. the enemy attacked in two strong waves from the direction of Vaulx-Vraucourt. The attack was ultimately stopped by British artillery and rifle fire, but a small enemy party managed to take cover in the shattered remains of a cemetery. There they remained pinned down for the remainder of the day, providing useful targets for the 10th Battalion's Lewis gunners and snipers. At 11 a.m., after a light barrage lasting less than half an hour, the Germans again advanced, but on reaching the edge of the wire they were once more stopped by rifle fire. After a slight pause, however, the enemy advanced again and managed to push two machine guns through the furthest belt of wire on D Company's front, and another on A Company's front, setting them up behind mounds some 100 yards in front of the Battalion's main positions. A Company also came under rifle-grenade fire from a sunken track, but enemy activity then petered out until 6 p.m., when a weak attack was made against the barricade opposite D Company. A Vickers gun soon dealt with this attempt and an uneasy calm then settled for the evening. Second Lieutenant Record had been snatched and taken prisoner and Lieutenant-Colonel Clark, after only a few days in command, had been hit and wounded. His place was taken by Major Chichester, the Battalion's second in command.

Relative quiet heralded the night of the 23rd/24th until at about 1.30 a.m. when a heavy bombardment fell on the front and support lines. After a couple of hours the barrage ceased in order to allow a strong attack on the Battalion's front and right. The Cheshires began to

German Stormtroops sweeping through the British lines during the Kaiser's Spring offensive.
Taylor Library

fall back and a platoon of B Company of the 10th Queen's withdrew when the Germans were seen working round their flanks and rear. The remainder of B Company subsequently fell back some 800-900 yards to the line it had occupied on the night of the 22nd, but A and D Companies held out for another half-hour before also pulling back. The enemy then entered B Company's old position and successfully bombed their way up it, driving A Company out of their trenches to the north-west. By the time A Company retired, the Germans had taken possession of a number of commanding positions on the flank and rear and were able to inflict severe casualties on the retreating British. Major Chichester and two experienced company commanders, Captains Robson and Hart, were among those wounded, leaving Captain Mellor to take command.

Shortly afterwards the re-grouped 10th Battalion, now consisting of three companies each 113 strong, bravely counter-attacked. Supported by the 26th Royal Fusiliers, The Queen's managed to reoccupy the original front line, but orders were then received to withdraw. At around 6.30 p.m. the scattered remnants of the Battalion dug in on a line running north-west from the western edge of Favreuil to Sapignies. During the day of the 25th a further withdrawal was ordered to a new line between Bihucourt and Achiet-le-Grand and that night the Battalion was ordered to again move back to

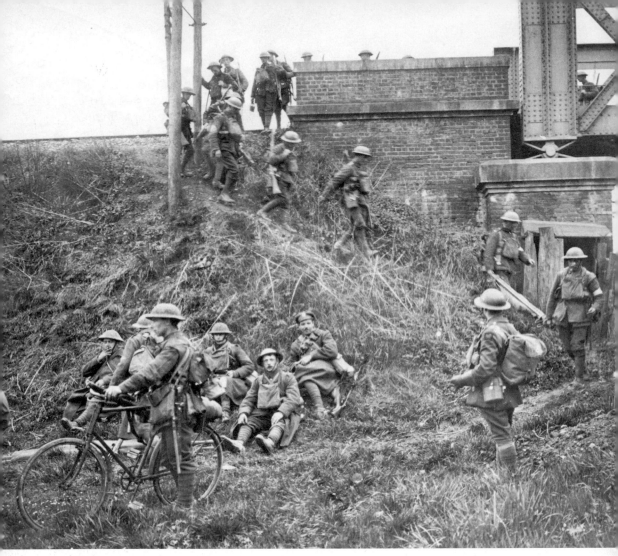

British troops moving forward to a position to try and stem the German advance. Taylor Library

Gommecourt. A hot meal was served at 6 a.m. the following morning, but only 125 men of the 10th Queen's were able to line up for the much-needed nourishment. Perhaps the most critical losses were those of the two senior company commanders, Captain James Hart and Captain Albert Robson, whose wounds had proved fatal. Captain Hart was a 24-year-old from East Dulwich who had twice been decorated with the Military Cross. The death of 25-year-old Robson, who had been with the Battalion since it was formed, was particularly tragic. At Flers in September 1916, the popular former teacher of Sir Walter St. John's School, Battersea, had been fortunate to survive despite being wounded in both thighs and one arm. At Messines in 1917 he had been hit again and cheated death by a few inches when a piece of shrapnel passed through his cheek and shattered his jaw. Promoted to Captain, the young officer's luck finally ran out on the 24th when he was dashing from one trench to another, urging his men on and shouting "You can give it them, A Company". He fell, shot through the head, and died instantly. Having married only a few months before he sailed for France in 1916, Robson left a young widow, Winifred Alice, and a little daughter at 53 Wroughton Road, Clapham Common. The Adjutant, Captain Mellor, wrote:

> *Everyone says the same of his courage and splendid example. I came up with him in the same carriage. It was the first chance I had of knowing him. He was a great companion, full of good temper and cheerfulness. He will be a great loss to the battalion.*

Such losses were not only difficult to replace in the middle of a battle,

Dead and wounded British casualties during the German advance. Taylor Library

but also hit the morale of the men. Nevertheless, there was little time for reflection and the Battalion's survivors took up positions in trenches south of Gommecourt, reinforcements being arranged by orders which required every available man at the transport lines to be armed and sent up to the firing line. The majority of these men were, however, unable to reach the Battalion and were instead held as a reserve for any emergency that might arise.

Apart from some strafing fire from enemy aircraft the 26th proved fairly quiet and most of the men managed to snatch at least a couple of hours' sleep, despite the bitter cold which was such a contrast to the warmth of Italy only a month before. Early on 27 March the Battalion's surviving strength marched back for a day's respite to Bienvillers-au-Bois, north-west of Gommecourt. At midday on the 28th they were recalled to Gommecourt to take up a position to the north-east of the village, just behind the front line. The next morning passed peacefully, but in the afternoon a heavy enemy bombardment began. This, coupled with torrential rain, an icy wind and uncertainty as to the whereabouts of the advancing Germans, completed a bleak picture. Orders were received to relieve a battalion of the 42nd Division near Bucquoy, but to do so, almost the entire strength of the shattered 124 Brigade had to be used. B Company of the 10th Queen's found itself attached to the 20th Durham Light Infantry and A Company to the 20th Royal Fusiliers. In effect, the 10th Queen's temporarily ceased to exist as a separate fighting unit.

Fortunately, this state of affairs did not last long. On 31 March the two detached companies rejoined C Company and took over a 400 yards centre sector of the brigade front. The next day the Battalion was at last relieved from the front line and marched back to Halloy. As if to mirror the relief of the men, the weather at last improved and a fine Spring evening did much to lift spirits as the troops stepped out.

During March, 1918, the losses of the 10th Queen's had been crippling. From a total strength of 902 all ranks at the beginning of the month, bitter fighting had left only 379 – losses of 58% and mostly in a period of just ten days. But if the survivors thought they were now to be given an opportunity to lick their wounds, they were much mistaken.

Back to the Salient

After just twenty-four hours' rest at Halloy the Battalion moved on by bus and entrained for Poperinghe, the reserve area back on the Flanders front in Belgium. Here, another two days' rest was snatched

The bitterly contested ground on the approaches to the village of Passchendaele. By the Spring of 1918 it was near impassable during wet weather. Taylor Library

before the men marched eastwards to Brandhoek and on 7 April went into the front line in the Passchendaele [Passendale] sector, north-east of Ypres. Still in the face of the continuing German offensive, B and D Companies were responsible for 1,200 yards of front, consisting of fourteen posts south of Passchendaele village, while A Company was held in support at Mosselmark [Molenaarelst], and C Company remained in reserve at Bellevue [Bellewaerde].

The 10th Queen's remained in these positions until 14 April, but that night, owing to the German advances south-west of Ypres, it was decided to hold the Passechendaele sector only lightly and the Battalion therefore took over a two-battalion front of some 2,200 yards. Reinforcements had brought strength up to a total of twenty officers and 577 other ranks, but these numbers were still nothing like sufficient for the length of line held.

By 16 April the Germans' capture of the important position of Mont Kemmel meant that Allied lines had to be drawn back to a line closer to Ypres. During the very early morning of this day, the Battalion therefore fell back quietly and unnoticed by the enemy and joined the defences in front of Ypres. The Battalion's companies were allocated to the Intermediate Zone defences from the Sally Port to the St Jean [St-Jan] road, a distance of 1,200 yards and including a line running

Germans capture the high ground at Kemmel forcing the Allies to withdraw.

through a cemetery which was later to become the main line of resistance. Conditions here were reasonably quiet, apart from mustard gas shelling which occurred two or three times a week and caused most of the casualties incurred.

The 41st Division remained in defence of Ypres until early in May, when it moved back by rail to Watten, and then marched on to Audrehem, where open-warfare training was undertaken and a little time was even found for recreation. Another move was then made to Oudezeele, north of Cassel where Lieutenant-Colonel E. B. North DSO, another former Royal Fusilier, assumed command on 29 June and the 10th Queen's acted as a reserve battalion to a division of the French Army. Edward Bunbury North could certainly claim a wide variety of military experience before joining the 10th Queen's. Originally from Lancashire, he was forty-eight years old and as a Regular Army officer had already seen long service around the globe. First commissioned in 1890, he had been decorated for his service with the Egyptian Army from 1898 to 1899, joining the Nile Expedition of 1898 and participating in the Battle of Khartoum where he was mentioned in despatches. He had then fought in South Africa with the Royal Fusiliers from 1899 to 1900, taking part in the relief of Ladysmith, and from 1907 to 1909 was attached to the Imperial Japanese Army before returning to Britain. He had come to France as Brigade Major to the West Riding Division in 1915 and was promoted to command the 4th Battalion, Royal Fusiliers in 1916, winning the DSO with this unit before his move to the Battersea battalion.[67]

Among the occasional losses during this period was a recently-arrived replacement officer, Second Lieutenant Charles Proughten,

who had landed in France only five weeks before. A thirty-three-year-old former businessman and stockbroker, Proughten had joined the Inns of Court Officer Training Corps (O.T.C.) in January 1917 and upon receiving his commission, had eventually been posted to the 10th Queen's in April 1918. Killed in action after just five weeks on the continent, Proughten was nevertheless glowingly described in the letter written to his wife and daughter by his company commander: 'He had proved himself one of the most efficient and trusted officers in the Company. He was a man who knew no fear. He had endeared himself to us all, and died like a soldier.'

The Battalion largely spent June of 1918 on and about the Scherpenberg position south-east of Poperinghe, in daily anticipation of further enemy attacks. Fortunately, as the enemy's offensive ran out of steam, these attacks did not materialise, although a steady flow of casualties continued, including Captain Alfred Hale who was killed on 8 July. Later in July, an American Army unit, the 106th Infantry Regiment of the 27th U.S. Division, was attached for training and the Battalion then took the initiative and participated in several raids during the following weeks. Lieutenant Girling won the Military Cross for one such operation on the night of 8/9 August when he managed to bring back a captured German NCO from the enemy's trenches. Second Lieutenant Harold Marshfield was among the dead on 14 August and on the 20th Private Charlie Young was wounded during the advance along the Menin Road. The German bullet that knocked him flying would have been a fatal one had it not been slightly deflected by a spare clip of Charlie's own bullets. Despite this good fortune, the wound still almost proved to be the young soldier's undoing. In the haste and confusion of the advance, Charlie was left for dead and for three days lay alongside a dying German boy who kept calling for water. A little way off another badly wounded German watched Charlie for some time, but then recovered enough to start shooting at him. Luckily this drew the attention of a passing Scottish soldier who shot the German and came to Charlie's rescue. A three weeks' stay in hospital in Abbeville followed before Charlie returned to the Battalion. Little of note, other than the Battalion Sports Day, then followed until 28 September when the Battalion took part in the fourth and final Battle of Ypres. By this date the 10th Queen's had been brought back up to the Brandhoek area where the 41st Division was part of a force under the command of HM The King of the Belgians, consisting of the Belgian Army, a number of French Divisions, and General Plumer's Second Army.

At 5.30 a.m. on the 28th the massive Allied attack commenced on a front of some four and a half miles south of the Ypres to Zonnebeke road. Without any preliminary bombardment the element of surprise was successfully achieved and on both the British and Belgian fronts the attack was soon being hailed as a brilliant success. The 10th Queen's moved up in heavy rain as part of a support force consisting of the 41st and 36th Divisions and reached their assembly point at Hill 60 in time for a 3 p.m. zero hour. With A and B Companies in front and C and D in reserve, the Battalion advanced and met with only slight opposition in 'mopping-up' operations – clearing out concrete dug-outs, rounding up prisoners, securing arms dumps etc. There was little or no shelling by either side, with only rifle and machine-gun fire being exchanged and many men had to think hard for the last time they had fired their rifles standing up in the open. This continued until the Battalion reached Opaque Wood where positions were established as part of a line running through Kortewilde to Zandvoorde. For a loss of no more than sixteen casualties, the 10th Queen's had captured sixty-three prisoners, sixteen machine guns, a battery of field guns, a howitzer and a bus. The Germans, who had maintained less than five divisions in the sector, had been driven from the whole of the high ground east of Ypres, the area which had been so bitterly contested during the battles of 1917.

The following morning, in a day of rare sunny weather, A and C Companies of the Battalion were detached to guard the flanks of 123

Men of the Battersea Battalion on the front line near Passchendaele. G. Richardson

Brigade during an attack along the Ypres-Comines canal. This Brigade's progress stalled, however, due to an unexpectedly strong enemy counter-attack and consequently the 10th Queen's and 20th Royal Fusiliers were pushed forward to give fresh impetus to the advance. By 10 a.m. on 30 September the Battalion had reached the banks of the River Lys between Comines and Wervicq [Wervik] and consolidated positions after taking twenty-nine prisoners and twenty-five machine guns. The next day the 10th Queen's were relieved to form brigade reserve in the Kruiseecke [Kruiseke] area, suffering not only from a fair amount of enemy shelling, but also from persistently bad weather. On the evening of 7 October the Battalion marched to Birr Cross-roads on the Ypres to Menin road where it was to entrain for Abeele. The trains were considerably delayed and it was not until 9 p.m. on the 8th that the Battalion eventually reached Douglas Camp at Steenacker. Four days' respite was managed here until the Battalion once again packed up in preparation for its part in the Battle of Courtrai [Kortrijk].

On 13 October, and most appropriately for a Battersea-raised battalion, the 10th Queen's detrained at a point named 'Clapham Junction' east of Ypres on the Menin Road. They remained there in bivouac until the evening when an advance began as reserve to the other two battalions of 124 Brigade. The Belgian, French, and British forces in Flanders were now attacking on a front between the Lys River at Comines and Dixmunde. The British sector ran for some ten miles from Comines to the hamlet of Sint Pieter on the Menin to Roulers [Roeselare] road and on the night of 13 October the 10th Queen's had reached the cross-roads at Au Rossignol Cabaret when the tail of the column was heavily shelled, causing several casualties and a good amount of temporary confusion. The Battalion's position of assembly was reached early on the 14th at Rifle Farm, but when the Allied barrage fell at zero hour the enemy put down a heavy retaliatory bombardment, lasting for two hours and causing several casualties, including Second Lieutenants Edward Goss and J.A. Laing who were killed. The morning was very misty and this, together with the smoke from the barrage, caused a dense fog which caused severe disorientation among the attacking formations. When the fog eventually lifted several units were found to be hopelessly mixed up and the situation deteriorated further when an enemy field battery and several machine guns opened up at extremely close range. For a while the advance ground to a complete halt and numerous casualties were suffered. Units were soon reorganised, however, the objective was captured and consolidated and the enemy battery put out of action. On the 15th the Battalion was relieved and marched back for a few days' rest to the Gulleghem [Gullegem] area.

On the morning of 21 October, 1918 the 41st Division was again called to the front to attack the line of the River Scheldt east of the Courtrai-Bossuyt [Bossuit] canal between Bossuyt and Autryve [Outrijve], and the 10th Queen's moved to an assembly position near Vamoennacker Farm. The attack, which commenced at 7.30 a.m., was successful until a tunnel along the Courtrai-Bossuyt canal was reached. It had been intended that on crossing the canal near Keibergmolen [Keiberg], the 10th Queen's whould advance with their right on the canal, but the tunnel could not be passed as it was heavily wired and defended by strong enemy positions. All movement here was impossible, the area not only being swept by machine-gun fire, but also by enemy mortars. The next day, 22 October, the Battalion was therefore marched back to the eastern side of the canal, but here too they found themselves still under heavy machine-gun fire. During the early afternoon orders arrived to resume the attack and though these instructions were later cancelled, some of the companies had already begun to advance. The Battalion therefore continued and the attack eventually proved successful, the tunnel being taken with twenty-six prisoners and six machine guns captured. A rest was then permitted until the morning of the 25th when there was a general advance to reach the line of the River Scheldt near Avelghem [Avelgem]. The 10th Queen's followed the advance in support of 124 Brigade's other two battalions, but on arrival at the line Kattestraat-Ooteghem [Otegem], found that the leading battalions had been halted by strong enemy positions on the left flank. At 4.30 p.m. the Battalion was ordered to advance, but B and C Companies on the left were soon stopped after only 300 yards by heavy machine-gun fire from just east of Ooteghem. On the right the advance was met with only short-range gun fire and managed to continue. At dusk patrols were sent out and reported Ooteghem and Driesch [Dries] clear of the enemy and the Battalion then moved forward to the line of the road between these two villages. Unopposed patrols again pushed forward the next day to Kloosterhoek, Bosch, and Kaphoek, but the 10th Queen's were then relieved from the front line and returned to the Courtrai area where a welcome rest was granted. In addition to the two officers, Goss and Laing, twenty-six other ranks had been killed in this campaign, one officer and 142 men were wounded, and one man was missing.

Chapter 14

VICTORY AND OCCUPATION

The fourth Battle of Ypres proved to be the last general action in which the 10th Queen's took part. Although the Battalion helped in the general pursuit of the retreating enemy, there was little direct confrontation and casualties were few and far between. In such circumstances it is perhaps not surprising that a small minority of the men became determined not to risk their lives any further and Charlie Young recalled a number of ruses. One trick was to put a needle through one's knee, which caused the joint to swell dramatically. Other men smoked cordite, which temporarily made them appear drastically ill. One even went so far as to shoot himself through the hand.

But for the vast majority of the men it was simply a case of trudging onwards and keeping one's head down as much as possible. On 11 November 1918 the Battalion had reached Terbosch, some twenty-five miles west of Brussels, when news of the signing of the Armistice was received. With the war apparently over[68] the men celebrated with great relief and thoughts instantly turned to the prospect of how soon they would be sent back home to England. Almost immediately, however, news arrived that the 41st was to be one of the eight British divisions forming the Army of Occupation in Germany and the Battalion's advance was therefore ordered to continue. At the beginning of December the 10th Queen's had reached Viane where headquarters were sited in an empty chateau and battalion photographs were taken. In the middle of the month they became the first British troops to be billeted at Waterloo, seven miles south of Brussels, since the famous battle there in 1815. With scant regard for the historic site, the men made a nuisance of themselves by scratching their initials on the commemorative lions there.

Leave was granted for sight-seeing in Brussels, but the Battalion's stay at Waterloo proved to be a short one. On the 16th they marched past King Albert I of the Belgians and a few days later continued on to Wanze, fifteen miles south-west of Liège, where Christmas Day and the New Year passed peacefully.

On 6 January 1919 the Battalion were spared further marching and entrained at Huy to follow the Meuse river before crossing the frontier into Germany at Herbesthal. They left their train at Hoffingsthal for a

The 10th Battalion's officers in Germany as part of the Army of Occupation, January 1919. D. Inkster

march of some twenty-three kilometres into the Cologne bridgehead where billets were found in the village of Lindlar. An outpost line, eleven kilometres on from Lindlar, was the Battalion's responsibility, but it was here that demobilisation began in earnest. The men of the 10th Queen's had been given the option of signing on for another year as part of the Army of Occupation, and while most were still happy to be repatriated, there were many who decided otherwise. Most of those who chose to continue were NCO's who could expect to lead a fairly privileged peace-time existence in the Army. But there were also those private soldiers who had nothing better to return to in England. Charlie Young was one such soldier who volunteered for the extra twelve months, a decision he had no cause to regret as he spent most of his time playing football when freed from his duties as a mess waiter.

On 10 February 1919 the entire Battalion marched from Lindlar to Ehreshoven to receive, from their Army Commander, their King's Colour which had been sent from England. The next day the 10th Queen's moved to Engelskirchen and later in the month back to Ehreshoven for the whole of March and April. In the latter month another new commanding officer took over on the 18th, Lieutenant-Colonel Robert O'Hara Livesay being a forty-two-year-old Regular

238

officer with long service in The Queen's Regiment. Commissioned in 1896, he had served in South Africa from 1899 to 1902 where, unusually for a junior officer, he had managed to win the DSO as well as being mentioned in despatches. He had left the Army in February 1914, but the outbreak of war had seen him recalled from the Reserve in August of the same year. In October 1915 he had been re-gazetted in the Regular Army as a junior captain in The Queen's Regiment and went on to serve successfully and be promoted throughout the war.[69]

At the beginning of May and with a full strength of sixty-five officers and 1,275 other ranks, the Battalion returned to Lindlar and moved into tents. There was then no further move until 17 July when the Battalion relocated to Bensberg and later again to Siegburg, seven miles south-east of Cologne. The unit diary recorded little of interest for the remainder of the year, training of all kinds, recreational activities and sight-seeing being the norm. The local people were generally friendly, but at times there was the expectation of civil disturbance for one reason or another and the Battalion remained on-call for any such problems. Eventually, on 31 December 1919 the following entry appeared in the unit diary: 'Preparations started for disbandment of the Battalion.'

On 5 January, 1920, the Battalion's King's Colour was escorted by B and D Companies to Siegburg Railway Station and in the care of Lieutenant Cadman, left for Holy Trinity Church, Guildford, where it remained until relocated to St. Mary's Church, Battersea, in 1933. The Battle Honours listed on the Colour are:

Ypres, 1917; Ypres, 1918; Somme, 1916; Somme, 1918; Flers-Courcelette, 1916; Morval, 1916; Le Transloy, 1916; Arras, 1918; Messines, 1917; Pilckem, 1917; Menin Road, 1917; St Quentin, 1918; Bapaume, 1918; Lys, 1918; Kemmel, 1918; Courtrai, 1918; France and Flanders, 1916-1918; Italy, 1917-18.

In February 1920 the 10th Queen's moved to Muhlheim Barracks, Cologne, to help with salvage work. Finally, the beginning of the end commenced on 25 February 1920 when an advance party of the 2nd Battalion, Loyal North Lancashire Regiment arrived to begin relieving the 10th Queen's. Two days later a notice appeared in orders that 'The Battalion will move to No. 1 Concentration Camp for dispersal on the afternoon of March 6.'

On 5 March, two officers and 199 other ranks moved to this designated camp in Cologne for demobilisation and were followed the next day by the remainder of the Battalion. Before leaving, Lieutenant-Colonel Livesay addressed his men for the last time on the parade ground, the Battalion gave the Royal Salute to the Union flag and the band of the 1st Battalion, Durham Light Infantry played a final hymn. The Army Commander then made a farewell speech before the Battalion marched past and set off for the concentration camp and ultimately, home. The proud tally of decorations won by the Battalion read:

CMG:	1 officer
DSO:	5 officers (one with bar)
MC:	30 officers (six with bar)
DCM:	7 NCOs
MM:	83 other ranks
MSM:	6 other ranks

plus foreign decorations.

Yet the cost had been high. Forty-four officers and 640 other ranks were killed or missing, and sixtyofficers and 2,200 other ranks had been wounded. The total number of casualties roughly equalled *three times* the original strength of the Battalion.

PART FOUR

Chapter 15

A LAND FIT FOR HEROES?

On 24 December 1918, Prime Minister David Lloyd George declared 'What is our task? To make Britain a fit country for heroes to live in'. To the modern-day reader or researcher, however, the Wandsworth and Battersea newspapers of the time displayed a strange and almost total silence on the achievements and fate of the boroughs' battalions and their local heroes, coupled with a notable lack of celebration over the signing of the Armistice on 11 November 1918. The 10th Queen's, of course, were still busy in Germany as part of the victorious Army of Occupation, but there was only passing mention in the local press of the hundreds of prisoners of war of the 13th East Surreys who were then being released and shipped home.

For the majority of them, still held in the Dülmen prisoner of war camp, news of the Armistice had come swiftly when, only a half hour or so after the ceasefire came into effect at 11 a.m. on 11 November 1918, a French orderly ran up shouting that the war had ended. Even the Germans were excited, the officers went home or out for the day, while the camp guards took their regimental badges out of their caps and wore them the wrong way round. They left the former prisoners to their own devices, they were free to roam as they pleased and there was little or no animosity between the British and the Germans – only relief and joy. A few days later, a level of order returned for a lengthy march of three or four hours to a railhead where a cheery surprise awaited the released men since the train for their journey out of Germany had been decked by their former captors with laurels and other evergreens. Before long a frontier post was reached, the train halted and after a few handing-over formalities, the German officers politely took their leave. This done, and when a Dutch railway engine was coupled on to the troop train in place of the German one, several Dutch officers came along the train and spoke to the men in English "You are out of the hands of the enemy now and will soon be in

Holland". This friendly greeting almost made the men feel at home already and this impression was strengthened as soon as the train crossed the border into Holland where, though the country had managed to remain neutral throughout the war, pro-British sentiment still ran high. Everywhere along the line there was a hearty reception, all the Dutch people were at the trackside or up at their windows, the little Dutch girls wearing short full skirts, clogs and bonnets, and the older men sporting traditional baggy trousers and blouses and smoking long pipes. This type of reception continued all along the line until the train reached the town of Enschede where the released Tommies were to stay for three nights in a large cotton factory while the Dutch authorities arranged the remainder of the journey through Holland. For the short march from the station to the factory, a Dutch army band played and all along the route Dutch troops and policemen lined the streets as a guard of honour. The East Surreys felt like dignitaries and the Dutch civilians seemed as pleased to see them as if they had been their own troops. The local people simply could not do enough for their visitors and the men's spirits were further raised by a concert part provided by the Red Cross. It was in the style of a fine old British concert hall production, with all the songs that the men knew and could sing along to. The local population again turned out, joined in and were keen to talk and hear of the privations of prisoner-of-war life, particularly in respect of food, as they knew the Germans had little. The Dutch apologised for not being able to give the hungry soldiers as much food as they would have wished, explaining that the British sea blockade had also hit their supplies hard and that, as a consequence they, too, were severely rationed. They nevertheless invited many of the British into their homes and were genuinely pleased to be able to welcome them back from German captivity and to do anything they could for their visitors, even if it were as little as helping to carry any personal property or parcels that the troops had.

In the factory, clean straw had been provided for the men to lie on and the Red Cross officials distributed postcards for the men to send home and notify their friends and families that they were out of Germany and on the way home. In many cases, the postcards arrived after the men. After their three nights in the factory, the men were paraded in preparation for the next stage of their journey, to the port of Rotterdam. That morning, it looked as if the entire town of Enschede had turned out to give the troops a hearty send-off, calling out good wishes and "a speedy journey home" in English. Another long troop train collected them and pulled out of the station to an accompaniment of loud cheering and much waving of hands, hats and handkerchiefs. It took the entire day to reach Rotterdam, the route continuing to be lined by waving Dutch people standing by their houses, canals and barges. At Rotterdam, an English officer met them with new uniforms into which they changed before boarding their ship, the men being happy to once again be wearing khaki and to be able to throw away their tattered blue POW uniform. The change of clothing also entailed the luxury of a bath and an issue of clean underwear.

The North Sea crossing was not without drama. Thick fog, the German and British minefields and a very rough sea were among the challenges and few of the 560 men aboard were not sea-sick, meaning that conditions on the tightly-packed ship left much to be desired.

At last the shelter of the Humber estuary was reached and after a calm night at anchor the ship got under way again the next morning and eased into the busy docks at Hull. The harbour was full of ships sounding their sirens and flying signal flags in greeting, while the river banks and dockside were crammed with wives, sweethearts, mothers and fathers, many with photographs of the boy they were hoping to welcome home.

Once disembarked and breakfasted in a large warehouse, the men entrained for the large military camp at Ripon in Yorkshire, about seventy miles from Hull. Here, a fine, hot roast dinner was waiting, along with beer, stout and mineral water. Another hot bath and more clean underwear followed, together with the welcome news that all were being granted two months' prisoner-of-war leave. After a day and night at Ripon, the men paraded once more, numbered off and marched back down to the station. A few hours later and the Londoners were at King's Cross.

Most of those who had been captured were repatriated by the end of December 1918, but there was only muted local reporting of their return and it was to take the better part of a year before many of the troops who had avoided capture at Fleurbaix were released from service. Most had been spread far and wide when the 13th Battalion was disbanded, not only throughout the East Surrey Regiment, but also throughout the Army in general. Demobilisation proceeded only at a plodding pace and vociferous, or even sometimes violent, protests from those anxious to return home were therefore not uncommon.

The reticence of the press to trumpet the Armistice was undoubtedly also linked to the fact that the Great War was not truly considered to have ended on 11 November 1918. The treaty negotiations at Versailles were to continue long into the following year, with the Germans struggling against the Allies' aim to gain as much as possible from war reparations. But in November 1918, although there was some celebration of the Armistice, there were still those who feared that it might yet be no more than a temporary ceasefire.

In addition, there were other pressing national domestic issues which served to relegate news of the battalions. A hotly-contested General Election was fought in December 1918 with, for the first time, a limited number of women permitted to vote. It was also the occasion when all men over the age of twenty-one were allowed to vote. Until then, only male house owners were enfranchised and it is sobering to remember that the vast majority of those who had volunteered to serve their country in the Great War had unhesitatingly done so when they were not even allowed to vote for their own government.

Lieutenant Hedley Payne DCM died of wounds back in England, 21st February 1919.
Author

A world-wide epidemic of deadly Spanish influenza was also headline news and well on its way to claiming more lives than the war. The statistics of this were staggering. At the beginning of November 1918 there were 150 deaths in one week from influenza in Battersea alone. This was a particularly dangerous development for any of the Wandsworth and Battersea Battalions' men recovering from wounds. Private J. Brookes of the 10th Queen's died in a Boulogne hospital in such circumstances just four days after the Armistice. Of the 13th East Surreys, the popular former Fulham footballer, Sergeant Billy Barton, died in St. Omer in December, having been transferred to the 8th East Surreys and then to a unit guarding German POWs. Private Sidney Ricks, from the Causeway, Wandsworth and one of the 13th Battalion's earliest volunteers, succumbed in January 1919, soon after returning to

Wandsworth. So too did Lietenant Hedley Payne, son of the Reverend Arthur Payne of The Grove, Earlsfield. Payne, who won the DCM earlier in the war before being commissioned, had been wounded, captured and hospitalised, but photographs sent home had shown him in good spirits. After his return to England, however, he died 21 February 1919 and was buried in Wandsworth Cemetery.

But while the home population therefore had much to preoccupy them without being over-concerned for the returning troops, an occasional local event or news articles nevertheless served to keep memories fresh. In Wandsworth, Alderman Dawnay was knighted for his efforts in raising the 13th Battalion and for his patriotic leadership of the Council throughout the war. This achievement was, however, tempered by personal tragedy when his son, a doctor, died in the influenza epidemic. Dawnay nevertheless continued as Mayor and Chief Magistrate of the Borough and on 22 January 1919, proudly announced to a meeting of Wandsworth Borough Council that he had received two enemy machine guns from the War Office. The 13th Battalion had captured these weapons in France and the British government was now donating them to the Borough of Wandsworth as a gesture of thanks for having raised the Battalion in 1915. While neither the War Office nor the Council appears to have commented on the fact, it is at least possible, if not probable, that the guns came from the Battalion's attack on Villers-Plouich in April 1917, when ten enemy machine guns were

Payne had only recently received a letter from King George V welcoming him home from captivity.
Author

245

captured. If the East Surrey Regiment had kept these as war trophies, then were the two donated examples the very two guns overwhelmed by Corporal Foster when winning his Victoria Cross? The Council agreed that one gun should be displayed in Streatham Library and the other in Putney Library, but sadly, their subsequent whereabouts have long since been forgotten.

In 1919 Alderman Lieutenant Commander Cooper Rawson became Mayor of Wandsworth when Sir Archibald Dawnay died in office.[70] As committed as his predecessor to honouring the survivors of the Wandsworth battalion, Cooper Rawson made it one of his first duties to arrange a dinner for them. The new Mayor was also quick to forge links with Villers-Plouich, the village temporarily freed from German occupation by the 13th East Surreys in 1917.

In Battersea, civic thanks to the men of the Battersea battalion were given on 20 June 1919, by which time those who had declined the offer of further service had left the Battalion in Germany and returned home. On this evening, the Mayor of Battersea hosted a dinner and presented Colonel Oakley DSO with a Sword of Honour from the grateful Council. The occasion also led to the attendees deciding to form the 10th Queen's Old Comrades' Association. Colonel Oakley was President, while the Vice-Presidents listed included the familiar names of Colonel North, Lieutenant-Colonels Gwynne, Jarvis and Hayley Bell and Captain Inkster served as Treasurer. An annual reunion dinner continued until at least 1949.

Yet, though these early celebrations were tempered by a note of caution, in reality it was only a matter of time before the Versailles Treaty was signed and the British government therefore started to consider how best to mark the official end of the war. Lloyd George created a Peace Committee that met for the first time in June 1919, under the chairmanship of Foreign Secretary Lord Curzon. A man who loved pomp and ceremony, Curzon led the Committee in drawing up plans for a four-day celebration at the beginning of August 1919, including a Victory March through London, a day of Thanksgiving services, a river pageant, and a day of popular festivities. At the end of June, however, the Versailles Treaty was signed and the arrangements had to be quickly brought forward to 19 July. For many people in Battersea and Wandsworth, the events planned for central London were close enough to be a greater attraction than most local ceremonies.

The Victory parade in particular was an unforgettable spectacle and a huge success. Nearly 15,000 troops took part in the march, led by the victorious Allied commanders Haig, Pershing, Foch, and Beatty who saluted their 'glorious dead' comrades as they passed Lutyens's impressive new Cenotaph[71] in The Mall. Later in the day there were entertainments staged by the League of Arts in St James' Park; Shakespeare was performed by the National Organisation of Girls' Clubs in Regent's Park; there was a concert in Green Park; and an Imperial Choir of 10,000 voices sang in Hyde Park, supported by the massed bands of the Brigade of Guards. To the latter, the King and Queen paid a surprise visit during the afternoon and a lavish firework display followed later in the evening.

Locally, the Boroughs of both Battersea and Wandsworth saw a great number of celebratory street parties and small parades. But not everyone joined in. Around the country there were several instances of ex-servicemen refusing to take part in celebrations or processions, fearing that they ran the risk of being 'ornaments for one day' at a time when claims for better pensions for ex-servicemen and their dependants were a much more pressing issue. The most serious challenge to the celebrations came in Luton, where there was already bad feeling over the Council's refusal to allow discharged soldiers to hold their own memorial service in a park. The Town Hall was burnt down by rioters before a detachment of soldiers arrived and for several days afterwards Luton was, ironically, under military occupation. Fortunately there were no such problems in Wandsworth or Battersea, though some unrest might have been expected in the latter borough, due to its history of anti-war feeling.

The sense of injustice felt by some ex-servicemen was heightened by Lloyd George's declaration 'To make Britain a fit country for heroes to live in'. Keeping the Prime Minister's pledge should have been simple in a country that had been spending £7 million a day on the war effort – surely only a fraction of that amount would be needed to provide properly for the returning troops? Yet for the soldiers who survived to come home, the thanks of a grateful country were often no more than a suit of civilian clothes, two or three medals, and a small cash payment. A Private received the equivalent of only a few weeks' wages, though officers got more. Many of those returning received a little extra by means of a disability pension, but this, of course, entailed the drawback of being disabled. Many viewed the money, like the country's gratitude, as only temporary. Resentment was also wide-spread that those who had done best out of the war were the industrialists who had remained at home and made large profits out of the conflict. Large numbers of demobilised soldiers, irrespective of their wartime rank and decorations, therefore soon realised that the dream of coming home to a secure job, which they believed to be their right, was not going to come true. Some of the survivors of the Wandsworth and Battersea battalions were reduced to selling cards, matches and mementoes. Soup kitchens and food distribution centres became familiar ports of call for many, even for the seriously wounded[72], who often found that medical tribunals discharged their disability rights far too soon. In light of the disappointments of civilian life, many men understandably clung to any possibility of staying on in the Army.

Private W. Grantham was one such former soldier of the 13th East Surreys. A pre-war regular in the Royal Navy, Grantham had been serving in HMS *Tiger* at the outbreak of war and was wounded during the Battle of the Dogger Bank in early 1915. He was discharged from the Navy in April, but managed to promptly re-enlist in the Army where he served in both the Wandsworth Battalion and the 2nd King's (Liverpool Regiment), gaining the Military Medal for conspicuous bravery. Again wounded, he succeeded in remaining in the Army with the Royal Army Service Corps as an Instructor until his release in February 1919. Perhaps not surprisingly for such a man of action, Grantham spent only four restless months in civilian life before re-enlisting in the Royal Navy, but his military career finally came to an end when his old wounds rendered him unfit for further service the following year.

Another example was Reggie Maxfield of the 10th Queen's. In April 1918, only just commissioned and trained, Maxfield had been rushed out to the Somme on his nineteenth birthday to join the Battersea Battalion on its return from Italy to help stop the Germans' spring offensive. He had spent the remaining seven months of the war as a front-line soldier with the rank of second lieutenant, but then had no great experience of work in civilian life to help him compete with the hundreds of thousands of job-hungry demobilised men returning to England. Clutching at the straw of continued Army service offered by the inclusion of the 10th Queen's in the Army of Occupation in Germany, in April 1919 he succeeded in finding a niche as a clerk in the canteen at divisional headquarters in Germany. His temporary wartime commission came to an end and he soldiered on with the rank of Private.

Yet while Britain was still struggling to come to terms with its own bitter memories of the war, and at the same time was slipping inexorably into the recession and disappointments of the 1920s, it is heartening to discover that the people of Wandsworth found the time to consider those who had suffered even more. The British League of Help was a scheme whereby British towns and cities could 'adopt' and help to fund the restoration of a devastated French or Belgian community. On 25 September 1920, Wandsworth Council formally adopted Villers-Plouich, the village where Corporal Foster won his Victoria Cross and which had been left utterly ruined by the war, under the scheme. Not one building in the small French community had been left intact and the returning civilian population was reduced to living in temporary hutted accommodation while they planned for reconstruction. Several visits to the village were made by members of the Council, commencing with Mayor Cooper Rawson in October 1920, accompanied by former Lieutenants Harker and Lanham who had both served at Villers-Plouich [see Appendix IV]. Despite high unemployment and lean times generally, some £1,200 (around £200,000 at 2009 rates) was collected from private donations in Wandsworth and sent to the French Mayor to assist with rebuilding. Substantial contributions were also made in terms of clothing, shoes and the other necessities of life. The latter included seeds and items for Monsieur and Madame Delecourt who ran the village school. The first consignment, however, suffered as a result of the criminal activity then endemic in post-war, devastated France. Despatched via the Walford Steamship Company's SS *Jolly Esmond*, the packing case reached Boulogne docks on 29 November, but was then not cleared by customs onto the French railway network until 9 December. Thereafter it disappeared into thin air, a fate shared by no less than five of the six cases sent from Wandsworth between November and December. The only one to reach Gouzeaucourt (the nearest railhead to Villers-Plouich) contained children's toys for Christmas.

This sorry state of affairs was set out in a letter from Wandsworth Council to Lord Derby in time for his visit to France in January 1921 and thereafter conditions appear to have improved. Mayor Cooper Rawson's own contribution of four footballs for boys at the village school safely reached Villers-Plouich in July 1921, and fund-raising efforts continued throughout the year, including a charity football match in Wandsworth in November. The link with Villers-Plouich was also strengthened by Wandsworth's schoolchildren. The pupils of two London County Council schools in the borough, Miss Glover's girls at Aristotle Road, Clapham, and the children of

Southfield School, wrote many letters to their Villers-Plouich counterparts commencing over the 1920 Christmas season, practising their written French while sending news and best wishes.

And finally, on 16 July 1921, a fitting epitaph to the 13th East Surreys came when a ceremony at the 'Frying Pan' site on Wandsworth Common put right a great disservice to the battalion. In the presence of the Mayor of Wandsworth, Alderman T. E. Comins, JP and the Members of the Borough Council, a Service of Consecration was held and Major-General Sir John Longley KCMG CB, Colonel of the East Surrey Regiment, then presented the King's Colour to over 350 former officers and men of the Battalion. Among those present were Major Taylor, Captains L. J. Deacon, G. E. Deacon, J. R. Hucker MC, T. W. Hucker MC, King and Dodd, Lieutenants Lanham, Saville, W. B. Parker MC, Batch, C. J. de Beaurepaire, and Dobb and RSM Lee DCM. This King's Colour was the Battalion's standard which had never been received due to the demands of active duty overseas and the hasty disbandment which followed the disaster at Fleurbaix. The ceremony was closed by a speech from the Mayor, who stressed how proud were the people of the Borough in the achievements of the Battalion. The Colour Party and detachment from the Regimental Depot at Kingston-upon-Thames, led by Lieutenant Lanham, then marched to All Saints Church in Wandsworth High Street and placed the King's Colour in the care of the Vicar.[73]

Chapter 16

IN MEMORIAM

T hough memories of the two battalions have gradually faded over the years, there are still several reminders today of their service. Battersea Council held true to its pledge and in the Town Hall in Lavender Hill (now Battersea Arts Centre) a commemorative plaque was unveiled in 1919, recording the battle honours of the 10th Queen's and a memorial board was erected listing those local men who had given their lives for King and country.

Also in 1919 a committee of past and present officers and NCO's of the Queen's Regiment met to consider providing a fitting war memorial. It proved impossible to obtain a suitable outdoor site and it was therefore decided that the memorial should be placed on the north wall of Holy Trinity Church, Guildford, home to the regimental chapel. The total amount raised was £3,000 and several alternative designs were considered before the committee accepted that submitted by Captain E. Stanley Hall, an officer who had served with the 10th (Battersea) Battalion and who was also a distinguished architect, later to become President of the Royal Institute of British Architects.

Holy Trinity Church, Guildford – the QRWS regimental chapel and the 10 QRWS memorial window.
Author

The memorial was completed and unveiled on 4 June 1921. It consists of a central niche in which rests a bronze and glass casket, containing the book that lists the 8,000 all ranks of the Queen's (Royal West Surrey) Regiment who gave their lives during the First World War. Over the niche is a tympanum supported by columns and showing the regimental badge, the Paschal Lamb. Above the memorial are three stained glass windows, subscribed for by the 3rd, 8th, and 10th Battalions. The one of the Battersea Battalion, on the right, contains the figure of St. Catherine making her choice between the Crown of Laurels and the Crown of Thorns – the Victory over the Flesh. Access to the chapel is still possible today through the church.

The equivalent regimental chapel for Wandsworth's 13th Battalion is that of the East Surrey Regiment, in All Saints Parish Church, Kingston-upon-Thames, Surrey. The Chapel dates back to the 15th Century, but was restored by relatives, friends and comrades of the Regiment in memory of those who lost their lives in the First World War and whose names are commemorated in the Book of Remembrance there. The Bishop of Southwark dedicated it as the Regimental War Memorial in 1921 and in 1924 impressive memorial gates were added leading to the church. Oak panels on the walls of the Chapel serve as memorials to officers who served in the Regiment, while a section in the north wall is reserved to commemorate the Regiment's Victoria Cross holders, including Corporal Foster of the 13th Battalion.

Further memorials blossomed in the 1920's and 1930's when private fund-raising enabled many divisional symbols to be set up in France and Belgium. The 40th Division's former members gave money for a new altar in the church at Bourlon and a marble plaque there still commemorates the men of the Division, including those of the 13th East Surreys, who fell in and around Bourlon wood in November 1917. For the 41st Division, it was the former officers of the 10th Queen's who were among the most active in raising funds for an appropriate memorial. Lieutenant-Colonel Jarvis was the chief organiser and succeeded in raising a large sum for a statue in the village of Flers, the community liberated by the Division in 1915. The result, a full-size bronze statue of a British soldier in full battle order and rifle at the trail, has become one of the most evocative and well-known memorials of the Western Front. Raised on a granite plinth at one end of the village's main street, it was handed over to the Mayor of Flers on 15 May 1932 by Lieutenant-General Sir Sidney Lawford. Almost 400 of the 41st Division's former members were present, including a good contingent from the 10th Queen's.[74] The same old comrades of the 10th Queen's were instrumental in another act of remembrance just over a year later. In January 1920, shortly before the Battalion's disbandment, its King's Colour had been escorted back to England and delivered into the care of Holy Trinity Church, Guildford. There had been strong feelings and representations, however, that the Colour's rightful home was in Battersea, the community that had given birth to the Battalion. The justice of this was eventually accepted, but it was not until Sunday, 25 June 1933 that the King's Colour was returned for laying up in the parish church of St. Mary's, alongside the River Thames. Lieutenant-Colonel Oakley led the parade from the Clapham Junction drill hall of the 23rd London Regiment to St. Mary's and Lieutenant-Colonel Jarvis led the return. Bands of the 22nd and 24th London Regiments (The Queen's) played as Oakley first presented the Colour to Councillor Strange JP, Mayor of Battersea, who in turn delivered it into the safekeeping of Reverend Maxwell. This historic reminder of the exploits of the 10th Queen's still lies in St. Mary's church.

Eventually and inevitably, however, memories of the First World War were eclipsed by those of the Second. No veterans remain from the events of 1914-18 from the Wandsworth and Battersea battalions. By and large, few personal reminiscences of the conflict appeared in print, a situation very much in contrast to the present era. Participants of the Falklands and Gulf conflicts, for example, have been able to produce best-selling first-hand accounts within months of the end of hostilities. But from the average Tommy, or even officer, of the First World War, such efforts were rare.

For the Wandsworth Battalion, some echo of past glory was periodically heard thanks to their VC holder, Tiny Foster. Tiny had returned to ordinary life in Tooting after being invalided out of the army in 1918, shortly before the Armistice, as a result of his injury at Bourlon Wood in November 1917. A grateful Wandsworth Council held a dinner in his honour and offered him the position of Dusting Inspector, overseeing the Refuse Collection contract on which he had previously worked as a dustman. In June 1920 he attended a Buckingham Palace garden party and on 11 November that year he was present at the Cenotaph in Whitehall for the burial of the Unknown Warrior. A formal VC holders' dinner followed in November 1929 at the House of Lords and in 1931 Tiny was presented to Prince Albert, (later King George VI) at the opening of Wimbledon Town Hall. Thereafter Tiny was content to limit his formal appearances to participation in the annual Armistice Day Parade at the Cenotaph, marching in the ranks of the VC recipients. In 1934, however, the local press noted that for the first time since the parades began after the war, Tiny had been unable to attend due to poor health. This was a portent of things to come, for Tiny had suffered a reoccurrence of pneumonia, worsened by weakened lungs which were a legacy of his wartime service. For a while, Tiny recovered and continued to be a regular sight pedalling about Wandsworth's streets on his Wandsworth Council duties. By and large he was content to let his wartime achievements be forgotten – 'My V.C.?' he told the *Daily Express* in 1937, 'I want to forget it. But it did me a bit of good all the same.' Sadly, in January 1946, another sudden attack of bronchial pneumonia gripped Tiny. After just two days off work, he rapidly worsened and died on 22 January. His funeral and burial, in Streatham Cemetery, Garratt Lane, Tooting, attracted national Press coverage and was attended by many local dignitaries.[75]

But Foster's relatively early death meant that even his name and exploits faded and it was then not until 1964 that anything more was heard of the 13th Battalion. On Saturday, 26 September 1964, Wandsworth Council unveiled a commemorative tablet alongside the Town Hall in Wandsworth High Street. Depicting the unique Wandsworth version of the regimental badge, the tablet reads:

> *In proud commemoration of the 13th (Service) Battalion of the East Surrey Regiment known as "The Wandsworth Regulars". Raised in the Borough of Wandsworth in 1915, the Battalion served with distinction in France from 1916 to 1918.*

Fittingly, music for the ceremony and 'Beating Retreat' was performed by the Band and Drums of the 4th (T.A.) Battalion of the Queen's Royal Surrey Regiment. This regiment had been formed on 14 October 1959 by an amalgamation of the East Surrey Regiment with The Queen's (Royal West Surrey) Regiment. The 4th (T.A.) Battalion had been formed from the former territorial units of the 6th Battalion, East Surrey Regiment and the 23rd Battalion, London Regiment.

It was then more than thirty years before memories were again refreshed, prompted by an unnamed writer to the local *Wandsworth Guardian* newspaper. The correspondent recalled the exploits of Ted Foster VC and the letter caught the attention of the author who, together with two colleagues from Wandsworth Council, travelled privately to Villers-Plouich in November 1994 to re-establish contact with the village. From the Mairie's records the three visitors discovered that for many years after the war the Secretary to the Mayor of Wandsworth had continued to correspond with prominent residents of Villers-Plouich and cordial relations had clearly been maintained. In 1928 the Mayor of Villers-Plouich gratefully wrote that reconstruction of the village had been completed and that a tablet had been set in the wall of the Mairie to commemorate Wandsworth's help. This tablet remains today, as do the community's files holding all correspondence with Wandsworth dating back to the 1920's, including the letters sent in 1920 and 1921 from Wandsworth's schoolchildren. On a less favourable note, curt reminders are still held on the file from Wandsworth Council's Borough Treasurer, stressing that receipts were expected for all monies forwarded.

The three Council officers were met with enthusiasm in 1994 by the then Maire of Villers-Plouich, Jean Leterme, and his wife Elisabeth. This brought about a one-day visit in April 1995 by Councillor Beryl Jeffery, Mayor of Wandsworth, calling at the Villers-Plouich Mairie, Fifteen Ravine military cemetery and the Louverval Memorial (on the N30 Bapaume-Cambrai road) where the names are recorded of over 7,000 men of Third Army who have no known grave from the Battle of Cambrai.

The increased awareness of Corporal Foster's heroism at Villers-Plouich then led to the discovery that his civilian grave, in Streatham Cemetery, Tooting, had no headstone. Public subscription soon put matters right and in June 1994 a fine black marble headstone was erected before Councillor Jeffery as Mayor of Wandsworth, the Foster family, Council officers, a standard bearer from the East Surrey Regimental Association and an honour guard from the 5th (TA) Battalion, The Princess of Wales's Royal Regiment. This was followed by an event, on the evening of Monday 8 May 1995, when a new footpath through King George's Park in Wandsworth was named 'Foster's Way' by Mayor Councillor Jeffery. In front of some 40 descendants of Ted Foster (including son, grandson and great grandchildren) Mayor Councillor Jeffery also unveiled another commemorative tablet as a tribute to Foster's bravery. And finally, as she relinquished her one-year's term of mayoral office on 17 May 1995, Councillor Jeffery officially welcomed Monsieur and Madame Leterme to Wandsworth. During this first-ever official visit to Wandsworth from the Borough's adopted French village, Monsieur and Madame Leterme laid a floral tribute at the Town Hall's memorial to the Council employees killed in both World Wars.

The interest generated by these exchanges and events continues. Wandsworth Council, in a scheme of 'Green Plaques' to mark the houses of notable persons and historical locations in the Borough, selected the former homes of both Corporal Foster VC and Private Twyford to be among the first recipients of such plaques.

Councillors and officers, local Rotary groups, representatives of the Wandsworth Historical Society and many individual borough residents have made privately-funded visits to Villers-Plouich, to Ypres and to Flers, the latter being the Somme village captured by the Battersea Battalion in September, 1916. Moving even further afield in 2002, a party of twenty-nine flew to northern Italy to tour the former operational area of the 10th Queen's overlooking the Piave River. Here, the Mayor and community of the small town of Giavera del Montello welcomed the Wandsworth Council group and a commemorative service was held at the nearby British military cemetery where the Battersea Battalion's two fatalities from the campaign are buried.

The British Army unit that had formed the honour guard over Tiny Foster's grave in 1994 was an appropriate choice as it had played a part in keeping alive the memory of Foster's valour. A Guildford-based company of the 5th (TA) Battalion, The Princess of Wales's Royal Regiment[76], honoured the action of Corporal Foster and Lance-Corporal Reed each year in a 'Villers-Plouich Dining Night' hosted in the Junior NCOs' mess. Lamentably, the 5th Battalion fell victim to a Defence review in 1999 and their annual cricket match against Wandsworth Council for the Villers-Plouich Cup could no longer be held.

By way of replacement, however, an annual Villers-Plouich award was then instituted for the Mayor of Wandsworth's Charity Golf Day on 24 April 2007, the 90th anniversary of the capture of Villers-Plouich by the 13th East Surreys, the action in which Corporal Foster won his Victoria Cross. Two weeks later, the Mayor of Wandsworth, Councillor Jim Maddan, and a party of Wandsworth Councillors visited Villers-Plouich to a warm welcome from the village's current Mayor, Raymond Machut. Monsieur Machut and his wife, Nadine, have also been visitors to Wandsworth. Touchingly, the French have, in recent years, named the square outside their Mairie 'Place de Wandsworth', the sign bearing the coat of arms of both communities.

Most recently, in February 2008, two additional stone tablets were laid outside Wandsworth Town Hall alongside the 1964 original, described above, that records the service of the 13th East Surreys. The new tablets commemorate all the volunteer and Territorial units raised or based in the borough and include the 13th East Surreys and 10th Queen's in the listing. The sacrifice is not forgotten.

NOTES

1 Haig took over as Commander-in-Chief of British Expeditionary Forces in France and Flanders in 1915.

2 Alderman Dawnay, of Cedars Road, Clapham, was head of A. D. Dawnay & Sons, a large company of construction engineers with steelworks in both London and Cardiff. He was subsequently granted the honorary rank of Lieutenant-Colonel for his efforts in raising the 13th Battalion and his leadership as Mayor of Wandsworth throughout the war led to a knighthood in 1918.3 Upon local government reorganisation in 1965, Clapham and Streatham were transferred to the London Borough of Lambeth and were replaced in the reshaped Borough of Wandsworth by the area previously covered by the Borough of Battersea, the latter then ceasing to exist.

Upon reorganization of the Army's Territorial Forces in 1908, the 4th (Volunteer) Battalion of the East Surrey Regiment became the 23rd Battalion of the County of London Regiment. This unit was still affiliated to the East Surrey Regiment and continued to be based at the St John's Hill drill hall at Clapham Junction. Today, the hall still flourishes as a Territorial Army centre for the London Regiment and, high on the centre's facade, the coat of arms of the East Surrey Regiment remains.5 The Volunteer Forces were the First World War equivalent of the Home Guard.

6 Confusingly, it was the Queen's (Royal West Surrey) regiment who were Guildford-based, yet it was the image of Guildford castle that appeared as part of the badge of the Kingston-based East Surrey Regiment, due to the links between Guildford and the old 1st Surrey Militia.

7 13th Battalion badges (only true examples carry the manufacturer's name, Geo. Starr, Putney on the reverse) are today collectors' items of considerable value, due to the unique change of the regimental crest.

8 Surviving records suggest that there were several pairs of brothers or other close relatives who served as officers in the Battalion. In addition to the Huckers, other examples would seem to have been Second Lieutenants L. I. Deacon and G. E. Deacon, C. J. de Beaurepaire and P. G. de Beaurepaire, Captain L. B. Mills and Second Lieutenant T. B. Mills. 9 The recruiting personnel of this office included Private Faires who later transferred to the training staff of Wandsworth's second battalion, the 14th East Surreys. On 18th April 1916, Faires died in the Army hospital housed at the Royal Victoria Patriotic Building on the edge of Wandsworth Common. He was buried in Wandsworth Cemetery, Magdalen Road.10 Catchpole was to be invalided home after being wounded with the Battalion, but subsequently joined the 1st Wiltshires and returned to the Front. He was killed in Flanders during the Germans' offensive in April 1918 when ironically he at last was 19 and officially old enough to serve overseas.

11 The revolver, suitably inscribed, survives today as an exhibit in the Imperial War Museum.

12 Bandsmen were designated to act as stretcher bearers when on active service.

13 This gift, specially crafted by Wilkinson Sword, was sent on to Burton. In 1998 it resurfaced in the ownership of a collector in New Zealand.

14 At this time, the 13th East Surreys' transport was still predominantly horse-drawn, though the schoolchildren of the borough had presented a motor ambulance to the Battalion. Capable of taking stretcher cases as well as walking wounded, it was presented by Alderman Dawnay and, once the Battalion was in France, was used at Divisional Headquarters, attached to the RAMC.

15 The term 'bomb' refers to what we now call a grenade, 'bombers' therefore being the specialist grenade throwers. Experienced cricket bowlers and fielders were natural first choices.16 See History of the 40th Division by Lieutenant-Colonel F. E. Whitton CMG, pp 17-18. Though the narrator is unidentified, there are indications which suggest it was Lieutenant Beecroft, the Battalion's Transport Officer.17 The 41st Division was likewise home to Battersea's 10th Battalion, The Queen's (Royal West Surrey) Regiment.

18 It became clear that single men were no longer responding adequately to the calls to volunteer and therefore, in January 1916, compulsory service was approved.

19 The 40th Division was originally one of two divisions, the 35th and 40th, which were called 'Bantam' divisions, being largely comprised of men of small stature. In the case of the 40th Division, these men were mainly Welsh miners. As Brigade and Battalion changes were implemented, and also as the war progressed, the Division's 'Bantam' status diminished. 20 Whitton op. cit. pp 13-14.21 RSM Birch, an old soldier, was replaced by RSM E. J. Seymour before the Battalion left for active service.

22 Kitchener had drowned on 6th June 1916, when the cruiser HMS Hampshire struck a mine and sank off the Orkneys en-route to Russia. 23 It was said that the state of discipline of a battalion could be told by simply looking at their trench line and that the unit's fighting efficiency could be gauged by the record of night patrols and raids undertaken. The latter were considered to be particularly important, since it was feared that trench warfare could make men lazy, or disinclined for fighting in the open. 24 Less than two weeks later the 13th Battalion also lost Private William Twyford of Earlsfield, killed in action. While remaining records are not conclusive, it is possible that William and Reginald Twyford were related.25 Sadly, Bert Bell's warm clothing did

not prevent him suffering from inflammation of the middle ear later that winter. On 27th December1916 a telegram from the Army warned Mr and Mrs Bell that their son was dangerously ill from what should have been a relatively minor infection. A War Office notification confirmed this the next day, but in fact, Private Bell had already died on the afternoon of the 27th in No. 6 General Hospital, Rouen. He was buried in St. Sever Cemetery, Rouen where he is described as having died of wounds, contradicting the information given to his family.

26 A Bangalore torpedo was an explosive device used to blow up barbed wire defences.

27 Lieutenant Buckland, the 25 year old who had come from Argentina to fight for his country, was buried in Philosophe Cemetery, close to young Reginald Twyford. By a remarkable coincidence, his niece was many years later to marry the son of Captain Jim Hucker MC, also of the 13th Battalion.

28 Venereal disease, in particular, was a great cause for alarm among the military authorities. By 1917, 20% of the British troops in France had contracted V.D. and for the first time, the Army began to issue the men with contraception. Sociologists acknowledge that this 'encouragement' was to have far-reaching effects in Britain in the post-war decade.

29 Early in December 1916, the Asquith Government had fallen and Lloyd George had become Prime Minister. The new British leader was under no illusion that the battles on the Somme had been a costly failure and he was determined that 1917 would be the year of victory.

30Atkins, of Baskerville, Leicestershire, survived the war. He later became High Sheriff of Leicestershire and Honorary Colonel of the Leicestershire Regiment. Colonel Ernest Clive Atkins CB DL died in January 1953.

31 On 16th June 1917 Foster was also awarded the prestigious Médaille Militaire decoration for this act by a grateful French government.32 Three reminders of the East Surreys' courage remained around Villers-Plouich. The spot where Corporal Foster won his VC became 'Surrey Ravine' and until the end of the war trench maps also showed a communication trench as 'Foster's Lane' and a track named 'Surrey Road'. In the spring of 1918 the area again fell under German control. In September 1918, however, Villers-Plouich was permanently liberated in the early stages of the Allies' final victorious advance of the war. The first unit to reach 'Surrey Road' was the 1st Battalion of the East Surrey Regiment.

33 Lieutenant Victor William Scott MC later left the 13th Battalion to join the Royal Flying Corps. He was killed while flying in March 1918. 34 In August 1917, Major-General Harold Ruggles-Brise of the Grenadier Guards had been promoted and returned to England on the 24th. His successor as commander of the 40th Division was Major-General John Ponsonby, formerly of the Coldstream Guards. 35 Divisional headquarters had overlooked Third Army's orders that all tanks were to be temporarily withdrawn on the 24th for refitting. 36 Battlefield communications were still relatively primitive during the First World War. In established positions telephone lines could be laid, but many messages, particularly during offensive actions, had to be transmitted by runners - with all the uncertainties that such methods involved. Several of the scrawled communications sent during the 13th Battalion's fighting in Bourlon Wood survive with the unit's war diary in the National Archives, Kew. 37 Captain Lowe, like Captain Burton, had been attached from the 14th Battalion, Highland Light Infantry since July 1917.38 Captain Jim Hucker MC had been fortunate to survive. Twice, on previous occasions, shells had landed at his feet, but failed to go off. As a result of his wound received shortly after Bourlon Wood, however, he was not to return to active service with the 13th Battalion. He spent a year recovering in hospital before being sent for civilian employment in the Ministry of Pensions. Demobilised in May 1919, he returned to his career with the bank of Coutts and Co.

39 See 'A Brass Hat in No Man's Land', Brigadier-General F. P. Crozier, 1930.40 Crozier, op. cit.41 Lieutenant Berney was the Battalion's third Medical Officer, replacing Lieutenant R. D. MacGregor who had taken over from Captain Spence in September 1917.

42 In an action close to Ervillers on the 25th, Lance-Corporal A. H. Cross of the Machine Gun Corps won the Victoria Cross in recovering two of the 40th Division's machine-guns that had been captured by the enemy. Cross survived the war, but until an imposing and appropriate headstone was erected in 2001, his last resting place was an unmarked plot in Streatham Vale Cemetery, south-west London. 43 Almost 80 years later, Mrs Carole Henderson found her grandfather's final resting place in Etaples Military Cemetery. Accompanied by a standard bearer of the Royal British Legion, she and her mother were at last able to lay a wreath of remembrance on Lance-Corporal Sellers's grave.

44 Private Warman DCM was taken prisoner just a couple of weeks after his courageous act. He died after the Armistice while still in a P.O.W. camp in Germany on 4th December 1918, and was buried in Hamburg Cemetery.

45 They were still not quick enough. In this battle 398 Portuguese died and 6,585 were taken prisoner, spelling the end of the Portuguese Expeditionary Corps as a fighting unit.

46 There are discrepancies between the regimental history and other sources. The officer POW records which were meticulously maintained and published by Cox & Co.'s Bank during the war list 11 officers of the 13th Battalion as captured on 9th April: Major West; Captains Ainger and Linge; Lieutenants Allason, Pinnick, Morris and Pedrick (RAMC - USA); Second Lieutenants Webb, Parker, Cant and Blatch. The regimental history omits Lieutenant Morris but adds Captain Price and Second Lieutenant

Buck.47 Fort MacDonald was named after Jacques MacDonald, one of Napoleon's generals and later made a Marshal of France. His father's Jacobite family had fled western Scotland to settle in France.

48 Herbert Warden CBE DSO and bar DL JP was by far the Battalion's most successful commanding officer. He returned to Edinburgh post-war to become Director of Pensions for Scotland from 1919 to 1925 and died in 1946.

49 At the time of the signing of the Armistice on 11th November, 1918, the Wandsworth Borough News reported that 414 NCOs and men of the 13th Battalion were recorded as POWs, with a further 58 men still missing and known not to have been captured. 13 officers were believed held in captivity, while six remained unaccounted for. Prisoners of war were repatriated from the end of November 1918 onwards, the last officer returning by the end of December 1918.

50 Colonel Inglis had inherited, from an uncle who had also served in the Queen's, a segment of the old regimental colours which had been replaced in 1847.

51 Abbott acted as a company commander with the 12th Queen's from April 1916 to April 1917 when his ill-health prevented him from continuing. Even so, he remained with this Reserve battalion for a further three months as Messing Officer before being posted to staff duties In January 1918, Abbott was finally declared unfit for further military service of any kind and was gazetted out of the Army. He returned home to Battersea in March 1918 to a hearty welcome from the Council and local community. He resumed his duties as a Councillor and later served as Mayor of Battersea.

Contrary to expectations, Captain Brereton survived, while poor Hoggett died of his lesser wound in July 1916, after repatriation to a hospital in Manchester, close to his home and wife Ada, in Sale.

52 The naming of Joubert Street gives a vivid example of the history of radical politics and anti-war sentiment in Battersea, honouring as it did one of the enemy Generals in the Boer War.

5. Delville Wood, or more correctly the Bois d'Elville, had been almost totally destroyed when the area was captured by the South African Brigade after a bitter struggle in mid-July, 1916. It had become known as 'Devil's Wood' to the Allied troops who suffered there. Today, only a single, shrapnel-riddled trunk remains of the original wood among the many later replacement trees.5354 The attack on Flers was the first occasion that tanks were used in battle by the British Army.

55 Oakley's wounds eventually brought him back to the Battersea area as he was evacuated to the 3rd London General Hospital in the Royal Victoria Patriotic Building on Wandsworth Common.

56 Major Jarvis was not to return to the 10th Battalion, but despite the ill omen of his horse stumbling as he had set off from Battersea, he recovered from his wounds. He returned to 124 Brigade to command the 21st Battalion, The King's Royal Rifle Corps, who fought alongside the 10th Queen's. This battalion not only boasted Captain Bruce Bairnsfather, the celebrated cartoonist, but also a young Lieutenant Anthony Eden, later to enjoy a high-profile political career and ultimately become Prime Minister. Jarvis survived the war as a Lieutenant-Colonel with the DSO and bar and a Mention in Despatches. His medals are displayed in the Queen's Royal Surrey Regiment Museum, Clandon Park, Surrey.

57 Fortunately, both Parkes and his artistic efforts survived the war and the latter, together with other personal papers, are now held in the Liddle Collection at the University of Leeds.

58 Lieutenant-Colonel Oakley had been called upon to take temporary command of a brigade. He went on to serve as an acting Brigadier-General and survived the war, reverting to the rank of Colonel. He was to remain a good friend of his successor, Roland Gwynne, and Gwynne was made godfather to Oakley's youngest daughter, Barbara Gwynne Oakley, in 1918.

59 Gwynne's wounds were severe and back in England it was feared that he still might lose his leg. Thankfully, the limb was ultimately saved, but Gwynne's active service was finished and he would always carry a limp. He was convinced that Inkster had saved his life, but was frustrated in obtaining another decoration for the young officer since there had been no direct enemy action during the rescue. Gwynne was later to send nine 20 franc notes for the men who had helped find him, and an inscribed silver cigarette case for Inkster.

60 Some of these dugouts still remain to be seen today in the side of the railway embankment near the village of Hollebeke.

61 After the war, Parkes went up to Oxford University and subsequently took holy orders, a move prompted by his experiences in the war. A man of unconventional thought, he was among the few in Britain to take seriously the plight of German Jewry in the 1930s. He helped with Jewish emigration from Germany and was eventually warned by the Swiss police that the Nazis had ordered his assassination. From the 1940s onwards he was a prolific and best-selling author, both on religious questions and the future of the Jewish people. His autobiography 'Voyage of Discoveries' was published by Gollancz in 1969.

62 The site of this mass grave was named the Royal West Surrey Cemetery, Flètre and only one further burial took place there in 1918. After the war, however, the Royal West Surrey Cemetery ceased to exist when the dead of the 10th Battalion were exhumed and re-interred in individual graves at Bertenacre Military Cemetery, Flètre, just 500 yards to the north-west. There they still lie today in a peaceful rural setting disturbed only by the noise of passing traffic on the nearby A25 motorway.

63The bodies of Andrews, Webb and Adams were never recovered after the battle. Their names are therefore among those of the

Queen's Regiment listed on the Tyne Cot memorial to the men missing in the Ypres Salient with no known grave. There are 34,888 soldiers thus commemorated at Tyne Cot.

64 In this action Busby won the Military Medal for capturing an enemy machine gun single-handed and bombing ten German gunners. From a photograph among the papers of Lawrie Inkster, it would seem that Sergeant Busby later received a commission as a Second Lieutenant.

65 Prior to departure for Italy, the Battalion had a Medical Officer from the United States Army - Lieutenant T. W. Hales. But since the Battalion expected to face the Austrian army in Italy, and the United States had yet to declare war on Austria, Lieutenant Hales had been replaced by Captain Clark RAMC, a British officer.

66 Frank Hayley Bell remained with the 10th Queen's for the remainder of the war, reverting to the substantive rank of Major.

67 Lieutenant-Colonel E. B. North CMG DSO retired from the Army in 1923 and died in his native Lancashire in 1944.

68 Though the Armistice brought the fighting to an immediate halt on 11th November, it was still not certain that the war was over, pending peace talks.

69 Livesay's rejoining the Regular Army was to serve him well as a career. He retired as a Brigadier-General in 1920 and eventually settled in Hailsham, Sussex, only a few miles from one of his predecessors with the 10th Queen's, Lt-Col. Sir Roland Gwynne. Brigadier-General Livesay CMG DSO died in 1946.

70 On the evening of 22nd April 1919, Sir Archibald slipped and fell while leaving the Council House in East Hill, Wandsworth. Although it was initially thought he had suffered no more than a grazed leg, his condition worsened overnight and he died at 5 a.m. the following morning. Sir Archibald Dawnay JP CE, honorary Lieutenant-Colonel to the 13th Battalion, was buried in the family vault at Forest Hill.

71 This original Cenotaph was a temporary structure, which quickly began to deteriorate. Lutyens also designed its permanent replacement, which was the centrepiece of the ceremony on 11th November 1920 when the body of the Unknown Warrior was returned to Britain for a state funeral in Westminster Abbey.

72 The problem worsened for many ex-soldiers as the results of their terrible wounds continued to make themselves felt. Even ten years after the Armistice, there were over 6,000 new issues in one year of artificial limbs as a result of war wounds. Almost two and a half million men were in receipt of a pension for war disabilities of some sort (approximately 40 per cent of the soldiers who served in the war) and 48 special mental hospitals still tended 65,000 shell-shock victims.

73 Sadly, the King's Colour of the 13th East Surreys disappeared from All Saints, probably during redecoration in the late 1970s/early 1980s.

74 In addition to unit, community and church war memorials, a number of other organisations ensured that their members or staff would be remembered for the ultimate sacrifice. One such company is Harrods store which created a Great War roll of honour. The first panel of the memorial lists three men of the 13th East Surreys who worked for Harrods before joining up. Sergeant Harry Page, killed at Mory on 23rd March, 1918, worked in the Removals Department; Private Henry Harvey of the Meat Department was killed at Bourlon Wood on 26th November 1917 and Private John Goldsbrough, formerly of the Grocery Department, died of wounds from the same engagement on 6th December 1917.

75 In 1989 Tiny's adopted son, Dennis, reluctantly decided to sell his father's medal group in order to help his own retirement. Auctioned at Christies in London, the medals were bought for £11,000 by an Australian collector, but in recent years have been patriotically purchased and returned to Britain by the Michael Ashcroft Trust.

76 In 1921 The Queen's (RWS) Regiment was retitled The Queen's Royal Regiment (West Surrey) and in 1959 amalgamated with The East Surrey Regiment to form The Queen's Royal Surrey Regiment. This became The Queen's Regiment in 1966, together with the Queen's Own Buffs, The Royal Sussex Regiment, and the Middlesex Regiment (Duke of Cambridge's Own). In 1992 The Queen's Regiment then joined with The Royal Hampshire Regiment to become the present-day The Princess of Wales's Royal Regiment (Queen's and Royal Hampshires).

THE 14TH (RESERVE) BATTALION (WANDSWORTH) EAST SURREY REGIMENT

As noted in Chapter 2, recruitment to the 13th Battalion was so successful that a second Wandsworth unit, the 14th (Reserve) Battalion, was created. Its purpose was to act as an overspill unit to the 13th Battalion and to train and supply replacements for the parent battalion when reinforcement drafts were wanted.

The 14th Battalion was not only the last of the East Surrey Regiment's battalions to be raised, but also proved to be the last of Kitchener's New Army battalions. It was unique in that out of the twenty-eight London Boroughs, it was the only instance where the formation of a second infantry service battalion proved possible. It remained in Wandsworth after the departure of the 13th Battalion and Lieutenant-Colonel Burton and his Adjutant, Captain Alexander, were subsequently transferred from the 13th in order to repeat their earlier success in organising a new unit. The 14th's structure was largely the same as that of the 13th, with the same headquarters and parade ground.

The 14th Battalion remained at Wandsworth until 1 November 1915, when it moved to Gravesend with a strength of almost 600 men. There it proved to have its share of recruits with an eye for the black market. On 28 January 1916, Liberato Declaniz, an Italian ice cream vendor, was fined £10, with £30 costs, by the South Western Police Court for buying military clothing from two of the 14th Battalion's soldiers. The press report of the proceedings did not cover the military sentences which were undoubtedly passed on Privates Weightman and Newman.

At the end of June 1916 the 14th was the first battalion to be disbanded upon reorganisation of the Draft Finding Units. Responsibility for sending reinforcements to the 13th Battalion then became the job of the 5th Battalion, the latter already being well known to the 13th and 14th Battalions since its headquarters were in the neighbouring Borough of Wimbledon.

APPENDIX II

NOMINAL STRENGTH OF THE 13th BATTALION, EAST SURREY REGIMENT, ON DEPARTURE FOR FRANCE, 3 JUNE, 1916
OFFICERS

Headquarters:
Lieutenant-Colonel W. C. Newton (Commanding); Major F. S. B. Johnson (Second in Command); Captain C. E. Linge (Adjutant); Hon. Lieutenant F. Foster (Quartermaster); Lieutenant G. R. Spence RAMC (Medical Officer); RSM E. J. Seymour; RQMS F. C. Webb.

A Company:
Major R. S. Taylor; Captain E. Crocker; Lieutenants R. H. Harker, T. F. Davis; Second Lieutenants R. W. H. King, F. W. Lanham (Bombing Officer), A. F. Senior.

B Company:
Captain M. Pemberton; Lieutenants C. R. Blackburne, F. S. Ainger; Second Lieutenants A. L. Anderson, W. F. C. Embley, J. R. Hucker (Signalling Officer), L. F. Menzies-Jones.

C Company:
Captains L. R. Merryfield, H. P. Naunton; Lieutenants F. J. T. Hann (Machine Gun Officer), M. Stanford; Second Lieutenants G. K. Fielding, G. E. Head, T. W. Hucker, V. W. Scott (Sniping Officer).

D Company:
Captains L. B. Mills, O. G. Norman; Lieutenants E. S. Beecroft (Transport Officer), F. E. Buckland, F. N. Corben; Second Lieutenants G. E. Deacon, L. I. Deacon.

The above were joined by 968 other ranks to achieve a full battalion strength of 1,003 men.

APPENDIX III

NOMINAL STRENGTH OF 10th BATTALION, QUEEN'S (ROYAL WEST SURREY) REGIMENT ON DEPARTURE FOR FRANCE, 5th MAY, 1916
OFFICERS

Headquarters
Lieutenant-Colonel R. Oakley (Commanding);
Major T. McL. Jarvis (Second in Command);
Major A. K. D. Hall;
Captain A. Lawrence (Adjutant);
Hon. Lieutenant G. King (Quartermaster);
Lieutenant T. W. Sweetman RAMC (Medical Officer).

Companies
Captains M. Bessell, D. C. Johnston, J. A. Worthington, G. F. Collyer,
W. Barclay, F. Sutherland, J. B. Dodge;
Lieutenants L. J. Petre, H. A. Dawson, A. F. Robson, E. H. S. Barter,
C. H. Hastings, T. W. Brereton;
Second Lieutenants G. A. Webb, G. N. Gibbs, L. E. Andrews,
H. G. D. Ereckson, H. V. Shortman, H. Raynham, F. L. W. Darling,
W. A. Pope, R. A. Hawes, F. R. Hoggett, W. G. B. Ellis, F. J. Heath,
L. Inkster, J. W. F. Burgess, R. C. Burr, L. Bain, H. S. Brown,
S. J. Ranson, E. H. Bord.

(Author: this description of a Wandsworth Council Mayoral visit to Villers-Plouich appeared in the *Wandsworth Borough News* in 1920).

'A little bit of Wandsworth'

VILLERS-PLOUICH, October 1920

by Robert H Harker (*Wandsworth Borough News*)
Lieutenant in the Wandsworth Battalion

Villers-Plouich! What a wealth of memories the name revives in the minds of those of the Wandsworth Battalion of the East Surrey Regiment who took part in its capture, who assisted in the subsequent consolidation of the position, or who manned its protecting trenches in the succeeding months until the time of the first Cambrai battle. Memories gay and sad – unfortunately and necessarily more sad than gay, for the Harvester of Death demanded a heavy toll in those intervening months between April and November 1917. It is but little that the French villagers can do in return for the great and supreme sacrifice. They preserve in their hearts imperishable gratitude for those valiant soldiers; they have made it a sacred duty to take care of the graves. In the serenest spot of that once beautiful, now terribly scarred village, a piece of land has been consecrated, and here lie those gallant fellows who fell on the field of honour, their graves tended with wonderful care and pride by a venerable French fossoyeur. It is, in paraphrase of Rupert Brooke,

'A corner of a foreign field that is forever – Wandsworth.'

For all time it will prove an inseparable link between our great Borough and that village of Villers-Plouich, near the Somme.

Wandsworth, through its fighting sons, was associated with many villages and towns in France. Armentières, Hulluch, Loos, Calonne, Hébuterne, Bourlon and Villers-Guislain, are but a few of a long list that falls readily to the mind. But with none of these is it so intimately linked as Villers-Plouich. Not only was the village recaptured from the Germans by the men of Wandsworth, but the greatest military honour was earned there by a Wandsworth man as the result of a most gallant action. And so, when the Wandsworth Borough Council, at the suggestion of the Mayor, decided to 'adopt' a part of devastated France, it was fitting that their choice should fall on Villers-Plouich.

To the people of Villers-Plouich, the news that Wandsworth had decided to assume the role of 'godmother' came as a ray of hope. It means so much for them to have someone taking a sympathetic interest in their welfare. They are not putting off until a later day the things which need immediate attention. Bravely they have set themselves to reclaim the land from its wartime aspect of waste and ruin, and to re-establish their domiciles. *A demain, c'est du faineant la refrain* is the motto they have constantly in mind and in view, for 'tomorrow is the lazy man's song' is printed in large letters and hung in conspicuous places throughout the village. Having recovered from the first shock of discovering a blackened ruin where once stood a substantial homestead, a heap of debris marking the site of some well-known and well-loved building, a torn and broken land where once all was bright and green, they have commenced the heavy work of reconstruction, if not light heartedly, at least with steadfastness of purpose which in time must reap a deserved reward.

But in the meantime, before the traces of war have been completely obliterated, if such a thing be possible, the residents of Villers-Plouich will be called upon to battle in the face of tremendous difficulties. They will not stumble with faintness of heart, but their task will be such as to call for exceptional powers of endurance. More or less poorly clad, they are but ill-fitted to resist the rigours of the coming winter and their temporary homes of wood, cleverly constructed though they be, will prove but indifferent places of shelter. It is because of the hardships they will be called upon to meet during the long and bitter winter months that they are overjoyed to learn that the people of Wandsworth are to extend a helping hand. And just as they are constantly mindful of those brave fellows who repose in the British cemetery nearby, so will they be ever grateful for any assistance which may be accorded in their grievous circumstances.

FRENCH MAYOR'S THANKS
Grateful Memories of Wandsworth's Gallant Men

The Mayor of Wandsworth (Lieut.-Commander Cooper Rawson) is to be congratulated on the kindly thought that prompted the suggestion that our Borough should succour Villers-Plouich. It will mean such a little effort on our part, but it will mean much, very much, to the French villagers in the gallant fight they are making. Read what Monsieur Farez, the Mayor of Villers-Plouich, said to Wandsworth's Chief Magistrate a fortnight ago, when, accompanied by the Mayoress, Commander Cooper Rawson paid a lightning visit to the village to discover at first hand the urgent needs of the villagers:

I am happy, on behalf of the inhabitants of Villiers-Plouich, to offer hearty welcome to the British delegation who are so kindly interesting themselves in us, and who wish to lend us their precious assistance. We are not lacking in courage. We wish to reconstitute the country, systematically destroyed by the barbarians, and it is in order to arrive at that result that the inhabitants returned here in the early months of 1919, and have resolutely commenced to work. The difficulties, however, are great; the resources are restricted; and the restoration can only proceed slowly. The decision of the Borough of Wandsworth to serve us in the role of 'godmother' has been welcomed with joy, and I am happy to express our gratitude.

Much fighting took place in our village, and a great number of your brave soldiers have wetted our soil with their blood. Their bodies repose here. It is with respect that we salute their mortal remains. We consider it as a sacred duty to take care of their graves, and we preserve in our hearts grateful memories of those valiant soldiers, who fell on the field of honour in the defence of civilisation and of right.

There was no rhetorical ebullition – just a few plain words of gratitude uttered with an air of quiet, dignified sincerity; an expression of thanks for those who helped to recover France and their little village from the barbarous Hun, and of a joy borne in the knowledge that while they are working strenuously to recover Villers-Plouich from its present aspect of terrible desolation they will not be left to their own meagre resources, but will be aided by those whose sympathies have been aroused. In well-chosen words Wandsworth's Mayor replied as follows :

May I say how grateful I am to you for the kind welcome you have extended to us. We have seen all along the great courage your fellow countrymen have displayed in rebuilding their villages and towns after the terrible desolation which has been caused by the Germans. I am speaking on behalf of the Borough of Wandsworth, which I represent, when I say we not only admire your great courage, but we feel the most sincere sympathy with you in the terrible times through which you are passing. If there is anything we can do to assist you during the period of reconstruction, you may rest assured that no effort will be spared on our part.

At this point the Mayoress was presented with a bouquet at the hands of M. Gratte Panche, a seventy-five-year-old soldier who fought near Péronne in the 1870 war. He was in Villers-Plouich at the time the Germans overran it in the early days of the Great War, and was made prisoner.

Mrs Cooper Rawson, in returning thanks for the flowers, said:

'I consider it a great honour to come to this village to meet you. In England we realise how much you have suffered here in France. I thank you very much indeed for the flowers you have so kindly given to me.

The ceremony of welcome at the little wooden town hall having been terminated with appropriate exclamations of 'Long Live England' and 'Long Live France', the members of the delegation were conducted through the village to the school, another wooden structure which has been erected in the last few months. Here the children were assembled under the direction of the headmaster (Monsieur Delacourt) and his wife, and on behalf of his fellow scholars, a little boy named Fernond Dubois read the following message of welcome:

Ladies and Gentlemen, in the name of all the children of the village of Villers-Plouich, I extend to you a hearty welcome to our dear little village. We have learned with pleasure that you are willing to interest yourselves in the reconstruction of our little country, and for that we thank you very sincerely. We shall not forget that you came to our help, and we shall always be grateful for all the good you may be able to do for our village and our schools. Will you please accept these modest flowers, the colours of a grateful France? These are the same flowers that we have placed on the graves of the brave English soldiers who fell in chasing the enemy from our village. To the representatives of our English 'godmother', in the name of all the children of Villers-Plouch – Thank you!

A BRAVE STRUGGLE.
Admiration for the Courageous French People

In reply, the Mayor of Wandsworth said:

> *May I thank the children of Villers-Plouich very much indeed for their pretty flowers, and for their very kind remarks. It has been a great joy to us to come here to see you, and to try to do something to help you in the brave struggle you are making to get on your feet again after the war. We have the greatest admiration for the courage displayed by the French people in the enormous losses they have sustained and the great hardships they have gone through, and who are striving so bravely to help themselves.*

This concluded the official programme of the reception, but at various points in the village inhabitants met the party and numerous bouquets were handed to the Mayoress, who suitably returned thanks. One bunch of beautiful flowers was presented by a French soldier who had served in the firing line throughout the war, and who expressed his joy at the fact that the Germans had been driven from his village, and that Wandsworth had decided to lend a hand during the work of reconstruction. On all sides there were obvious signs of the whole-hearted manner in which the returned inhabitants of Villers-Plouich have laboured since they re-entered the village. Wooden huts have been erected and rapid progress has been made in the direction of clearing the debris and repairing roads, while a temporary school, town hall, church, and other buildings essential to the public life of the inhabitants have been constructed. Here there is no labour trouble; no loss of time in arguing about how few hours a man should work in the course of one day; no costly strikes. The people are too busy to grumble; too eager in repairing the damage done as a consequence of the war to count the hours of their labour. From the first break of dawn until the darkness of night it has become so profound as to render further effort in the open air impossible, industry proceeds unchecked but for necessary brief intervals for refreshment, and then the task of improving the interiors of dwellings is resumed until the late hour for retirement. Many months of further effort will be necessary, and then this people will be able to look to the fruits of their labour with becoming pride.

Throughout devastated France the returning refugees are reconstructing with equal purpose. Péronne, Bapaume, Albert and other places rendered historic, are hives of industry, and in every hamlet and village and town throughout the length and breadth of the area the work of reclamation is proceeding at a remarkable rate. An outstanding example of the progress since the Armistice is to be found at South Maroc, a town near Lens. The whole of the houses have been rebuilt and refurnished, and the only traces of the war are the shell holes in the village wall, and a few trenches not yet completely filled in.

The 'adoption' of Villers-Plouich has caused a good deal of controversy in the Borough of Wandsworth. Many ratepayers, already groaning beneath the heavy burdens they are called upon to shoulder, have formed the wrong impression that the outcome will mean a further increase of the local rates. There is not the slightest need for alarm. The 'adoption' is purely a voluntary effort, and no one will be forced to assist against his or her wish. A subscription list has been opened by the Mayor and all who wish to give are cordially invited to do so. In conversation with Monsieur Farez, Commander Cooper Rawson learned that the inhabitants of Villiers-Plouich are urgently in need of articles of clothing, boots, seeds, furniture, and agricultural implements, and an urgent appeal is made to all to help in providing these necessities. The Mayor has already received some cheques, seeds and clothing. Much more is required. Will you help?

R.H.H.

'SOME IMPRESSIONS'
By Lieut.-Commander Cooper Rawson, R.N.V.R. (Mayor of Wandsworth)

In the hope that they may be of some advantage to those who are already interested in Villers-Plouich, which the Borough of Wandsworth has adopted, and to those who are willing to be interested in the future, I venture to record a few of the impressions gained during my recent flying visit to this devastated village.

I should, perhaps, explain, at the outset, that the decision that the Borough should act as 'godmother' to this unfortunate place does not involve any further burden upon the rates.

The adoption is on the lines laid down by the British League of Help, which was instituted to give people in this country, who are capable of appreciating how much we in England have been spared in the war, the opportunity of helping the occupants of the devastated areas of France to help them to re-establish their homes.

It is desired to assist with something more useful than sympathy the poor people who may have come back to find their homes and their entire belongings swept away.

My party comprised the Mayoress, Lieut. Harker, who actually served with the Wandsworth Battalion at Villers-Plouich, Lieut. F. W. Lanham, M.C., who also served there, and myself. The Wandsworth Battalion, which formed the 13th East Surreys, served with great distinction in this village, actually re-capturing it from the Germans, and it was here that Corporal Foster won his V.C., Captain H. P. Naunton the D.S.O., Lance-Corporal Reed the D.C.M. and Major L. Mills the M.C.

Unfortunately, many casualties were sustained, and the remains of our gallant representatives are at rest in the Villers-Plouich Cemetery, so it was felt that a more suitable place for adoption would be difficult to find. Leaving London at 8.00 a.m., via Folkstone and Boulogne, we arrived at Amiens in the evening, and at an early hour the following morning proceeded by car to Villers-Plouich, about 30 to 40 miles away, passing en route through several entirely demolished towns and villages.

Arriving at Villers-Plouich, we found the Mayor and his Council standing waiting for us outside the temporary Hôtel de Ville, and the first thing that struck me was 'how long have they been standing here?', as they had no idea of the time of our arrival. I appreciated subsequently how typical their attitude was of the rest of the

267

population; that is to say, very much in need of and very anxious for help, but willing to wait for it patiently and cheerfully. To say that our reception was impressive very inadequately describes the feeling displayed by those concerned. From the Hôtel de Ville we commenced our tour of the village, which space will not permit me to describe in detail, but what made a great impression upon me was the cheerful spirit of the people under such appalling conditions as to warrant the most extreme depression.

The whole village is smashed to pieces. Not a single house or building of any kind remains. The Mayor, who occupied a magnificent chateau (judging by the photographs), is now living or rather existing with his wife, son and daughter, in a wooden shanty of three rooms and a small kitchen, and the people generally are occupying huts manufactured out of wood and corrugated iron, retrieved from the battle area. There are two wells in the village, one being useless, owing to the fact that a German fell into it unfortunately (for the well); the other is one sunk by our soldiers, and worked by a motor which has been left behind for the use of the villagers.

The school children, numbering some eighty odd, naturally presented a pathetic picture, but like the remainder of the people they stood cheery and bright in the small square piece of ground cleared of bricks and rubbish outside their temporary school, and when they presented an enormous bouquet of wild flowers and shouted 'Vive l'Angleterre, as lustily as our boys at the L.C.C schools at home, one felt, coming straight from a land of strikes and grumbles, that these people really had something to grumble about, but appeared to find hard work a more profitable form of exercise, and, without making any odious comparisons, one could not help being impressed by the industry of the people generally, not only at Villers-Plouich, but throughout the whole of the many miles of devastated area through which we passed.

Our last visit was to the British Cemetery, containing the remains of our gallant comrades of Great Britain and our Dominions: officers and men of the Army, Marines and Naval Division; rows of little white crosses on scrupulously tidy graves reverently and gratefully cared for by a very picturesque and charming old French peasant. This is only one of the dozens of cemeteries containing the remains of thousands of British soldiers who have sacrificed everything for us who are still living; men whose claims upon us for some sort of material sacrifice and recognition appear to have been already forgotten by a great number of those at home for whom they died. I may have been a long while coming to the main point, but, having seen the appalling conditions under which these good people are cheerfully endeavouring to return to the status quo, it is impossible adequately to describe it, and one feels that there is much to be said, and it is so difficult to compress everything into a small space.

I am not, unfortunately, possessed of the gift of the writer's skill. I wish I could by my pen extract tears of gratitude and benevolence from those living safely and comparatively comfortably at home, but I regretfully realise my limitations. I can merely appeal to those who have some sort of home to try and realise what it would mean to them to have been driven from their homes by German artillery, and to have come back to find their houses entirely destroyed, and their furniture and other belongings vanished by destruction or theft, and they will then be able, but only in a small degree, to appreciate what these people have suffered.

Some will wish to help out of gratitude for those in whose village rests the care of the graves of their relatives. Others may, I hope, be disposed to help out of ordinary sympathy, and as a token of gratitude for what they have escaped. Whatever the motive may be, I want all I can get.

The inhabitants of Villers-Plouich require immediately, before the winter sets in and they have not a single shop –

Warm clothing, for adults, children and babies.

Boots and shoes (not worn out).

Vegetable and other seeds.

French educational books.

Agricultural implements.

Horticultural implements.

Chickens, and in fact anything.

Money will, of course, naturally be acceptable to buy educational books and other things, and I venture to hope that the inhabitants of this Borough, who responded so splendidly while the war was in progress, will now show that they are possessed of the spirit of human kindness, and send along everything they can spare, and some things they cannot spare, for the relief of their Allies, who are so hard hit.

Parcels, or money, can be sent to me at the Town Hall, Wandsworth, for the present, but it is hoped subsequently to have collecting or receiving depots in the various Wards.   A.C.R.

Ted Foster VC in later life doing his rounds as a
Dusting Inspector for Wandsworth Council.
D. Foster

The commemorative tablet, giving thanks to
Wandsworth, in the Mairie at Villers-Plouich.
Author

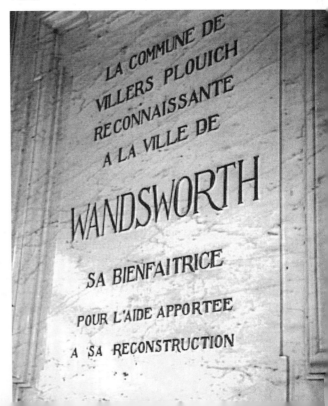

ONE MAN'S WAR

The following notes, kept safely over the years by Mrs Ivy Sharp, were written in pencil by her father in 1918. George Franks was a Battersea boy and joined the 10th Queen's on its inception in 1915. Discharged due to wounds in 1918 when he was then a lance corporal, he returned to civilian life as a Keeper on Tooting Bec common.

Landed in France May 6th 1916.

Arrived at Strazeele May 7th.

Left Strazeele May 20th.

Arrived at Le Bizet 22nd May & then proceeded in firing line.

Left Le Bizet Front on July 29th, arrived at Etaples in hospital August 10th 1916.

Left Etaples on September 13th and joined the Batt. at the Somme & in the attack at Flers village, September 15th 1916. Buried alive 15th. Made 3 attacks there. Buried alive 16th.

Flers village, Goudecourt, Le Sars to Sept 30th 1916.

5 bombing raids.

Left Somme October 1916.

Relieved Australians at St Eloi (Ypres Salient) October 1916.

Big bombing raid Xmas 1916 with snow on ground; gain machine guns and prisoners, lost about 4 men out of 82 men.

Patrol and covering wiring parties in No Man's Land night after night. Wounded 2.

The big attack June 7th 1917. Captured the Dammestrasse. Big mine exploded 3.10 a.m., reached the German 3rd line of trenches and was wounded. Run off to dressing station, blown flat down by German shell on the way down, thousands waiting.

Arrived Boulogne June 9th.

Arrived in England June 11th. Landed Folkestone, proceeded to Nottingham same day.

Left Nottingham for Eastbourne, Eastbourne to Shoreham on the mend.

From Shoreham to Sittingbourne. Then to Sutton and finally discharged at Sutton on May 30th 1918. Thank the Lord.

PWRR at Ceremony with the late Dennis Foster, son of Ted Foster VC.   Author

Edward Lister, Council Leader, joins the Mayors of Wandsworth and Villers-Plouich during a private visit. Liz Shaw

A LITTLE WAR TRAGEDY

The Royal Victoria Patriotic Building on Wandsworth Common was one of several premises requisitioned for use as a military hospital. Many wounded of the Wandsworth and Battersea battalions were brought back from France and Belgium to be treated there at the 3rd London General Hospital, alongside casualties from all the Empire's armies and other theatres of war. Those who did not survive their wounds and could not have a home burial were buried in the nearby Wandsworth Cemetery where several plots of headstones bear testimony to the countries who sent their men to fight for Britain: Canada, South Africa, New Zealand and Australia. Among the latter is at least one soldier who had been wounded at Gallipoli, evacuated to Egypt and then shipped to England for further treatment – all in vain.

The 3rd London General Hospital published its own *Gazette* and the following anonymously-penned poem, which appeared in May 1917, reminds us that for the women at home, the conflict involved the trauma of waiting for news of loved ones at the front, or of caring for those wounded who returned.

A Little War Tragedy

> I must not bewail,
> Falter or grow pale,
> Say I'm ill or sit wrapped in a shawl:
> He was not my brother, Nor acknowledged lover –
> No-one knew I cared for him at all.
>
> Just by chance they said,
> 'Have you heard he's dead?'
> As they handed me a cup of tea:
> One among so many, Guess they had not any –
> He was just the whole wide world to me.
>
> Life must still go on,
> Work is to be done –
> These things happen every day I know:
> I was nothing to him
> Have no right to rue him,
> Save the right of having loved him so.

[With thanks to the late Jon Catleugh]

May 1995 Jean Leterme, former Mayor of Villers-
Plouich, and his wife during an official visit to
Wandsworth. Liz Shaw

The Foster's Way footpath in King George's Park,
Wandsworth. Liz Shaw

The Mayor of Wandsworth, Cllr Leslie McDonnell, with the Mayor of Giavera in 2002. Author

BIBLIOGRAPHY AND INFORMATION SOURCES

A BRASS HAT IN NO MAN'S LAND.
> Brigadier-General F. P. Crozier CB CMG DSO. Jonathan Cape 1930.
ACROSS THE PIAVE.
> Norman Gladden. HMSO 1971. ISBN 0-11-290070-4.
A KITCHENER MAN'S BIT.
> Gerald V. Dennis. MERH Books 1994. ISBN 0-9524126-0-8.
A LAND FIT FOR HEROES: BRITISH LIFE AFTER THE GREAT WAR.
> Christopher Grayling. Buchan & Enright 1987. ISBN 0-907675-68-9.
ARMY BATTLEFIELD GUIDEBELGIUM & NORTHERN FRANCE.
> Richard Holmes. HMSO 1995. ISBN 0-11-772762-8.
A SHORT HISTORY OF WORLD WAR 1.
> James L. Stokesbury. Robert Hale Ltd 1982. ISBN 0-7092-9735-7.
A WOOD CALLED BOURLON.
> William Moore. Leo Cooper 1988. ISBN 0-85052-4822.
DEATH'S MEN.
> Denis Winter. Penguin 1979. ISBN 0-14-016822-2.
GUILDFORD IN THE GREAT WAR..
> William H. Oakley. Privately published 1934.
HISTORY OF THE 40TH DIVISION.
> Lt-Colonel F. E. Whitton CMG. Privately published 1926.
HISTORY OF THE EAST SURREY REGIMENT. Vol. II 1914-1917,
> H. W. Pearse & H. S. Sloman. The Medici Society Ltd. 1923. Vol. III 1917-
> 1919, H. W. Pearse & H. S. Sloman. The Medici Society Ltd. 1924.
HISTORY OF THE FIRST WORLD WAR.
> B. H. Liddell Hart. Pan Books Ltd. 1972. ISBN 0-330-23354-8.
HISTORY OF THE QUEEN'S ROYAL REGIMENT. Vol. VII.
> Colonel H. C. Wylly. Gale and Polden Ltd. Undated.
LIST OF BRITISH OFFICERS TAKEN PRISONER IN THE VARIOUS THEATRES
OF WAR BETWEEN AUGUST, 1914, AND NOVEMBER, 1918.
> First published by Cox & Co. 1919. Later published by The London Stamp
> Exchange Ltd 1988. ISBN 0-948-13081-4.
MONUMENTS OF WAR.
> Colin McIntyre. Robert Wade Ltd 1990. ISBN 0-7090-4027X.
REGIMENTS AND CORPS OF THE BRITISH ARMY.
> I. S. Hallows. New Orchard 1991. ISBN 1-85891-237-7.
RICHTOFEN.
> Peter Kilduff. Arms and Armour Press 1993. ISBN 1-85409-127-1.
SOLDIERS DIED IN THE GREAT WAR 1914-1919. PART 36THE EAST SURREY
REGIMENT. War Office. 1921.

THE ARMIES OF THE GREAT WAR. Contributions by Joe Sweeney and Sergio
   Coelho.
   http://212.67.202.71/~johnwhal/armies/portarm/portarm.htm
THE CROSS OF SACRIFICE OFFICERS WHO DIED. VOL. I. S. D. & D. B. Jarvis.
   Roberts Medals Ltd. 1993. ISBN 1-873058-26-8.
THE HISTORY OF THE 12TH (BERMONDSEY) BATTALION EAST SURREY
   REGIMENT.
   J. Aston and L. M. Duggan. Union Press 1936.
THE KAISER'S BATTLE.
   Martin Middlebrook. Penguin Books 1983. ISBN 0-14-017135-5.
THE NATIONAL ROLL OF THE GREAT WAR 1914-1918. SECTION VII.
   Published by the National Publishing Company. Date n/k.
THE WAR WALK.
   Nigel H. Jones. Robert Hale Ltd 1983. ISBN 0-7090-1174-1.
THE WESTERN FRONT THEN AND NOW.
   John Giles. After The Battle 1992. ISBN 0-900913-71-1.
THE 1916 BATTLE OF THE SOMME.
   Peter H. Liddle. Leo Cooper 1992. ISBN 0-85052-349-4.
VOYAGE OF DISCOVERIES.
   James Parkes. Victor Gollancz Ltd. 1969.

www.cwgc.org Commonwealth War Graves Commission

DOCUMENTATION SOURCES

National Archives, Kew, Richmond, Surrey:

   WO95/2605} 119 Brigade war diary.
      /2606}

      /2608}
      /2609} 120 Brigade war diary.
      /2612}

      /2640}
      /2641} 124 Brigade war diary.
      /2642}

The Queen's Royal Surrey Regiment Museum, Clandon Park, West Clandon,
Guildford:
   war diary of the 13th (Service) Battalion (Wandsworth), The East Surrey
   Regt;
   war diary of the 10th (Service) Battalion (Battersea), The Queen's (Royal
   West Surrey) Regt.

The Liddle Collection, Brotherton Library, University of Leeds:
Papers relating to,
Private R. A. Maxfield;
Captain George Beaumont (via the Rev. Arthur Beaumont).

Mr Tom Miles and the Western Front Association:
Taped reminiscences, Feb 1984, and photographs of Charlie Young, former Pte, 10th Queen's;
Correspondence of Private Herbert Bell, 13th East Surreys.

Mrs Carole Henderson:
Documents and photographs relating to L/Cpl Percy Sellers, 13th East Surreys.

Mr Donald Inkster:
Documents and photographs relating to Capt Lawrence Inkster, 10th Queen's.

Mrs Dianna Hucker and Mrs Pat Hucker:
Documents and photographs relating to Captains James Hucker and Thomas Hucker and Lieutenant Frank Buckman, 13th East Surreys.

Mrs Sabrina Harcourt-Smith:
Documents and photographs relating to Lt-Col Sir Roland Gwynne, 10th Queen's.

APPENDIX VIII

ROLLS OF HONOUR, CEMETERY AND MEMORIAL SITES
13TH (SERVICE) BATTALION (WANDSWORTH)
THE EAST SURREY REGIMENT

*(Appendices VIII and IX compiled by Mr Tom Miles,
son of the late Tom Miles Snr., former Private with the 13th East Surreys)*

ABBEVILLE COMMUNAL CEMETERY EXT, FRANCE.
Cpl J T Wooton 13413 06.03.17 died

ADDINGTON (ST MARY'S) CHURCHYARD, KENT.
Pte G Wright 13515 05.11.18 died

AIRE COMMUNAL CEMETERY, FRANCE.
Pte V S Wood 13451 17.04.18 dow

ALDERSHOT MILITARY CEMETERY.
Pte S Neale 13605 25.02.16 died

ANNEUX CEMETERY, FRANCE.
2/Lt F G Wheatcroft 26.11.17 kia (attd from 5th Bn)

ARRAS MEMORIAL, FRANCE.
Pte F Bowles 25706 26.03.18 kia
Pte A Burgess 202592 23.03.18 kia
Pte A Davis 204750 26.03.18 kia
Pte W R Dibble MM 1672 22.03.18 kia
Pte F Edington 36159 26.03.18. kia
Pte J Evans 35914 26.03.18. kia
Pte T Fennell 15514 17.09.16. kia
Pte W H Garner 14948 26.03.18. kia
Pte L F Green 33262 26.03.18. kia
Pte H Greenhalgh 35950 26.03.18. kia
Pte H A Horrex 25237 26.03.18. kia
Pte F L Johnson 8323 23.03.18. kia
Pte E Littlejohn 14581 23.03.18. kia
Pte R H MacEwan 34879 26.03.18. kia
Cpl W R G Mallett MM 6186 25.03.18. kia
Lt W V L Mallett 22.03.18. kia (attd from 5th Bn)
Pte A J Mann 18384 23.03.18. kia
Pte E Matthews 35846 23.03.18. kia
Pte R E McCraw 19875 23.03.18. kia
L/Cpl A J Morath 16293 23.03.18. kia
Pte D E Oakes 32938 26.03.18. kia
Cpl H J Papworth 9193 23.03.18. kia
Cpl H W Page 20005 23.03.18. kia
Cpl F W Perry 13871 17.09.16 kia
Pte G H Slawson 32170 26.03.18 kia
Pte H R Snook 18345 17.09.16 kia
Pte F Warren 1638 23.03.18 kia
Pte G W Weigold 14646 23.03.18 kia
L/Cpl A V Weston 9766 17.09.16 kia

BACAP (FAIRWELL) CEMETERY, LANCASHIRE.
Pte R Hitchen 18300 02.07.16 dow

BAC-DU-SUD BRITISH CEMETERY, FRANCE.
Pte T E Cockerill 33009 25.03.18 dow
Pte W Green 36109 24.03.18 dow
Pte S Ireland 241354 25.03.18 dow
Pte J W Sparling 20134 23.03.18 dow
Pte J R Thompson 15826 15.03.18 dow

BARLIN COMMUNAL CEMETERY EXT, FRANCE.
L/Cpl W J Cutmore 20056 14.08.16 dow

BOULOGNE EASTERN CEMETERY, FRANCE.
Pte G J Butcher 11570 27.05.18 dow
Capt L R Merryfield 28.08.16 dow
Pte C H Parkes 13681 29.08.16 dow

BRADFIELD (ST LAWRENCE) CEMETERY, ESSEX.
Pte W Hunebell 20079 11.07.17. dow

BRAY MILITARY CEMETERY, FRANCE.
Sgt H E Bailey 13999 07.05.17. dow
Pte W G Donaldson 19721 25.04.17. dow
Pte F J Foster 6845 28.12.16. dow
Pte R C Greenwood 14841 25.04.17. dow
2/Lt F C Johnston 23.04.17. dow
Pte L W Page 30555 19.03.17. dow
Pte A H Rogers 32642 25.03.17. dow
Sgt P Sheppard 9264 29.04.17. dow

BUCQUOY ROAD CEMETERY, FICHEUX, FRANCE.
Pte P C Turk 25699 13.12.17. dow

BULLY-GRENAY CEMETERY, BRITISH EXT, FRANCE.
Pte G Golding 20081 26.08.16. kia
Pte W Twyford 11039 25.08.16. kia
Pte T E Woollard 13384 25.08.16. kia

CABARET-ROUGE CEMETERY, SOUCHEZ, FRANCE.
Pte W Atkinson 28731 21.08.18. kia
Pte F Cole 11023 21.08.18 dow
Lt R H T Peacock 09.04.18 kia
Pte L H Richardson 24017 07.12.17 kia
Lt V W Scott MC 16.03.18 kia (attd. to RFC)

CAMBRAI MEMORIAL, LOUVERVAL, FRANCE.
Pte A J Adams 10935 26.11.17 kia
Pte W R Andrew 22768 26.11.17 kia
Pte J Aspey 28619 26.11.17 kia
Pte H H Austin 32316 26.11.17 kia
Pte A Bailey 33205 26.11.17 kia
Pte H S Ball 21016 26.11.17 kia
Pte A E Bance MM 230 26.11.17 kia
Pte F Barnett 34431 26.11.17 kia
L/Cpl B J Bennett 31828 26.11.17 kia
Pte S W Bennett 14654 26.11.17 kia
Sgt L Bleeze 11191 26.11.17 kia
Pte F A Bradley 25684 26.11.17 kia
Pte C R Bryant 20014 26.11.17 kia
Pte A Bunce 28627 26.11.17 kia
Pte M J Burton 34423 26.11.17 kia
L/Cpl E Clark 18248 26.11.17 kia
Pte W Clements 25694 26.11.17 kia
Pte E Collen 30250 26.11.17 kia
Pte F Connett 6200 26.11.17. kia
Pte G R Cufflin 28668 26.11.17. kia
Pte C N Curtis 17084 26.11.17. kia
L/Cpl G Dalton 204815 26.11.17. kia
Pte W A Dawson 20135 26.11.17. kia

Pte H Fox 28671 26.11.17. kia
Pte J Fuller 11618 26.11.17. kia
Pte C Gander 25707 26.11.17. kia
Pte H J Gates 15926 26.11.17. kia
Cpl H L Gray 10935 26.11.17. kia
Pte A Green 28635 26.11.17. kia
Pte H J Harbour 30551 26.11.17. kia
Pte B Harris 30436 26.11.17. kia
Cpl C T Harris 19176 26.11.17. kia
Pte S Harrison 28678 26.11.17. kia
Pte H Harvey 13305 26.11.17. kia
Pte R Hobden 30549 26.11.17. kia
Pte T Hope 16289 26.11.17. kia
Pte T W H Hunt 202004 26.11.17. kia
Pte F Lathey 30543 26.11.17. kia
Pte J Lee 31441 26.11.17. kia
Capt W N Lowe 24.11.17. kia (attd. from 14th HLI)
Pte F W Maher 31238 26.11.17. kia
Pte A Marsden 28642 26.11.17. kia
Pte W McFie 1837 26.11.17 kia
Pte F Mileham 32664 26.11.17 kia
L/Cpl E H Miller 13096 26.11.17 kia
Pte A Mitchell 35653 26.11.17 kia
Cpl G Moxon 11106 26.11.17 kia
L/Cpl G Needham 13165 26.11.17 kia
L/Cpl J Nicholson 28691 26.11.17 kia
Pte J Parkinson 28647 25.11.17 kia
Pte G Pollard 33753 26.11.17 kia
Pte E Quaife 19711 26.11.17 kia
Cpl H R Rathbone 18076 26.11.17 kia
Pte M T Rathke 32643 26.11.17 kia
Cpl V A Rooff 21184 26.11.17 kia
Pte H H Saunders 30587 26.11.17 kia
Pte D T Stephenson 28704 26.11.17 kia
Pte F Stevens 23730 26.11.17 kia
Pte F Thorpe 203711 26.11.17 kia
Pte G Tyler 30597 26.11.17 kia
CSM C Wagner 13404 26.11.17 kia
Pte A Watson 7331 26.11.17 kia
Pte F T White 28728 26.11.17 kia
Pte C Williams 11423 26.11.17 kia
Pte D J Williams 35677 26.11.17 kia
L/Cpl W Wright 11319 26.11.17 kia

COLBY (ST GILES) CHURCHYARD, NORFOLK.
Pte D Hardingham 27188 28.9.18. died

COUIN BRITISH CEMETERY, FRANCE.
Cpl W Rowe 18392 19.11.16. dow

CROIX DU BAC CEMETERY, STEENWERCK, FRANCE.
Pte A E Redgrave 26952 09.04.18. kia

DELVILLE WOOD CEMETERY, LONGUEVAL, FRANCE.
Pte A V Broughton 18407 08.01.17. kia

DENAIN COMMUNAL CEMETERY, FRANCE.
Pte J Coles 28665 07.12.17. dow

DOVER (ST JAMES) CEMETERY, KENT.
Pte F A Moon 11679 22.11.18. died

EBBLINGHEM MILITARY CEMETERY, FRANCE.
Pte D H Meadway 26933 13.04.18. dow
Pte F H Trenfield 27120 17.04.18. dow

ETAPLES CEMETERY, FRANCE.
Pte J Archer 3/10252 01.12.17. dow

Pte S C Chapman 30160 05.02.17 died
L/Cpl P H Sellers 8397 08.04.18 dow

EXETER HIGHER CEMETERY, DEVON.
Pte A W Hallett 30541 11.12.17 died

FIFTEEN RAVINE CEMETERY, VILLERS-PLOUICH.
(NB Fifteen Ravine cemetery holds 740 graves of unidentified soldiers. Many of these were reinterred at Fifteen Ravine after the First World War following exhumation from a German cemetery near Bourlon. Almost certainly among these unidentified were the 13th Battalion's 'missing' from the action at Bourlon Wood in November 1917).kia
2/Lt G R Alexander 24.04.17 kia (attd from 2nd R.Sussex)
Pte J W Atkinson 19756 24.04.17 kia
Pte H A Chowney 25708 24.04.17 kia
Capt E Crocker 24.04.17 kia
Pte C W Harvie 15920 24.04.17 kia
Pte F McKierman 13820 24.04.17 kia
Pte T G Norris 13477 24.04.17 kia
L/Cpl F C Payne 11261 24.04.17 kia
Pte A E Quenza 13509 24.04.17 kia
Pte A Shaw 13661 24.04.17 kia
Pte W Swann 14097 24.04.17 kia
L/Cpl S Swinfield 18229 24.04.17 kia
L/Cpl B White 11427 24.04.17 kia

FINS NEW BRITISH CEMETERY, SOREL, FRANCE.
Pte W H Bird 30591 14.07.17. dow
L/Cpl W Blackman 18363 04.07.17. kia
Pte J F Brown 8455 24.04.17. dow
Sgt J H Caisbrook 13027 27.07.17. kia
Pte T E Cane 13446 29.06.17. kia
Pte F L Faulkner 25872 31.07.17. kia
Pte H Grady 16221 29.07.17. kia
Pte S H Hurst 14937 27.07.17. kia
Pte A E Lambird 13298 14.07.17. kia
Pte S H Lee 13432 08.07.17. died
2/Lt M MacEwan 05.07.17. kia (attd from 5th Bn)
L/Cpl J H Melhuish 11936 02.07.17. kia
Pte R Pallent 33240 14.07.17. kia
Pte P D Sprackling 30553 18.07.17. kia
Pte D Trevett 20105 13.07.17. dow
Pte E Warren 22481 26.07.17. kia

FOURMIES COMMUNAL CEMETERY, FRANCE.
Pte C Fisher 21128 26.11.17. dow

GOUZEAUCOURT NEW BRITISH CEMETERY, FRANCE.
Pte G Dell 24323 30.05.17 kia
Pte D Goddard 13525 24.04.17 kia
2/Lt R N Goodyear 24.04.17 kia (attd from 6th Bn)
Pte A Holt 13410 30.05.17 kia
Cpl A Newble 9183 24.04.17 kia
Cpl R Points 62 30.05.17 kia
Pte W Potter 1321 24.04.17 kia
Cpl W A Williams 9444 24.04.17 kia

GRAND-SERAUCOURT BRITISH CEMETERY, FRANCE.
Pte R H Bainbridge 28623 20.12.17 dow/PoW

GROVE TOWN CEMETERY, MÉAULTE, FRANCE.
L/Cpl Hobbs 13148 20.01.17 dow
Pte G J Willshaw 8414 29.01.17 died

HALLE COMMUNAL CEMETERY, BELGIUM.
Pte A Barnes 241779 28.10.18 died

HAMBURG CEMETERY, OHLSDORF, GERMANY.
Pte G W Chivrall 15306 01.05.18 dow/PoW
Pte E T Humphrey 28741 19.04.18 dow/PoW
Pte W Warman DCM 11316 04.12.18 died/PoW

HAVERSKERQUE BRITISH CEMETERY, FRANCE.
Pte G Foster 2644 10.04.18. dow

HÉBUTERNE MILITARY CEMETERY, FRANCE.
Cpl G J White 14096 20.11.16. kia
Pte W H Wood 14820 17.11.16. kia

HEM FARM CEMETERY, HEM-MONACU, FRANCE.
Pte F Bennett 13051 20.01.17. kia
Pte W L Huxstep 19727 14.02.17. kia
Pte P Mann 13683 14.02.17. kia
Pte G Penfold 25789 14.02.17. kia

LA KREULE CEMETERY, HAZEBROUCK, FRANCE.
Pte J F Collis 27059 12.04.18. dow
L/Cpl G Stunell 10862 10.04.18. dow (gas)

LA NEUVILLE CEMETERY, CORBIE, FRANCE.
Pte G Treffrey 13942 05.02.17. died

LE GRAND BEAUMART, STEENWERCK, FRANCE.
Pte A S Basely 13421 09.04.18. kia
Pte W Wells 25680 09.04.18. kia

LEUZE COMMUNAL CEMETERY, BELGIUM.
Pte C W J Elson 14960 11.07.18 died
Pte A W Nailard 28225 13.07.18 died

LEWISHAM (HITHER GREEN) CEMETERY, LONDON.
Pte A F Wood 19932 25.03.19 died

LILLE SOUTHERN CEMETERY, FRANCE.
Pte R J Hawkins 25788 12.04.18 kia
Pte W A Hill 11086 19.04.18 dow
Cpl R H Newns 14589 10.04.18 died

LONGUENESSE SOUVENIR, ST. OMER, FRANCE.
Pte C King 13520 27.04.18 died

LOOS MILITARY CEMETERY, FRANCE.
Lt W J Chambers 18.08.16 kia (attd from 11th Bn)
Pte W L Felton 19870 28.07.16 kia
Pte G F Haggis 13393 17.08.16 kia
Pte F Harris 11254 18.08.16 kia (Cité Calonne Memrl.)
Pte F C Norris 9617 19.08.16 kia
Pte J Norris 14070 18.06.16 kia (Loos Memorial)
L/Sgt G A Randell 13677 28.07.16 kia
L/Cpl L R Taylor 9471 28.07.16 kia
Pte H Tullett 14959 19.08.16. kia

MAROC BRITISH CEMETERY, GRENAY, FRANCE.
Pte G M Goodwin 13797 11.09.16. kia

MONT HUON CEMETERY, LE TREPORT, FRANCE.
Sgt R E Gaynham 14001 03.04.18. dow

MORY ABBEY CEMETERY, FRANCE.
Pte W H Johnson 33928 11.01.18. kia
Pte G McCarthy 21724 14.01.18. kia
Pte W Nutley 10848 30.01.18. kia

NEUF-BRISACH COMMUNAL CEMETERY EXT, FRANCE.
Pte H J Barnard 11420 23.10.18. died

NIEDERZWEHREW CEMETERY, GERMANY.
Pte R Formby 20378 17.10.18. dow/PoW

NOEUX-LES-MINES COMMUNAL CEMETERY, FRANCE.
Pte T F Revell 16322 13.10.16. dow

ONTARIO CEMETERY, ORPINGTON, ENGLAND.
Pte L G Abrams 13053 16.04.18 dow rec'd Sailly, 10.04.18.

ONTARIO CEMETERY, SAINS-LES-MARQUION, FRANCE.
2/Lt C I Henderson 26.11.17 kia (attd from 1st Bn)
Pte S J Brookfield 25797 26.11.17 kia

ORIVAL WOOD CEMETERY, FLESQUIÈRES, FRANCE.
Pte G Latford 31398 26.11.17 dow
Pte W B Newman 28745 26.11.17 dow

PÉRONNE COMMUNAL CEMETERY EXT, FRANCE.
RSM E J Seymour DCM 3200 13.03.17 kia

PHILOSOPHE CEMETERY, MAZINGARBE, FRANCE.
Pte A J Barker 13967 08.08.16 kia
Pte T J Bird 19714 08.08.16 kia
Pte A G Brown 13271 13.10.16 kia
L/Cpl A M Bryan 18354 16.10.16 kia
Lt F E Buckland 05.10.16 kia
Pte J Denny 11416 07.08.16 kia
Pte T Holloway 14631 08.08.16 kia
Pte T J Long 13570 08.08.16 kia
L/Cpl F J Smith 15917 05.10.16 kia
Pte J D Sullivan 14784 06.10.16 kia
Pte W Thomason 13861 13.10.16 kia
Pte E Treeby 11122 07.08.16 kia
Pte R A Twyford 13064 08.08.16. kia (aged 15)

PLOEGSTEERT MEMORIAL, BELGIUM.
Pte G Ashby 204855 09.04.18. kia
Pte F T Babbage 19723 09.04.18. kia
Pte A S Bucknell 11210 09.04.18 . kia
Capt G Beaumont MC 09.04.18. kia (attd from 6th Bn)
Capt A B Burton MC 09.04.18. kia (attd from 14th HLI)
Pte E H Callan 9033 09.04.18. kia
Pte G K Cook 8140 09.04.18. kia
L/Cpl W R Davies 32547 09.04.18. kia
Pte G Elliott 13764 09.04.18. kia
Pte J Gourley 35521 09.04.18. kia
Pte W G Green 28673 09.04.18. kia
Pte J Grindey 7675 09.04.18. kia
Pte R H Grove 14642 09.04.18. kia
Pte E A Guy 11352 03.04.18. kia
Pte H J Hack 18334 09.04.18. kia
Pte M S T Hairs 22445 09.04.18. kia
Pte F G Harston 35082 09.04.18 kia
Pte A Hastings 241483 09.04.18. kia
Sgt R A Hinde 13558 09.04.18. kia
Pte C F Hopkins 11498 09.04.18. kia
Pte G G Horn 15510 09.04.18. kia
Pte G D W Hurcombe 24011 09.04.18 kia
L/Cpl F Jackson 19554 09.04.18 kia
Sgt A E Jarvis 7218 09.04.18 kia
Pte W Jenkins 13734 12.04.18 dow
L/Cpl F C Jiggens 16004 09.04.18 kia
2/Lt E Jordan 09.04.18 kia (attd from 7th Bn)
Pte J H Leaton 32098 09.04.18 kia
Pte J P Lynch 26921 09.04.18 kia
Lt J E M Michelmore 09.04.18 kia (attd from 6th Bn)
Pte W Mortimer 13672 09.04.18 kia
Pte J Moseley 11974 09.04.18 kia
Pte R E Muddle 204532 09.04.18 kia
Pte C J Newnham 14624 09.04.18 kia
Pte L Older 205965 09.04.18 kia
Pte R S Outram 1734 09.04.18 kia
Pte A J Page 16282 09.04.18 kia
Pte E W Palmer 13633 09.04.18 kia
Pte C Peskett 11094 09.04.18 kia
Pte J Pinion 26942 13.04.18 kia

Pte W T Plackett 26034 09.04.18 kia
Pte H Pocock 32663 09.04.18 kia
Pte F C Pratt 26944 09.04.18 kia
L/Cpl H Punter 10126 09.04.18 kia
Pte C H R Sayer 26859 13.04.18 kia
Pte A C Shippam 204600 09.04.18. kia
2/Lt H J Smith 09.04.18. kia (attd from 7th Bn)
Pte J E Summers 32106 09.04.18. kia
Pte S Thomas 28710 09.04.18. kia
Pte B G Took 21275 09.04.18. kia
Pte J A Wallis 24052 09.04.18. kia
L/Cpl E J Webber 20932 09.04.18. kia
Pte H H Wellington 28715 09.04.18. kia
Pte T E Wheeler 20012 09.04.18. kia
Pte G S Wilson 28718 09.04.18. kia
Pte G Worthington 19772 09.04.18. kia

PORTSMOUTH (KINGSTON) CITY CEMETERY.
Pte. G C Lenanton 201680 18.04.18. dow

RATION FARM MILITARY CEMETERY, LA CHAPELLE
D'ARMENTIÈRES, FRANCE.
Pte G H Godfrey 6878 09.04.18. kia

ROCQUIGNY-EQUANCOURT RD. BRITISH CEMETERY,
MANANCOURT, FRANCE.
Pte H Coombes 11496 23.08.17. dow
Pte E J Fisher 308 01.12.17. dow
Pte H Greenfield 33189 28.08.17. dow
Sgt G Jennings MM 17409 26.07.17. dow
Pte S Watson 30694 27.11.17 dow
Pte W C Watts 30577 28.11.17 dow

SAILLY-SAILLISEL BRITISH CEMETERY, FRANCE.
Pte C R Darkens 22446 15.03.17 kia

SOLRE-LE-CHÂTEAU CEMETERY, FRANCE.
2/Lt E E Richardson MM 09.11.18 kia (attd to 15 Sqn RAF)

ST HILAIRE CEMETERY, FREVENT, FRANCE.
Pte C Brown 33589 27.03.18 dow

ST-LÉGER BRITISH CEMETERY, FRANCE.
Pte A Filce 17390 12.12.17 kia
Pte J K Youlden 30078 12.12.17 kia

STE.MARIE CEMETERY, LE HAVRE, FRANCE.
Pte R H Bailey 30157 02.05.17 dow

ST. SEVER CEMETERY EXTENSION, ROUEN, FRANCE.
Pte H C Bell 15604 27.12.16 dow
Pte A F Derrick 30540 23.03.17 dow
Pte C Finch 14656 17.04.17 dow
Pte J Goldsbrough 31325 06.12.17 dow
Pte F B Hurst 3534 07.05.17. dow

STREATHAM CEMETERY, TOOTING
Pte A J Burrows 18144 25.09.17. died
Pte W J Durrell 13014 19.12.19. dow
(This cemetery also holds the civilian grave of the 13th Battalion's Victoria Cross holder,
Edward Foster).

THIEPVAL MEMORIAL, FRANCE.
Pte J A G Ashby 21676 24.04.17. kia
Pte B Bourner 13414 24.04.17. kia
Pte W Brambly 11201 24.04.17. kia
2/Lt L C Carey 04.09.16. kia (attd to 1st Bn)
Pte F A Chillmaid 14788 24.04.17. kia

Pte W Clark 13774 16.03.17. kia
Pte J Colvin 21757 24.04.17. kia
Pte A E Cooper 25861 24.04.17. kia
L/Cpl R Cornelius 13955 24.04.17. kia
Pte W A Edwards 25691 24.04.17. kia
Sgt P O Farley 9422 24.04.17. kia
Pte F J Foucher 20042 24.08.17. kia
Pte A Fox 11957 24.04.17. kia
Pte P C Hall 14731 24.04.17. kia
Sgt G Hewett 7396 24.04.17. kia
Pte J J Hurcomb 11386 24.04.17. kia
Pte G L Jenkins 31187 24.04.17 kia
2/Lt T B Mills 24.05.17 dow/PoW
Cpl F C Parsons 19388 23.04.17 kia
Pte C Percival 17627 08.10.17 kia
Pte A E Pryke 31336 24.04.17 kia
Pte J W Robinson 23993 24.08.17 kia
Pte W Scott 13258 24.04.17 kia
Pte G E Sharp 30118 24.04.17 kia
Pte F Smith 31411 24.04.17 kia
Pte H Tubman 23740 24.04.17 kia

TILLOY BRITISH CEMETERY, TILLOY-LES-MOFFLAINES.
Pte J R Coates 12483 26.11.17 kia

TINCOURT NEW BRITISH CEMETERY, FRANCE.
Pte W E H Davey 32656 08.07.17 kia
TOURNAI CEMETERY ALLIED EXTENSION, BELGIUM.
Pte A Coleman 30592 08.10.18 died
Pte S W Martin 35989 12.04.18 dow
Pte S Rowe 28698 10.10.18 died

TYNE COT MEMORIAL, BELGIUM.
Pte C Rawling 35655 09.04.18 kia
Sgt V Reade 4489 09.04.18 kia

VERMELLES BRITISH CEMETERY, FRANCE.
Pte H L Atwood 18249 26.06.16. kia
Pte J Ferrar 14095 23.06.16. kia
Pte J H Hayes 18304 23.06.16. kia
Pte G King 13956 20.06.16. died (accident in billets)
Pte F Walton 15912 25.06.16. kia
Pte W H Whyld 13158 25.06.16. kia
Pte T E Wilson 14526 21.06.16. kia

VEVEY (ST. MARTIN'S) CEMETERY, SWITZERLAND.
Pte A C Harris 204753 18.09.18. died

VILLERS HILL BRITISH CEMETERY, VILLERS-GUISLAIN.
L/Cpl E J Budge 3280 24.04.17. kia
L/Cpl W C Hammond 14006 28.04.17. dow
Pte A J Hearne 6788 19.12.17. kia

WAMBEKE CHURCHYARD, BELGIUM.
Pte R Barbour 32561 16.11.18. died

WANDSWORTH CEMETERY, LONDON.
Pte W Brackwell 11325 27.04.16. died
Pte F T Dart 11129 26.08.17. died
Pte H G Faiers 11013 18.04.16. died
Pte S G Ricks 13629 17.01.19 dow

WOOLWICH CEMETERY, LONDON.
Pte E G Cox 28732 15.05.18 dow

APPENDIX IX

10TH (SERVICE) BATTALION (BATTERSEA), THE QUEEN'S (ROYAL WEST SURREY) REGIMENT

ALDERSHOT MILITARY CEMETERY, HANTS.
Pte J Shepherd G/9601 24.01.16 died

ARRAS MEMORIAL, FRANCE
Pte D A Ayres 241895 23.03.18 kia
Pte H Bayliss T/207917 01.04.18 kia
Pte J S Blackett G/51768 26.03.18 kia
L/Cpl F Butler MM G/10189 26.03.18 kia
Sgt W Carter G/40191 26.03.18 kia
Pte W Cleave T/207880 01.04.18 kia
L/Cpl S G Cole MM G/21436 26.03.18 kia
Pte V J Collins G/69726 22.03.18 kia
Pte C G Cooper T/241290 01.04.18 kia
Pte F J Cooper G/2179 26.03.18 kia
Pte W Costain G/23049 21.03.18 kia
Pte G A Cox L/10644 21.03.18 kia
Pte A Ede G/23049 21.03.18 kia
L/Cpl R A Elmes T/207817 24.03.18 kia
Pte V Flutter G/1858 21.03.18 kia
Pte F G Garrard G/16062 24.03.18 kia
Pte T E Hannington G/23343 21.03.18 kia
Pte W J Harrison G/25009 21.03.18 kia
Pte J H Hart S/5017 21.03.18 kia
Capt J W Hart MC & bar 24.03.18 kia
Pte P C Higgins G/23331 27.03.18 kia
Pte H Hopper 207900 26.03.18 kia
Pte F B Horne 243133 26.03.18 kia
Pte E Ivison T/207904 26.03.18 kia
Pte G W Jerome T/241970 26.03.18 kia
Pte G A D Jones G/23352 26.03.18 kia
Pte W L Jones G/25012 21.03.18 kia
L/Cpl S Kenward T/242201 23.03.18 kia
L/Cpl T H B Little G/10162 26.03.18 kia
Pte C W Lumber T/243139 27.03.18 kia
CSM H Manning G/9642 26.03.18 kia
Sgt H J Manning G/9457 27.03.18 kia
Pte D B Meehan T/242782 24.03.18 kia
Pte C G Mills G/24904 26.03.18 kia
L/Cpl E A Mitchell G/8438 27.03.18 kia
Pte F Murrell L/10618 26.03.18 kia
Pte F Neaves G/7744 26.03.18 kia
Pte H W Oxshott L/10892 26.03.18 kia
L/Cpl P A Roberts T/207796 24.03.18 kia
Capt A F Robson 24.03.18 kia
Pte F Seymour G/1819 26.03.18 kia
Pte C Shapley G/6823 26.03.18 kia
Pte T Slaughter G/10066 22.03.18 kia
Pte A Smith T/241848 21.03.18 kia
Pte G W Smith G/6542 26.03.18 kia
Cpl E Sole G/10088 26.03.18 kia
Pte H B Stone G/23071 26.03.18 kia
L/Cpl H A Sutton T/207913 01.04.18 kia
Pte J Swift G/23034 01.04.18 kia
Pte C W Tharby G/9476 26.03.18 kia
Pte J Trinnaman G/60750 21.03.18 kia
Pte F W Tunstall G/23073 26.03.18 kia

Cpl W J Wadeson L/10815 26.03.18 kia
Cpl R H R Ward G/24249 26.03.18 kia
Pte F C Webb T/207902 01.04.18 kia
Pte A C A Wheeler T/243012 21.03.18 kia
Pte C Whiffin G/5492 23.03.18 kia
Pte C E White T/20789 26.03.18 kia
Pte G W White T/241060 01.04.18 kia
Pte H White G/3817 21.03.18 kia
Pte W E Wiffin G/7709 26.03.18 kia
L/Sgt C N Wilson G/14089 01.04.18 kia

BEDFORD HOUSE ENCLOSURE No 4, BELGIUM.
L/Cpl J E Burry G/9917 29.09.18 kia

BERKSHIRE CEMETERY EXTENSION, BELGIUM.
Pte C J Dumbleton G/9752 15.07.16 kia
L/Cpl W R Haycock G/10303 27.07.16 dow
Pte W J Speaight G/6287 27.07.16 kia
Pte G F White G/9753 12.07.16 dow

BERTENACRE MILITARY CEMETERY, FLÈTRE, FRANCE.
Pte A N Allen G/9786 18.08.17 kia
Pte P Ashton G/9911 18.08.17 kia
Pte W Atherall G/12740 18.08.17 kia
Pte A Blaber G/22957 18.08.17 kia
Pte A Bradford G/21594 18.08.17 kia
Pte J Bull G/51761 18.08.17 kia
Pte P Burkhill G/23011 18.08.17 kia
Pte G Butchers G/24101 18.08.17 kia
Pte F H Comber G/21604 18.08.17 kia
Pte T Cox G/21795 18.08.17 kia
Pte H Dalton G/52035 18.08.17 kia
Pte J Ford G/23050 18.08.17 kia
Pte A W Foster G/21806 18.08.17 kia
Pte C Goad G/9867 18.08.17 kia
L/Cpl F Hall G/1492 18.08.17 kia
Pte W R Hayler G/10070 18.08.17 kia
L/Cpl J Hennell G/10410 18.08.17 kia
Pte A P Hodge G/23022 18.08.17 kia
Pte E Ide G/1608 18.08.17 kia
Pte M M Milliam G/9625 18.08.17 kia
Pte H Molyneux G/23062 18.08.17 kia
Pte D Mumford G/6993 18.08.17 kia
Pte G Murphy G/5312 18.08.17 kia
Pte J E Plowright G/39678 18.08.17 kia
Pte D Robertson G/23068 18.08.17 kia
Pte G A Rowden G/39578 18.08.17 kia
Pte A Shepherd G/23070 18.08.17 kia
Pte G V Skeet MM G/12732 18.08.17 kia
Pte F S Slater G/13782 18.08.17 kia
Pte B W Smith G/10613 18.08.17 kia
Pte W G Smith G/22983 18.08.17 kia
Pte R J Watkinson G/22998 18.08.17 kia
Pte F A Watkives G/21863 18.08.17 kia
Pte R Wells G/9630 18.08.17 kia

BRANDHOEK NEW MILITARY No. 3 CEMETERY, BELGIUM.
Pte T A Dickerson G/25893 17.04.18 dow
Pte S C P Murkin G/25920 17.04.18 dow
Pte P S Waller G/25942 17.04.18 dow

BRIGHTON CEMETERY, SUSSEX.
Pte A C Drape G/21618 07.08.18.

CALAIS SOUTHERN CEMETERY, FRANCE.
Cpl W E Ingle G/10151 01.08.16 dow

CROYDON (MITCHAM RD.) CEMETERY, SURREY.
Pte W Tasker G/9850 06.02.16 died

DADIZEELE NEW BRITISH CEMETERY, BELGIUM.
L/Cpl E S Brown T/207787 14.10.18 kia
Pte W E Collins T/206868 14.10.18 kia
2nd/Lt J A Laing 14.10.18 kia

DICKEBUSCH NEW MILITARY CEMETERY, BELGIUM.
L/Cpl J Edwards G/3753 15.04.17 kia

DUNHALLOW A.D.S. CEMETERY, BELGIUM.
Pte F A Pond G/59928 24.10.18 died

ETAPLES MILITARY CEMETERY, FRANCE.
Pte W Bowles G/21020 27.09.17 dow
Pte J O Bryan G/10293 15.10.16 dow
Pte W Danks G/25896 03.11.18 died
Pte H Ellis G/40225 09.01.17 died
Pte A V Fenton S/6936 10.04.18 dow
L/Cpl F Gore G/7663 12.08.17 dow
Pte J C W Jenkins G/23353 09.04.18 dow
Pte C Kennedy G/198 04.03.17 died
L/Cpl T H Kirby G/22952 23.09.17 dow

FALMOUTH CEMETERY, CORNWALL.
Pte C Warmington 23299 06.03.20 died

FULHAM OLD CEMETERY, LONDON.
Pte E Middleton (served as Toms) G/9773 21.11.17.

GIAVERA CEMETERY, ITALY.
Pte S C King G/1232 07.01.18 dow
2nd/Lt H C Phillips 07.12.17 kia

GROOTEBEEK CEMETERY, RENINGHELST, BELGIUM.
Pte F G Church G/25743 04.09.18 kia
L/Cpl J J Daly G/10928 09.09.18 kia
Pte F Farr G/21810 04.09.18 kia
Pte R C Litchfield G/78509 04.09.18 dow
L/Cpl A W Medd G/24895 05.09.18 kia
L/Cpl W C Woods L/11992 04.09.18 kia

GUILDFORD CEMETERY, SURREY.
Pte W Greenfield S/1067 05.05.16 died
HARINGHE (BANDAGHAM) CEMETERY, BELGIUM.
Pte B W Albon G/25861 22.04.18 dow

HARLEBEKE NEW BRITISH CEMETERY, BELGIUM.
Pte C V Bignell G/25837 22.10.18 kia

Pte E C J Connelly G/68396 04.11.18 kia
Pte E Harbon G/30170 22.10.18 kia

HAZEBROUCK COMMUNAL CEMETERY, FRANCE.
2/Lt D W Jacques 24.12.16. dow

HEILLY STATION CEMETERY, FRANCE.
CSM A C Child G/10441 09.10.16 dow
Capt A Lawrence 19.09.16
Pte A J Mildenhall G/10016 20.09.16 dow
Capt W A Pope 07.10.16 dow
Pte R E C Roberts G/4635 24.09.16 dow
Cpl A J Stevens G/6598 15.09.16 dow

HOOGE CRATER CEMETERY, BELGIUM.
Pte A A Everett G/10500 22.09.17 kia
2nd/Lt E O Goss (attd from 4th Bn)14.10.18 dow
Cpl C Green L/11099 31.07.17 kia
Pte A E King G/21827 04.08.17 kia
Pte E A G Murfin G/21834 22.09.17 kia
Pte E A Price G/37530 20.09.17 kia

HORLEY (ST. BARTHOLOMEW) CHURCHYARD, SURREY.
Pte T Apps G/21577 11.11.18 died

KETTERING CEMETERY, NORTHANTS.
Pte G Kimberley G/10345 16.06.19 died

KLEIN-VIERSTRAAT CEMETERY, KEMMEL, BELGIUM.
Pte D I Andrews 206919 24.07.17 dow
Pte W G Burstow G/21586 20.07.17 dow
Sgt E F Cherry G/24105 24.02.17 kia
Pte A Crowther G/22517 24.02.17 kia
Pte S S Dobie G/10044 24.02.17 kia
Pte R Dowle G/7629 24.02.17 kia
Pte J Griffen G/13796 24.02.17 kia
Pte W H Hatt G/6889 (attd Trench Mortars) 04.02.17 kia
Pte P G Horne G/13894 24.02.17 kia
Pte R J Jarvis G/22529 24.02.17 kia
Pte J H Littlechild G/12873 24.02.17 kia
Pte E J Lucas L/10300 24.02.17 kia
Pte S W Matthews G/10385 24.02.17 kia
Pte R T Mole G/21831 24.02.17 kia
Pte H Newham G/21678 24.02.17 kia
Pte H N Parmenter G/10445 24.02.17 kia
Sgt J Payne G/9413 09.02.17 kia
Pte F Pearce G/2179 24.02.17 kia
L/Cpl E G Samme G/9853 24.02.17 kia
Pte J H Steele G/21853 24.02.17 kia
Pte A T Tomsett G/4645 24.02.17 kia

KEZELBERG CEMETERY, MOORSEELE, BELGIUM.
Pte H R Bigden G/68411 07.11.18 died

LA CLYTTE MILITARY CEMETERY, BELGIUM.
L/Cpl G A Barwick G/21790 05.01.17 kia
Capt E H Bird 24.02.17 kia
Pte A T Cheek G/10443 05.01.17 kia
Pte C D Chessell G/21607 05.01.17 kia
Pte G Chestney G/12748 05.01.17 kia
L/Cpl W A Hillyer G/18064 05.01.17 kia
Pte J M Keys G/7630 07.01.17 kia

Pte E Molin G/21674 05.01.17 kia
Pte C H Neale G/10408 06.08.17 kia
Pte C A Pearce G/11807 13.12.16 kia

LAMBETH CEMETERY, TOOTING, LONDON.
Pte F G Colyer G/11258 08.04.18. dow

LARCH WOOD CEMETERY, BELGIUM.
2nd Lt H T Batson (attd RFC) 11.09.17 kia
Pte P Long G/10446 20.09.17 kia

LIJSSENTHOEK MILITARY CEMETERY, BELGIUM.
L/Cpl J Austin G/25823 16.08.18 kia
Pte A Bland G/21535 23.07.18 kia
Pte S T Bone G/21591 23.03.17 dow
Pte E G Braybrook T/207804 13.07.18 kia
Pte R J Bridges G/69633 30.08.18 dow
Pte H Broughton G/25947 13.08.18 kia
Pte H G Buck G/11925 01.03.17 dow
Sgt C G Button G/9471 25.07.17 dow
L/Cpl H W Chastell G/29630 15.07.18 dow
Cpl G Donaldson G/2097 25.02.17 dow
Pte R Dooley G/7346 12.01.17 dow
Pte W R Field G/21807 10.12.16 dow
Pte E C Foster S/7142 15.07.18 dow
Pte R H Freestone G/25954 30.07.18 kia
Capt A L Hale 08.07.18 kia
Pte C Hibburt L/10921 26.02.17 dow
Pte F Lowe G/14734 25.02.17 dow
2nd/Lt H W Marshfield (from 9/E Surrey) 14.08.18 kia
Pte C A J Martin G/63627 04.08.18 dow
Pte G W Matthews G/18650 25.02.17 dow
L/Cpl J Moore G/24829 08.04.17 kia
Pte A C Morris G/63609 25.10.18 dow
Pte F J Munton G/39677 21.09.17 dow
Pte J Ottaway G/7714 08.06.17 dow
Pte C E Page G/14071 11.12.16 dow
Pte T Podmore G/25735 15.07.18 kia
Pte T C Prudden G/25926 28.07.18 kia
L/Cpl A Reynolds G/21688 14.06.17 dow
Pte B Rook G/25771 15.07.18 dow
Pte H C Savell T/25930 13.08.18 kia
Cpl H Seakins MM G/3217 25.02.17 dow
L/Cpl W F Sleath G/15377 25.02.17 dow
Pte A Smith G/25883 03.07.18 dow
Pte F J Speed G/21852 13.08.18 kia
Pte W H Stevens G/4384 21.01.17 died
Pte F G Talbot G/1522 20.09.17 dow
Pte A W Thody T/207893 30.09.18 dow
Pte J F O Thorp G/68425 26.07.18 kia
Pte W J Tindell G/68376 08.07.18 kia
Pte F C Whitenstall G/39285 13.07.18 dow

LONDON RIFLE BRIGADE CEMETERY, PLOEGSTEERT.
Pte F Alexander G/11759 12.08.16 kia
Sgt A H Cheeseman G/10058 02.08.16 kia
Pte J G Drew G/10137 27.07.16 kia
Pte E E Foster G/7725 30.07.16 kia
Pte R J W Green G/9946 23.06.16 kia
Pte A H Greenaway G/4923 29.06.16 kia
Pte H Ireson G/6946 07.06.16 kia
Sgt J Lennard G/9430 08.06.16 kia

Pte F W Milliner G/7719 28.07.16 kia
L/Cpl J T Moore G/10017 09.06.16 kia
Pte W H Moore G/9956 03.08.16 kia
L/Cpl A S Morris G/9837 21.06.16
Pte W E Rapson G/6773 27.07.16 kia
Pte F Smith G/10239 30.06.16 kia
Pte H Spence G/10170 21.06.16 kia
Pte G W Wakelin G/11762 27.07.16 kia

MAIDWELL (ST. MARY'S) CHURCHYARD.
Pte S J Iliff G/10405 14.01.17 died

MANCHESTER SOUTHERN CEMETERY, LANCS.
2nd/Lt F R Hoggett 18.07.16 dow

NUNHEAD (ALL SAINTS) CEMETERY, CAMBERWELL.
Pte G G Batchelor G/21541 15.03.17. dow
Pte H F Pearl L/6785 08.03.17. dow

NETLEY MILITARY CEMETERY, HAMPSHIRE.
L/Sgt J J Kitts G/6523 06.10.16 dow

OOSTTAVERNE WOOD CEMETERY, BELGIUM.
L/Cpl A C Bare G/13609 22.02.17 kia

OXFORD ROAD CEMETERY, BELGIUM.
Pte W C Tew G/25934 28.09.18 kia

PERTH CEMETERY, ZILLEBEKE, BELGIUM.
Pte F T F Hayes G/9381 04.08.17 kia
Pte T H Wiles G/23005 20.09.17 dow
Capt H C Willders-Lewis 04.10.17 kia

POND FARM CEMETERY, WULVERGHEM, BELGIUM.
Pte A C Muggleton G/7657 25.04.17 kia

POPERINGHE NEW MILITARY CEMETERY, BELGIUM.
Pte C H Lord G/23026 04.08.17 dow

RUCKINGE (ST MARY MAGDALENE) CEMETERY, KENT.
Pte R J Wightwick G/7645 09.11.18. died

TERLINCTHUN CEMETERY, FRANCE.
Pte J H Bromwich G/69647 05.11.18 died
Pte J Brookes G/69648 15.11.18
Pte N L Pattison T/242637 20.09.18 dow
Pte H A Wootten G/25940 11.10.18 dow
L/Cpl A F Wright G/22365 07.11.18 dow (gas)

THIEPVAL MEMORIAL, FRANCE.
Pte G H Baynes G/ 15.09.16 kia
Pte A Beckwith G/10192 03.10.16 kia
Capt M Bessell 15.09.16 kia
Pte B F Bird G/10306 17.09.16 kia
Pte E J Bond G/10497 03.10.16 kia
Pte G Boreham G/14133 09.10.16 kia
Pte R S Browning G/11767 15.09.16 kia
Pte S Burbery G/7526 17.09.16 kia
Pte S Butler G/10280 15.09.16 kia
Sgt C T Campbell G/9380 17.09.16 kia
Pte H W Campbell G/11012 17.09.16 kia
Pte W F Chambers G/10411 09.10.16 kia

Pte W Cole G/6242 15.09.16 kia
Pte A Cook G/7715 17.09.16 kia
Pte T Davis G/10069 17.09.16 kia
Pte W J Davis G/9826 17.09.16 kia
Sgt G W Dodson L/10060 09.10.16 kia
Pte A H Drake G/9931 17.09.16 kia
Pte W Dunn L/10867 17.09.16 kia
Lt A T Eaves 03.10.16 kia
Pte G H Edward G/9950 17.09.16 kia
Pte H Ellender G/7632 15.09.16 kia
Pte A Faulkner G/9755 15.09.16 kia
L/Cpl S Fendall G/9844 17.09.16 kia
Pte P Field G/7700 17.09.16 kia
Pte T G Finn G/7711 17.09.16 kia
Pte C T Fountain G/10068 17.09.16 kia
Pte J J Galvin G/9804 03.10.16 kia
Pte W Glitheroe G/10145 17.09.16 kia
Pte W W Goodchild G/10557 07.09.16 kia
Pte B W Hall G/7732 15.09.16 kia
Pte T E Harwood G/10030 15.09.16 kia
Pte A E Hentsch G/9800 17.09.16 kia
Pte A H Huggell G/9905 17.09.16 kia
2nd/Lt R C Javes 16.09.16 kia
L/Cpl W Knott G/6566 15.09.16 kia
Pte C G Lake G/9683 15.09.16 kia
L/Cpl F W Lewis G/9664 15.09.16 kia
Pte A Linkins G/7666 15.09.16 kia
Pte G H Loft G/10050 15.09.16 kia
Pte J W Macrow G/11912 03.10.16 kia
2nd/Lt H E Mance 15.09.16 kia
Pte H P Markwell G/9992 17.09.16 kia
Pte W J Martin G/10043 17.09.16 kia
CSM Pinnock G/9603 09.10.16 kia
Pte T V Powell G/6980 15.09.16 kia
Pte F Roberts G/10432 15.09.16 kia
Pte F Sartain G/10010 17.09.16 kia
L/Cpl J V Sheppard G/9906 17.09.16 kia
L/Cpl C B Smith G/9742 17.09.16 kia
Pte F Smith G/9957 15.09.16 kia
Pte T Smith G/10359 17.09.16 kia
Pte J H Spink G/9862 17.09.16 kia
Pte G W Standing G/6333 15.09.16 kia
Pte A L Stedman G/5496 17.09.16 kia
Pte W H Taylor G/9818 17.09.16 kia
Pte W H Torode G/9591 17.09.16 kia
Pte H K Vickery G/21719 07.10.16 kia
Pte G Waite G/10225 17.09.16 kia

L/Cpl N Walker G/9455 15.09.16 kia
Pte F Wilkinson G/7572 15.09.16 kia
Pte H Windsor G/9525 15.09.16 kia
Pte W H Woodward G/21461 09.10.16 kia
Pte G Wright G/10371 17.09.16 kia

TYNE COT CEMETERY, PASSCHENDAELE, BELGIUM.
2nd/Lt C H Adams 20.09.17 kia
Sgt C W Davey G/9755 22.09.17 kia
CSM A Gale G/9503 28.09.18 kia
Pte H G Knight G/13735 22.09.17 kia
Sgt W H Saunders MM G/9388 20.09.17 kia

VOORMEZEELE ENCLOSURE No. 3, BELGIUM.
Pte A O Armstrong 206913 24.07.17 kia
Pte G Butcher G/5894 15.06.17 kia
Pte D V George MM G/818 07.06.17 kia
Pte W Morris G/24906 05.09.18 kia
Pte W Parkhurst G/39330 07.06.17 kia
2nd/Lt W A Seeds 06-07.06.17 kia
Pte H A H Shepherd 7086 21.06.17

WANDSWORTH CEMETERY, LONDON.
Pte R E Griffiths G/10059 13.04.16 died
Lt H S Payne 21.02.19 died
Pte F Robinson G/9444 11.01.16 died

WICKEN CEMETERY, NEWMARKET, SUFFOLK.
Pte C W Rumbelow G/13263 02.06.17 died

YPRES (MENIN GATE) MEMORIAL, BELGIUM.
2/Lt E H H Woodward 24.12.16 kia

YPRES TOWN CEMETERY EXTENSION, BELGIUM.
Pte A McMann G/14934 28.04.18 kia
Pte J C Owen G/24913 27.04.18 kia

YPRES RESERVOIR CEMETERY, BELGIUM.
Pte G E Blewitt (Drummer) L/11259 20.05.18 dow
Pte J Ellis G/25749 14.10.18 dow
Pte W C Price G/6912 20.05.18 kia
2nd/Lt C E Proughten 23.05.18 kia
Pte W T Rance 22689 20.05.18

ZANTVOORDE BRITISH CEMETERY, BELGIUM.
L/Cpl T A Goodearl G/7634 01.10.18 kia
Sgt F G Hoy MM G/11750 22.09.17 kia

INDEX